Teaching Civics
in the Library

Teaching Civics in the Library

An Instructional and Historical Guide for School and Public Librarians

Reneé Critcher Lyons

McFarland & Company, Inc., Publishers
Jefferson, North Carolina

LIBRARY OF CONGRESS CATALOGUING-IN-PUBLICATION DATA [new form]

Names: Lyons, Reneé Critcher, 1961– author.
Title: Teaching civics in the library : an instructional and historical guide
for school and public librarians / Reneé Critcher Lyons.
Description: Jefferson, North Carolina : McFarland & Company, Inc.,
Publishers, 2016. | Includes bibliographical references and index.
Identifiers: LCCN 2015035349| ISBN 9780786496723 (softcover :
acid free paper) | ISBN 9781476620923 (ebook)
Subjects: LCSH: School libraries—Activity programs—United States. |
Civics—Study and teaching (Elementary)—United States. | Civics—Study
and teaching (Secondary)—United States. | Children's libraries—Activity
programs—United States. | Young adults' libraries—Activity programs—
United States. | School librarian participation in curriculum planning—
United States. | School libraries—Standards—United States. | Civics—
Juvenile literature—Bibliography. | Citizenship—United States—
Juvenile literature—Bibliography. | United States—History—
Juvenile literature—Bibliography.
Classification: LCC Z675.S3 L96 2016 | DDC 320.473071/2—dc23
LC record available at http://lccn.loc.gov/2015035349

BRITISH LIBRARY CATALOGUING DATA ARE AVAILABLE

ISBN (print) 978-0-7864-9672-3 (print)
ISBN (ebook) 978-1-4766-2092-3 (ebook)

Front cover images © iStock/Thinkstock

Printed in the United States of America

*McFarland & Company, Inc., Publishers
Box 611, Jefferson, North Carolina 28640
www.mcfarlandpub.com*

In honor of my daughter,
Faith Marie Lyons.

May your generation remember,
then keep, the Republic!

Table of Contents

Acknowledgments

First, I want to thank my publisher for allowing me to write two books that draw attention to the extreme sacrifice of our Founding Fathers and Mothers. We need to remember, and I hope these books, in the years to come, help many American and world citizens ponder, the values, political philosophies, and principles on which our country was founded: liberty, freedom, justice, equality, representation, participation, enlightenment, independence and individualism, and civic and personal responsibility. I also want to honor the leaders and scholars on whose shoulders we stand: Thomas Jefferson, Benjamin Rush, Noah Webster, Horace Mann, John Dewey, and Abraham Lincoln.

Second, kudos to those authors who are reintroducing civic role models and highlighting both the impressive and disturbing aspects of our nation's past for our children and young adults. I appreciate the fact such materials are available, and accessible, in support of civic education efforts. A special thanks to the National Children's Book Literacy Alliance and its executive and assistant directors, Mary Brigid Barrett and Geri Eddins, whose devotion to improvements in our nation's literacy levels, to include civic literacy, is endless. I am especially thankful for the NCBLA's resourceful print publication, *Our White House: Looking In, Looking Out*, as well as the accompanying website.

Third, I express my sincere thanks and love, once again, to fellow wordsmith and friend Helen Kampion, and three additional "always supportive" friends, Sara Palmer, Gidget Hernandez, and Mariette Winkler-Lisk. Also, how would I stand tall without the love and support I feel from my mentors and kind friends, Dr. Rosalind Gann and Dr. Linda Veltze? Thanks, Roz and Linda, so much!

Fourth, thanks to the academic libraries that support and provide materials for my scholarly efforts as well as the messages and stories I hope to share: East Tennessee State University's Sherrod Library and Appalachian State University's Carol Grotnes Belk Library.

Fifth, I want to acknowledge the gratitude, love, and special memories I hold for my politically active grandmother, Ethel Mae Hampton Holder, an exemplary American citizen, who cast one of the first ballots by a woman in the county in which I was born. Also, I want to remember, with honor, the legacy of my childhood librarian, Ms. Susie Buchannan, who engaged her students in a true interdisciplinary fashion.

Finally, all my love to my dutiful daughter, Faith, as well as to my mother, Anna, and stepfather, Tommy, who provide comfort, love, and those most important "You can do it" moments.

Preface

"Wherever Law ends, tyranny begins."—John Locke

I have always been interested in current issues and political affairs and cannot fathom the civic despondency evident in 21st-century American society, especially in light of the disconcerting political climate in which each and every citizen now lives and works. Perhaps those of us living in the mountains of Appalachia are closer to political issues, for politics continues to "hit us in the face" to the extreme, either nourishing or ravaging our environs and lifestyles. Nevertheless, several life experiences have fostered my increasing interest in civics education, as has been, and no doubt will be, promoted and delivered to a greater degree within our nation's libraries, the traditional bulwark of democracy, in coming years.

First, as I teach my graduate students in the School Library Media Program at East Tennessee State University, I continue to stand in awe of the profession I have chosen, one in which I must incorporate the precepts and principles of intellectual freedom, the right to privacy, and the freedom to read within student coursework. As these principles are challenged via widespread censorship efforts and even legislation based on fear rather than the rule of law (the Patriot Act), librarians must develop means of "combat"—that is, support networks, knowledge of supportive case law, and a grasp of the legal issues and social implications surrounding our First Amendment rights. In today's world, it is crucial that librarians be versed in civic tradition, discourse and advocacy efforts as well as means of combating Constitutional challenges.

Second, as I researched and wrote *Foreign-Born American Patriots: Sixteen Volunteer Leaders in the Revolutionary War*, my most recently published book (McFarland, 2014), I similarly stood in awe of the sacrifices and contributions made by the men and women who guaranteed our independence, freedom, and rights, sparking my inquiries into the manner in which these histories (civics education) are currently shared in American public schools. I was not awed by my findings; on the contrary, I was appalled.

Third, in my personal life, as I attempt to eat properly and avoid genetically-modified foods, vote for candidates uninfluenced by Super-PACs, plant heirloom seeds in my garden, and support the environmental efforts of such organizations as Appalachian Voices and the Sierra Club, I am appalled at the inculcation of corporate, rather than citizen-based, interests within legislative acts, public policy, and Supreme Court decisions.

Hence, I pitched the idea of creating an historical and instructional guide for the renewal of democracy-building efforts within our nation's school and public libraries, and the need for an increase in civics education efforts certainly supported by educational, political, public policy, legal and academic scholars and experts (as evidenced in the chapters to follow), to my publisher. McFarland, which has supported professional library materials throughout its publishing history, accepted my proposal.

Having created and presented a session dedicated to the collection of civics-related library materials at the 2013 American Association of School Librarians conference, I already had familiarity with the resources utilized for the activities included in this book. To learn more about the historical and modern-day civics education framework, as well as the level of civic literacy and health of American democracy in the 21st century, I primarily consulted the works of Feith, Campbell, and Hirsch, *Teaching America, Making Civics Count*, and *Making of Americans*, respectively, which convey the findings and recommendations of civics education proponents Peter Levine, David Campbell, James Youniss, and Sandra Day O'Connor. I encourage a thorough reading of all three of these resources.

While a plethora of primary sources conducive to civics education instruction are accessible in digital libraries via the Internet, I know of no other resource that utilizes acclaimed works of children's literature as thematic material for civic discourse, action, and service possibilities, or that defines and delineates all recommended "get out of the building" strategies. I hope this material will spawn civics education instructional opportunities delivered within our school and public libraries by trained and certified librarians, most appropriately in collaboration with social studies and civics education teachers (ultimately, in consultation with educators of all subject areas, pinpointing language arts integration and spearheading improvements in reading/language arts competencies and comprehension). I trust that the ideas and suggestions offered within this guide will serve as a starting point for the implementation of effective library civics education programming, and that library professionals will expand upon, customize, alter, and revise such activities and discussion prompts to fit their own community culture, localized resources provision, instructional contexts, and student learning characteristics.

As we enter days in which the constitutionally correct Freedom Act was not passed and the Patriot Act remains federal law, the *Citizens United* Supreme Court decision allows the demon of greed to infiltrate our political systems, voting rates among young adults remain at record lows, police brutality is overlooked and justified, Native American lands are being annexed to benefit foreign energy interests, and school and public librarian jobs are being culled as a result of oftentimes bogus federal and state budget cuts, let us, citizens of the United States of America, in the true spirit of our forebears, remain positive. Let us once again gather as a people to combat threats to our democratic republic form of government and foster educational offerings that inspire and direct our students to once again grab the reins of that steed called independence and guide the citizens of our Republic into voting booths, courtrooms, public forums, libraries stocked in civic materials, and the very halls of justice (Capitol Hill, the White House, and the Supreme Court Building) as impartial, service-oriented public servants (legislators, presidents, and justices), rather than ill-informed spectators taking only to the streets. Let freedom ring!

Chapter I

The Importance of
Civics Education

Are We a Nation of
Participants or Spectators?

"Those who cannot remember the past are condemned to repeat it."—Poet/philosopher George Santayana

In July 2013, former president Jimmy Carter announced to the world, "America does not have a functioning democracy at this point in time." He continued: "I think the invasion of human rights and American privacy has gone too far." In March 2014, Carter specified his concern that the National Security Agency (NSA) was monitoring and spying upon his own email. Though this opinion was voiced by a former president of the free world, after the initial news bite, neither outrage nor action on the part of the American citizenry followed. Thus, violations of Constitutional provisions guaranteeing privacy, in the form of wiretapping and phone surveillance, continued, with a voice or two arising here and there, to include Edward Snowden. Yet no community-based citizen organizations, charismatic leaders, or political representatives were making any "noise" about the purported violations. Indeed, many citizens instead touted the government's invasion of privacy as a means to fight the "war on terrorism," seemingly unaware of or avoiding Benjamin Franklin's admonishment: "Those who surrender freedom for security will not have, nor do they deserve, either one."

Why the complacent attitude in a nation whose very existence is based on questioning authority, asserting individual freedoms, trusting the balance of power, performing civil service, and holding representatives accountable for their actions? Why, in the words of Sam Nunn and William Bennett of the National Commission on Civic Renewal, are "too many of us … passive and disengaged. Too many of us lack confidence in our capacity to make basic moral and civic judgments, to join with our neighbors to do the work of community, to make a difference. Never have we had so many opportunities for participation, yet rarely have we felt so powerless…. In a time that cries out for civic action, we are in danger of becoming a nation of spectators" (Longo 8). Indeed, even Secretary of Education Arne Duncan understands that "a staggering number of Americans do not know much of the basic history and traditions of our nation" (qtd. in Campbell 35). Perhaps because our nation's emphasis on civics education experienced a debunking beginning sometime in the 1930s, taking a nosedive in the early 1970s, to the point that, as Thomas Patterson notes in *The Vanishing Voter*, "Today's young adults are less politically interested and informed than any cohort of young people on record" (qtd. in Longo 8). Ron Paige, former U.S. Secretary of Education, has even noted that today's student exhibits "neither an appropriate under-standing nor appreciation" of major historical movements in America, such as the civil rights movement. For example, according to a 2009 study conducted by the American Rev-olution Center, of 1,001 Americans surveyed, half believed the Civil War, Emancipation Proclamation, and War of 1812 happened before the American Revolution. One third did not know the right to a jury trial is in the Bill of Rights, yet 40 percent thought the right to vote was contained in these amendments.

Due to the neglect noted previously, which will be discussed in greater depth in Chap-ter II, by 1998 the American Political Science Association's Task Force on Civic Education noted that "current levels of political knowledge, political engagement, and political enthu-siasm are so low as to threaten the vitality and stability of democratic politics in the U.S.," foreshadowing President Carter's admonition nearly 15 years later. True to this admonish-ment, the Constitutional Rights Foundation's 2005 California Survey of Civic Education determined that only 47 percent of 12th graders agreed that "being actively involved in state and local issues is my responsibility." The following year, more than half of students taking the 2006 National Assessment of Educational Progress civics test failed, and only one in ten were as knowledgeable as they should have been. At that same time, on our nation's university and college campuses, "including Brown, Georgetown, and Yale, seniors knew less than freshmen about America's history, government, foreign affairs, and economy." Only about 15 percent of Americans aged 18 to 29 were attentive to political, international, and business news (National Assessment of Education Progress). Comparing these statistics to surveys targeting an older population, Martin Wattenberg asserted, "Regardless of whether the question concerned basic civics facts, identification of current political leaders, infor-mation about the presidential candidates, or knowledge of partisan control of Congress, the result was the same: young people were clearly less well-informed than the elderly" (qtd. in Campbell 15). Perhaps part of the blame for this diminution may fall upon "soft news" programming. Indeed, as Markus Prior wrote in the *American Journal of Political Science* in 2005, "Powerful evidence suggests that the enormous expansion of non-news programs has transformed some viewers into entertainment specialists, with negative consequences for their knowledge of political news" (qtd. in Campbell 20). Alarmingly, these statistics merely scratch the surface, as numerous assessments, surveys, and studies continually report evidence of decades of inattention to civic literacy standards within our nation's education infrastructure:

- Among students who demonstrate literacy advantages and who plan to attend college, only 56 percent expect to vote; among those students without literacy advantages and who do not plan to attend college, only 18.7 percent plan to vote (Democracy Prep— NYC 107).

- Only 22 percent of eligible Americans aged 18 to 29 voted in the 2010 midterm elections. In 2012, 80 percent were unaware of their state's voting registration requirements.

These statistics confirm a disturbing and disconcerting analysis: For 42 years, since 1972, voter turnout among youth (ages 18–24) has never reached 50 percent, with percentiles hovering in the 41–43 percent range even during presidential election years.

- Only 36 percent of college freshmen talk frequently about politics (LA Higher Education Research Institute).

- Only 24 percent of Latinos reference themselves as Americans (Pew Hispanic Center).

- Only 43 percent of eighth graders "appropriately" understand why citizens participated in the 1963 March on Washington.

- Only 28 percent of 12th graders can identify the social policy reflected by the picture of a sign "Colored Entrance" above the door of a theater.

The destructive nature of the lack of emphasis on civics education became especially evident in 2010, when a civics test administered by the federal government revealed two thirds of tested students scored below proficiency. Not even one-third could identify the historical purpose of the Declaration of Independence.

The federal government itself, perhaps due to inattention, ignorance, globalization, corruption, or political hashing, has contributed to the continuing decline in civic literacy. In 2011, Congress cut all federal funding for civic education, having provided only limited funding since the turn of the 21st century. And, in 2012, the "We the People" program initiated by Chairman Bruce Cole of the National Endowment for the Humanities (NEH)— a program founded in 2002 to fulfill the NEH's role in "celebrating American cultural achievement"—was discontinued and replaced by the program Bridging Cultures. (Cole's program included civic promotion in the form of three divisions: Landmarks of American History, Culture Workshop, and Bookshelf.) Cole noted, "The administration effectively assumed Americans have sufficient knowledge of their own culture to draw comparisons with others ... a faulty assumption, as numerous reports and tests have shown. If Americans are woefully ignorant of their own history and culture, how then can they be expected to sufficiently compare and understand other cultures? The NEH's changes in priorities do not bode well for its role in encouraging civic literacy" (Cole, qtd. in Feith 86). In fact, in a recent poll, participants believed that, on average, 27 percent of the U.S. budget is spent on foreign aid, when in reality that percentage is less than 1 percent.

Though fewer than half of eighth graders knew the purpose of the Bill of Rights, and only one in ten could correctly pick the definition of the system of checks and balances on the 2010 National Assessment of Educational Progress, administration of these exams (NAEP civics, U.S. history, and geography) has been indefinitely postponed for fourth and 12th graders. President Barack Obama's administration says this is due to a $6.8 million sequestration budget cut. The three exams will be replaced by a single, new test: Technology and Engineering Literacy. "Without these tests, advocates for a richer civic education will not have any kind of test to use as leverage to get more civic education in the classrooms," says John Hale, associate director at the Center for Civic Education. He continues, "Students must be prepared to think for themselves as independent citizens. Civics and government is as generative as math; we are not born as great democratic citizens. We aren't born knowing why everyone should have the right to political speech, even if it is intolerant speech" (Hale, qtd. in Center for Civics Education, preface).

Thus, a government "which has afforded Americans a degree of freedom and opportunity unparalleled in history" (Ross, qtd. in Feith 117) is effectively, due to a viewpoint which looks outward rather than inward, to private interest rather than public interest, impeding what was—and still can be—the world's most effective government. In doing so, it is producing, as noted by Nunn and Bennett, a complacent citizenry, a nation of bystanders rather than productive advocates. A study by Nina Eliasoph of ethnographic groups confirmed this complacency, as subjects were observed bringing a sudden stop to "ongoing talk among adults" when politically controversial topics were introduced, boding "poorly for democracy because if individuals keep views to themselves, they miss opportunities to learn from others and to reflect critically on their own views" (Youniss, qtd. in Campbell 75).

Another detrimental trend affecting civics education and literacy is the fact that young people, according to the Higher Education Research Institute, are increasingly "equating community service with civic service or political engagement." In truth, this apolitical notion of volunteerism does not consider community organization, civic knowledge (remaining aware of governmental processes and public affairs), political action, or public dialogue. Quantitative data indicates that 83.2 percent of college freshman volunteer occasionally during their senior year in high school and 70.6 percent on a weekly basis (indeed, colleges will rarely admit students without evidence of volunteer service). As a result of this honorable, yet flawed emphasis, America's youth "tend to think engagement with [the] political process is unimportant and irrelevant for change and that community service is a more effective way to solve public problems" (Boyte, qtd. in Feith 18). Harry Boyte, Founder of Public Achievement, reflects upon the weighted imbalance and disassociation between volunteerism and civic awareness, which "does not teach the political skills that are needed to work effectively toward solving society's problems: public judgment, the collaborative exercise of power, conflict resolution, negotiating, bargaining, and holding others accountable" (qtd. in Feith 18). Meira Levinson describes today's service work as "a weak, even eviscerated, conception of civic engagement" (qtd. in Campbell 300). Boyte argues, "We need bold, savvy, and above all political citizens and civic institutions if we are to tame a technological, manipulative state, to transform an increasingly materialistic and competitive culture, and to address effectively the mounting practical challenges of a turbulent and interconnected world" (Boyte, qtd. in Feith 20).

An emphasis on vocation and performance, rather than the traditional well-rounded approach to serving as a "productive citizen," is also taking root. Wendell Berry, advocate, writer, and environmental activist, has certainly chastised America's higher education model. At a 2007 commencement address, he observed, "The great and the would-be-great 'research universities' increasingly formed on the 'industrial model' no longer make even the pretense of preparing their students for responsible membership in a family, a community, or a polity" (Berry, qtd. in Feith 156), as evidenced by their rote, methodical testing practices, their neglect of civics education and assessment, and the presidentially mandated international focus of the National Endowment for the Humanities. The development of democratic citizens actually seems to be under attack, a dangerous consideration in the 21st century, "an epoch defined by profound debate over the state's authority in areas such as health care and the economy, and the propriety of U.S. efforts to combat Islamist radicalism on the world stage—with schools devoting remarkably little intellectual energy to questions of citizenship or the formation of democratic citizens" (Hess, qtd. in Feith xii). Hess believes, "A focus on academic performance, along with concerns about being branded controversial or intolerant, have in many places demoted talk of citizenship to assemblies, ceremonies, or the occasional social studies lesson. Although vocational citizenship fosters some essential social values, it often ignores other values that are crucial to civic health. These include such 'subversive' habits as questioning authority and searching for one's own truths.... Students must learn enough to be able to obtain and analyze the information that underlies our public debates" (Hess, qtd. in Feith xii).

President James Earl "Jimmy" Carter (1977–1981), the official presidential portrait by Herbert B. Abrams, 1982.

What is an American citizen's charge at a time when the U.S. Supreme Court asserts that corporations are citizens and the Voting Rights Act is no longer needed? What are our duties as American citizens at a time when the National Security Agency invades our privacy and collects our personal data? At a time when Congress increases the interest rates on student loans and shuts down our government on the basis of political whims and favors? At a moment when an American citizen can be detained without a right to trial? As John Dewey noted, "It is no disrespect to the founders of the nation to say that while they won freedom for themselves, they did not for their posterity. Every generation must fight for its own freedom, which with each generation will come in a new form" (Dewey, qtd. in Feith 331).

Perhaps the wisdom of the Founding Fathers and founding educators in our country will shed light on our need to return to the "true aim of democracy," defined by adult educator Harrison Elliott as "securing the active participation of every individual up to the limit of his capacity in the conduct of all his social, vocational, and political affairs" (Elliott, qtd. in Feith 11). David Campbell, director of the Rooney Center for the Study of American Democracy, points out that this definition requires the development of citizens adept in the following four areas:

- An understanding of the nation's political system

- A capacity for involvement in the political process

- Participation in public-spirited collective action

- Respect for the civil liberties of others

This writer asserts that the development of adept American citizens cannot be accomplished without enlightened, engaging, hands-on civics-based lessons, community involvement, and field experiences offered within and sponsored by our public school systems. The soul of liberty must continually be rekindled in students via civic instruction and discourse so that each generation, from one age to the next, may lay claim to the principles of the Declaration of Independence, in the words of Abraham Lincoln, "as though they were blood of the blood, and flesh of the flesh, of the men who wrote that declaration" (qtd. in Feith 177).

The Founding Fathers, especially Benjamin Rush, Thomas Jefferson, and Noah Webster, admonished that the principal purpose of education, the crucial mission of America's schools, is to form a productive, judicious, and civic-minded populace. First and foremost, students should grasp the magnitude of the agonizing sacrifices and hard-fought battles endured by America's founders. (John Adams proclaimed, "Posterity! You will never know how much it cost the present Generation to preserve your Freedom! I hope you will make good use of it. If you do not, I shall repent in Heaven, that I ever took half the Pains to preserve it.") These men were surrounded and oppressed by tyranny, and their contemporaries in Europe were experiencing all sorts of abuses of power, both by government and organized religion. Yet they rose to the occasion, largely due to their enlightened, rational, philosophical, and historically informed viewpoints. They realized such mindsets must be cultivated from generation to generation. For instance, Jefferson, upon the Revolutionary victory, noted, "Experience hath shewn, that under the best forms of government those entrusted with power have, in time, and by slow operations, perverted it into tyranny; and it is believed that the most effectual means of preventing this would be, to illuminate, as far as practicable, the minds of the people at large, and more especially to give them knowledge of those facts, which history exhibiteth, that, possessed thereby of the experience of other ages and countries, they may be enabled to know ambition under all its shapes, and prompt to exert their natural powers to defeat its purpose" (Jefferson, qtd. in Feith 2). Indeed, as noted in Feith (83–84), we must understand how tyranny was turned on its head by our Founders, then fall on our knees in gratitude for the freedoms and rights so easily taken for granted in the 21st century. As Bruce Cole, senior fellow at the Ethics and Public Policy Center, writes, "America was not a nation before the Revolution. It was a collection of thirteen little disparate seaboard colonies, each itself a miniature state. What united us, what forged the country, was the Revolution—the event that made the U.S. and the modern world. The Revolution led to another earthshaking event: a constitutional revolution that created a new system of government 'of the people, by the people, and for the people.' The Declaration of Independence provided its creed, and the Constitution outlined its form with genius. These documents enshrined the liberties and rights that Americans have exercised over the last two centuries. Knowledge of them is vital for the survival of our republic because we are united not by blood, land, or common religion, but by our founding principles— our 'ancient faith,' as Lincoln called it. Unlike other countries, whose origins are lost in the mist of time, the U.S. has a start date and a blueprint" (Cole, qtd. in Feith 83–84).

We the people should never lose sight of these principles. Indeed, we are charged with ensuring their survival. "Only by understanding our rich and complex history—with its proud and not so proud moments, with its great leaders and simple everyday heroes—can we strengthen what holds us together and create 'unum' from 'pluribus.' Without a solid understanding of history, our next generation of leaders will lack the critical understanding of what brought our nation to where it is now" (Cole, qtd. in Feith 77). Moreover, as Arthur Schlesinger, Jr., has noted, "History is to the nation as memory is to the individual. An individual without memory cannot distinguish between friends and enemies, nutrients and poisons, safe paths and perilous ones" (Schlesinger, qtd. in Feith 72).

Students must also understand the outline of our governmental system—that is, the three branches of government, the distribution of power between the three branches, the checks and balances associated with that structure, the manner by which bills become law, the Constitution and its amendments (Bill of Rights), and the means by which the Constitution may be amended. Benjamin Rush said, "The business of

Daguerreotype of Horace Mann (1796–1859), father of American public education; Whig and Free Soil congressman from Massachusetts, 1848–1853; president of Antioch College (Library of Congress).

education has acquired a new complexion by the independence of our country; the form of government we have assumed has created a new class of duties to every American. It is only by rendering knowledge universal that a republican form of government can be preserved in our country" (Rush, qtd. in Feith 171). A part-time educator himself, Rush supported "hands-on" learning and directed that each student "frequently attend the courts of justice, where he will have the best opportunities of acquiring habits of arranging and comparing his ideas by observing the secretion of truth in the examination of witnesses and where he will hear the laws of the state explained" (qtd. in Feith 4). In the mid–1800s, the father of modern-day education, Horace Mann, determined, "Citizens of a Republic must understand something of the true nature and functions of the government under which they live, for without education into the three branches of government and their roles and responsibilities, a republic is merely a 'political solecism'" (qtd. in Feith 5). Alan

Dershowitz echoes Rush and Mann's wisdom in the present day, noting, "No right is more fundamental to a democracy than the right to know your rights. No matter how powerful they may appear in print, rights are mere parchment pronouncements unless informed citizens are fully aware that they have them and are sufficiently knowledgeable to exercise them" (qtd. in Feith 27).

To preserve the Republic and the rights guaranteed in our Constitution (which is, as discussed previously, currently under attack), students must develop a sense of civic duty and the capacity to keep watch over elected officials, check the power of government, and force accountability. Otherwise, without an understanding of the "ideas and principles, heroes and villains, triumphs and catastrophes of the past, they judge the present on present concerns alone. When the time comes to exercise their freedoms, they think only, 'Is this good for me? Do I like it?… The outcome of civic illiteracy—the opposite of civic duty" (qtd. in Feith 167–168). In contrast, civic "health" fosters political participation, an understanding of political events, the habit of questioning authority and searching for one's own truth, and an analysis and investigation of information heard in public debates or read in commentaries, editorials, or media reporting. Our Founding Fathers well understood the urgency associated with the ever-present need to inculcate, generation by generation, a sense of civic responsibility and the need to avoid the trappings of a manipulative and/or power-hungry state. Noah Webster, the great compiler and teacher of the English language,

Portrait of Noah Webster, father of American scholarship and creator of *Webster's Dictionary* (1758–1843), by James Herring (1794–1867).

aptly conjectured, "If the citizens neglect their Duty and place unprincipled men in office, the government will soon be corrupted; laws will be made, not for the public good so much as for selfish or local purposes; corrupt or incompetent men will be appointed to execute the Laws; the public revenues will be squandered on unworthy men; and the rights of the citizen will be violated or disregarded." John Dewey, writing in the 1920s, reiterated Webster's concerns: "Education should cultivate the habit of suspended judgment, of skepticism, desire for evidence, appeal to observation rather than sentiment, discussion rather than bias, inquiry rather than conventional idealizations, for the purpose of constructing a 'Great Community'" (qtd. in Feith 141).

Likewise, a sense of empathy for the civic liberties of others must be instilled in America's students. Not only should America's Bill of Rights be inculcated, discussed, simulated, and demonstrated, but the United Nations' Universal Declaration of Human Rights should also be addressed. Empathy is defined as the ability to understand, relate to, and, in turn, affect the emotions and life experiences of a fellow human being. The development of empathy ensures humanity's survival: When behaving ethically as a result of our understanding of the other, we act and react to ensure the survival of the whole, rather than the part. Thus, as technology progresses in the form of nuclear weaponry, drones, and digital terrorism, if a democratic government is to endure and peace is to spread across the globe, students—our future leaders—must display the ability and willingness to uphold the ideals and values contained in the Bill of Rights for American citizens, as well as the universal rights of all global "neighbors." Accusations regarding U.S. violations of privacy rights, for example, in such powerful nations as Brazil and Germany, and the granting of asylum to such individuals as Edward Snowden by human rights–challenged nations such as China and Russia, would not be a three-minute news item to such an educated generation, but rather a call to demand ethical foreign relations accountability from our elected officials.

In summary, to quote Noah Webster, "It is an object of vast magnitude that systems of education should be adopted and pursued which may not only diffuse a knowledge of the sciences but may implant in the minds of the American youth the principles of virtue and of liberty and inspire them with just and liberal ideas of government and with an inviolable attachment to their own country." From an intellectual engagement with the principles and dilemmas of American democracy are born countrymen and countrywomen who welcome civic responsibility—citizens who take joy in discussion and debate, virtue and public service. "When the people are the primary decision makers for public matters, the virtue of the people is the virtue of the country. Civic virtue is the chief concern of a republic. And civic virtue cannot be cultivated without civic literacy. As the French enlightenment thinker Charles de Montesquieu argued, "The tyranny of a prince in an oligarchy is not so dangerous to the public welfare as the apathy of a citizen in a democracy. Citizens of a republic have not only political rights but duties as well, and our historical amnesia requires *immediate attention*. More than ever in our increasingly diverse nation, we need well-educated citizens with a shared knowledge of our history and a common understanding of our rights and responsibilities as Americans" (qtd. in Feith 84).

Chapter II

History and Current Status
of Civics Education in
Public Schools

"If a Nation expects to be ignorant and free, it expects what never was and never will be."—Thomas Jefferson

As mentioned in Chapter I, our Founding Fathers foresaw the need, and set the parameters, for generalized and uniform civics education based in standardized literacy and a common knowledge base. Well versed in world history and political philosophy, Jefferson, Adams, Madison, and Franklin all understood the precipitous nature of a Republic, many times citing the instructive example of ancient Rome, destroyed from within by unscrupulous Caesars and conflicting factions, in colonial times exemplified by "Germans against English, state against state, region against region, local interests against national interests" (Hirsch 4). They understood the newly created Republic required institutionalized education for all classes as an attempt to create "civic personalities," or loyal Americans who would subordinate their local interests to the common good and share common knowledge, virtues, ideals, and fervor for liberty and human rights and freedoms. Madison explained this aim: "As there is a degree of depravity in mankind which requires a certain degree of circumspection and distrust: So there are other qualities in human nature, which justify a certain portion of esteem and confidence. Republican government presupposes the existence of these qualities in a higher degree than any other form" (Hirsch 4–5). George Washington fretted over the fragile nature of the new government to the point he bequeathed a part of his estate to education for the purpose of spreading "systematic ideas through all parts of this rising Empire, thereby to do away with local attachments and State prejudices." Has American society forgotten the fragility of Republican forms of government in the midst of its current state of well-being and excess?

Benjamin Rush, writing the first essay on American education, suggested developing a common elementary curriculum that would produce "Republican machines." Jefferson, of course, believed all children—rich and poor, elite and non-elite—should receive an elementary education to ensure the welfare and longevity of the Republic. Moreover, he asserted, such a system would provide equal opportunity and the development of a "natural" aristocracy, rather than an artificial one, "to bring into action that mass of talents which

lies buried in poverty" and to eliminate the "artificial aristocracy
founded on wealth and birth, without either virtue or talents." He continued, "The natural aristocracy I
consider as the most precious gift of
nature for the instruction, the trusts,
and government of society.... The
artificial aristocracy is a mischievous
ingredient in government, and provision should be made to prevent its
ascendancy" (qtd. in Hirsch 87).

The idea of a common school,
in which "early grades were to have
a common core curriculum that
would foster patriotism, solidarity,
and civic peace as well as enable
effective commerce, law, and politics
in the public sphere" (Hirsch 6), was
legislated as early as 1825 by the state
of New York. The aim was not to
"make our children and youth either
partisans in politics, or sectarians in
religion; but [rather] to give them
education, intelligence, sound principles, good moral habits, and a free

Portrait of Founding Father and education proponent
Benjamin Rush (1746–1813), attributed to John Neagle
from a painting by Thomas Sully (Library of Congress).

and independent spirit; in short, to make them American free men [and women] and
American citizens, and to qualify them to judge and choose for themselves in matters of
politics, religion, and government.... [By such means] education will nourish most and the
peace and harmony of society be best preserved" (Hirsch 8). Indeed, Alexis de Tocqueville,
who toured America in 1831 and eventually wrote *Democracy in America*, noted, "In the
United States the general thrust of education is directed toward political life; in Europe its
main aim is to fit men for private life.... I concluded that both in America and in Europe
men are liable to the same failings and exposed to the same evils as among ourselves. But
upon examining the state of society more attentively, I speedily discovered that the Americans had made great and successful efforts to counteract these imperfections of human
nature and to correct the natural defects of democracy" (qtd. in Hirsch 9).

Early education leaders such as Noah Webster and Horace Mann reiterated that education's primary goal was to emphasize a child's future duty and responsibility as a citizen
of the Republic, which in turn would call upon the student's individualism and talents.
Without such education, they asserted, the Republic—an environment in which individual
development might be accomplished—would be forgotten. In fact, Mann defined public
schools as "nurseries of a free republic," whose role was to ensure "citizens of a Republic
... understand something of the true nature and functions of the government under which
they live" (qtd. in Feith 4). Classic educator and philosopher John Dewey "asserted that to

learn active citizenship, one must be an active citizen: civic education must be experiential" (Campbell 37).

Lincoln also espoused this philosophy. In an early speech (1838), "The Perpetuation of Our Political Institutions," he warned of the precarious nature of a Republic, admonishing parents, pastors, and schools to "teach the common American creed." He duly emphasized that without a "political religion," there would be no private freedom of religion or speech, nor freedom of person, equality, or civic peace. Lincoln conveyed the extreme urgency of instilling a sense of "devotional" patriotism in America's children as a means of preserving our ideals:

> Let reverence for the laws, be breathed by every American mother, to the lisping babe, that prattles on her lap—let it be taught in schools, in seminaries, and in colleges;—let it be written in Primmers, spelling books, and in Almanacs;—let it be preached from the pulpit, proclaimed in legislative halls, and enforced in Courts of Justice. And, in short, let it become the political religion of the nation; and let the old and the young, the rich and the poor, the grave and the gay, of all sexes and tongues, and colors and conditions, sacrifice unceasingly upon its altars [qtd. in Hirsch 68].

America's common, or public, schools rose to these ideals as proposed by America's early political and educational leaders. Their achievements supported the success of our Republic, a multicultural, yet peaceful melting pot that welcomed differing viewpoints and practices, all the while instilling a sense of loyalty and patriotism in its citizens, a "civil religion antagonistic to racism, sexism, jingoism, or injustice," and, remarkably, a society in which "When America falls short of its own ideals, idealistic Americans can become anti–American" (Hirsch 91).

Why, then, do such alarming 21st-century statistics, as delineated in Chapter I, indicate a present dearth of civics knowledge within American society? It seems the change may have begun in the early 20th century. By 1915, the U.S. Bureau of Education had embraced a "community civics" movement in which children were encouraged to understand community life, the benefits derived from it, and what the community has a right to expect in return, "cultivating ... the essential qualities and habits of good citizenship" (Levine qtd. in Campbell 40). There is nothing inherently wrong

John Dewey, father of progressive education, as a young scholar, University of Chicago, 1902 (photograph by Eva Watson Schütze [1867–1935]).

with this promotion, yet it seemed to lead to aseptic courses centered on "community welfare," rather than political participation and collective activism. As historian Julie Reuben notes, "Upright behavior, not political participation, became the defining mark of a good citizen.... The new community civics course was designed as a radical departure from earlier forms of citizenship education.... The most striking change was its new political philosophy inherent in its apolitical definition of citizenship.... Despite their desire to prepare students for their political responsibilities, the educators who designed civics programs could not envision both an active citizenry and a strong, active state" (qtd. in Campbell 50).

E.D. Hirsch, Jr., founder of Core Knowledge schools, and author of *The Making of America*, believes the problem began, on a macro level, in

Abraham Lincoln (1809–1865) and his son, Tad, February 9, 1864. Lincoln was a proponent of a "political religion" and "common American creed" (photographer Anthony Berger [1832–18??], Library of Congress).

the 1930s and 1940s when "child-centered pedagogy," rather than a core curriculum and teacher-centered classroom, was introduced into public education. He explains, "Twentieth-century Americans had become optimistic about America. They no longer worried that the very stability and peace of the Republic hinged on diffusing shared knowledge and preparing virtuous, loyal citizens who would subordinate private aims to the good of the whole. By the turn of the twentieth century, educators confidently believed that the public cohesion of the country was firm, and that schools should therefore concentrate on the growth and development of individual children by means of activities, without letting a lot of book learning get in the way. The needed knowledge would arise incidentally from immersion in concrete projects and 'hands-on learning' rather than from deadly 'rote memorization of mere facts'" (Hirsch 31). According to Hirsch, this philosophy was (and is) flawed in that it relied too heavily on "natural" development, rather than prescribed subject matter; did not contemplate the fragility of a Republican form of government, no matter the civic strength of a particular generation of citizens; and did not consider societal needs. George Counts of Columbia University warned that this movement "elaborated no theory of social welfare, unless it be that of anarchy or extreme individualism."

In contrast, one progressive movement during the Great Depression, now being heralded by modern visionaries, was that driven by sociologist George Counts, who dared educators to "build a new social order" without fear of the "bogeyman of indoctrination." Most demurred to conviction, but educators Ward, Hanifan, and Covello "managed a distinctive

middle ground, with the school serving as public problem solver, a community utility in studying and acting upon shared challenges. It mirrored practices in voluntary associations of various stripes, provided hands-on opportunities for civic participation, and actively linked community organizations representing distinct local interests" (Johanek 57).

Niemi notes that a considerable change in civics teaching occurred in the 1960s, with "Civics" and "Problems of Democracy" courses giving way to a more sterile course on governmental structure rather than courses that encouraged civic participation. Curricular changes accompanied this course change: a reduction in the number of social studies courses required to graduate from high school, the length of governmental courses changing from one year to a semester, increased availability of electives such as economics and psychology, and student-designed course selection. According to Niemi, "One cannot argue that changes in civics classes account for a post–1960s decline in political knowledge" (qtd. in Campbell 21).

Other philosophical movements followed: the "open" classroom of the 1970s, constructivism and critical thinking in the 1980s, and individual learning plans in the 1990s. Thus, for more than half a century, Hirsch contends, the American classroom has lacked a coherent curriculum of any sort, to include civics education, resulting in incompetent employees within the national economy, as well as ill-prepared participants in the American form of government. Examining the issue from a societal basis, former Justice of the U.S. Supreme Court, Sandra Day O'Connor, believes civics declined in our public schools due to disastrous political decisions: the Vietnam War, the Watergate scandal, and No Child Left Behind.

Turning to a pedagogical focus, Jason Ross of the Bill of Rights Institute identifies three specific impediments to the delivery of broad-based instruction in civic principles: poorly conceived state requirements, a mindset within the social studies discipline that emphasizes globalism and multiculturalism rather than democracy and constitutional government, and the inability of civics educators to receive adequate sup-

Sandra Day O'Connor (1930–), former justice of the Supreme Court; founder of iCivics; honoree of civics education act in the state of Florida (Justice Sandra Day O'Connor Civics Education Act CS/HB 105) (Library of Congress).

plemental training. Other points of "blame" include the Fordham Foundation's criticisms, as reiterated in the 2003 study, *Where Did Social Studies Go Wrong?*, which chastised the educational establishment for "embracing multiculturalism and for tolerating poorly trained teachers, ineffective teaching methods, and weak curriculum materials" (Feith 72). A similar study by the Fordham Foundation in 2007, confirming Ross's beliefs, determined that U.S. civics standards "run the gamut from impressively comprehensive to uselessly vapid" (Feith 75). Likewise, the Bradley Commission on History in Schools faulted textbooks "overstuffed with facts, distracting features, and irrelevant graphics" (Feith 72). Harvard University's David Campbell, conversely, believes the fault lies in the propensity for "lip service," in which all agree civics education is important, yet it is neglected in practice, receiving "little sustained attention from education reformers, policymakers, teachers' union, and so on" (Campbell 5). A survey of administrators by the Center for Education Policy revealed their opinion as well: Social studies and civics receive little attention due to testing pressure in other fields, with Secretary of Education Duncan citing this survey as a troubling indication of a narrowed curriculum (Campbell 40). Finally, in 2011, Charles N. Quigley, director of the Center for Civics Education, told reporters from the *New York Times*, "During the past decade or so, educational policy and practice appear to have focused more and more upon developing the worker at the expense of developing the citizen" (qtd. in Campbell 32).

On a micro level, the points discussed previously are confirmed by statistics compiled from studies, examinations, and observations conducted in, or about, America's classrooms:

- In North Carolina, U.S. history standards force teachers to begin social studies instruction on the period 1790–1820 with only one competency goal identified for this entire 30 years of strategic U.S. development, and a total neglect and inattention to studies from the Revolutionary period.

- Forty states permit students to graduate with just one semester of U.S. government or civics instruction. The remaining ten states do not require even one course, leaving the assessment to local decisions, a single demonstration of proficiency, or less than one semester of coursework.

- Civics education is pushed into the corner due to standardized testing, despite the fact that 40 state constitutions mention the importance of students' civic literacy and 13 cite civic education as the primary purpose of education.

- The Center for Civics Education determined that 50 percent of high school government teachers could not adequately explain key concepts such as popular sovereignty, habeas corpus, judicial review, federalism, and checks and balances. Only ten states require civics instructors be certified in the subject area.

- Only eight states conduct mandatory civics exams. Of these eight, only two require the test be passed to graduate high school: Ohio and Virginia. All of these tests are multiple choice rather than inquisitive short answer, essay, or project-based assessments.

- Administrators, professors, and students have too few incentives to pursue rigorous civic learning. In the current climate, parents and students tend to seek a concrete monetary payoff after graduation—a focus on landing jobs and paying bills rather than on supporting the Bill of Rights.

- One fourth of teachers surveyed thought parents would object if they covered politics in a government or civics class, and only 38 percent thought their district would give them strong support.

- Of 100 universities polled in 2009 by the American Council of Trustees and Alumni, only 11 required students to take a U.S. history or government course, confirming "the decades long slide of liberal education into pre-professional and vocational training."

Given these facts, there is little wonder that the statistics enumerated in Chapter I have been recorded, reflecting danger signals and corroborating President Carter's statement as quoted in this book's opening paragraph. Effectively, U.S. public schools, which were traditionally a bulwark of civility, are now committing civic malpractice, cheating students of their future freedoms. Yet, the story of America remains unfinished, as individuals, newspapers, nonprofit and governmental organizations, and institutions continue to publish factual information regarding the status of civic literacy among American citizens. Thus, educators and public policy experts across the country are taking note, diligently addressing civic learning needs, effecting change, and demanding reform and rejuvenation of civics education learning.

Chapter III

Anticipated 21st Century Progression

"We cannot be said to live in a true democracy if individuals or members of groups systematically possess unequal civic and political power, if some votes and voices count more or less than others, or if some stand either above or below the law.... Without civic knowledge, skills, identity, and propensity toward engagement, some students are essentially disenfranchised and disempowered. Civic learning opportunities are thus essential for promoting civic equity as a democratic ideal."

—Guardian of Democracy:
The Civic Mission of Schools
(Campaign for Civic Mission of Schools)

Civics education in the second decade of the 21st century is somewhat modeled after national standards written for the purpose of fulfilling Goals 3 and 6 of the Educate America Act of 1994:

Goal 3: Student Achievement and Citizenship

By the year 2000, all students will leave grades 4, 8, and 12 having demonstrated competency over challenging subject matter including ... civics and government ... so that they may be prepared for responsible citizenship, further learning, and productive employment.

All students will be involved in activities that promote and demonstrate ... good citizenship, community service, and personal responsibility.

Goal 6: Adult Literacy and Lifelong Learning

By the year 2000, every adult American will be literate and will possess the knowledge and skill necessary to ... exercise the rights and responsibilities of citizenship.

These national standards serve as an example for state curricula and are voluntary, intended to "help schools develop competent and responsible citizens who possess a reasoned commitment to the fundamental values and principles that are essential to the preservation and improvement of American constitutional democracy" (NCCE, Preface). The standards consider K–4, 5–8, and 9–12 leveled learning. Basic questions for each leveled set include:

- What is government, and what should it do?

- How do we define civic life, politics, and government?

- What are the basic values and principles of American democracy?

- How does the government established by the Constitution embody the purposes, values, and principles of American democracy?

- What is the relationship of the United States to other nations and to world affairs?

- What are the roles of the citizen in American democracy?

A more recent, authoritative development is the introduction of the National Council for Social Studies National Standards (2010). These standards are organized around thematic strands, two of which are conducive to civics education: (1) power, authority, and governance; and (2) civic ideals and practices.

For the first strand, students are asked to learn the foundations of American political

PREROGATIVES DEFEAT or LIBERTIES TRIUMPH

A political cartoon ("Prerogatives Defeat or Liberties Triumph") published in London, 1780, portraying the "Power, Authority, and Governance" abolished as a result of the victory accomplished during the American Revolution (Library of Congress).

thought, varying power, authority, and governance structures; the evolving implementation of these structures in contemporary times; and the manner in which others establish order and resolve conflicts across the globe. Essential questions associated with this strand include the following: What are the purposes and functions of government? Under which circumstances is the exercise of political power legitimate? What are the proper scope and limits of authority? How are individual rights protected and challenged within the context of majority rule? Which conflicts exist among fundamental principles and values of constitutional democracy? What are the rights and responsibilities of citizens in a constitutional democracy?

Teachers concentrating on the second strand should deliver content on the ideals, principles, and practices of citizenship in a democratic republic; the historical documents that articulate such ideals; the basic freedoms and rights emerging within the rule of law; the manner in which governmental institutions and private organizations support republican practices and principles; and the ways these ideals have been implemented across time and within differing societies. Essential questions are as follows: What are the democratic ideals and practices of a constitutional democracy? What is the balance between rights and responsibilities? What is civic participation? How do citizens become involved? What is the role of the citizen in the community and the nation, and as a member of the world community?

While answering these questions, students will explore how individuals and institutions interact. They will also recognize and respect different points of view, learning by experience how to participate in community service and political activities as a means of influencing public policy.

Together with 14 other civic-minded organizations, as well as scholars from across America, the National Council of Social Studies also developed the College, Career, and Civic Life (C3) Framework for Social Studies State Standards, the purpose of which is to prepare students not only for higher education and economically sound occupations, but also for civic life, or a person's ability to recognize changing physical and governmental environments; read, think, write, and discuss deeply; and act in ways that promote the common good. As the framework reads, "Now more than ever, students need the intellectual power to recognize societal problems; ask good questions and develop robust investigations into them; consider possible solutions and consequences; separate evidence-based claims from parochial opinions; and communicate and act upon what they learn. And most importantly, they must possess the capability and commitment to repeat that process as long as is necessary. Young people need strong tools for, and methods of, clear and disciplined thinking in order to traverse successfully the worlds of college, career, and civic life" (Framework 6).

The compelling question in the framework is this: What does liberty look like (within the disciplines of civics, geography, history, and economics)? Productive civic engagement, civic virtue, and the ability to deliberate are emphasized. Fifty-five specific indicators of excellence are divided among three broad subject areas:

- *Civics and Political Institutions*: The understanding of important institutions within society and the principles they reflect, requiring a mastery of knowledge in association with law, politics, and government.

What does liberty look like? "Liberty Enlightening the World," published in New York, 1884, with the caption "The colossal statue by Bartholid. Presented by the French People to America. As it will appear on its pedestal on Bedloes Island in New York Harbor" (Library of Congress).

- *Participation and Deliberation*: The application of civic virtues of democratic principles, such as the principles that guide the three branches of government (consent of the governed, limited government, legitimate authority, federalism, and separation of powers), the virtues of a citizen (honesty, respect for others, cooperation, and attention to multiple perspectives), and overarching values (liberty, freedom, equality, respect for individual rights, deliberation of issues and political concerns).

- *Process, Rules, and Laws*: A conceptualization of the political system and the rules, processes, and laws by which they work, along with a foray into working within such systems for the purpose of addressing public problems (civic action).

States, on paper at least, have utilized varying portions of these standards as a guide in some instances. For example, at the time of this book's publication, the theme of power, authority, and civics/government was included in all 50 states' and the District of Columbia's social studies standards. The theme of civic ideals and practices is found in every state's standards except Missouri. Forty states require at least one course in American government or civics, yet only nine require students to pass a standardized social studies test to graduate from high school. Eight states have statewide, standardized tests, yet only three such states test specifically in civics/American government. Also, all states have shifted to multiple-choice testing, rather than performance assessments, with the exception of Tennessee. That state recently passed Public Chapter 1036, a progressive piece of legislation that requires civics-based assessments once in grades 4–8 and again in grades 9–12. The assessment is considered "student influenced," and based upon an inquiry process that results in carefully designed products and tasks which determine if students can "demonstrate understanding and relevance of public policy, the structure of federal, state, and local governments, and both the Tennessee and United States Constitutions." Also, in 2014–2015, as a result of Florida's Sandra Day O'Connor Civics Education Act, sixth-grade students will be required to pass a state-mandated civics assessment based on civics education content in language arts/reading delivery, a one-semester civics course taught in sixth grade, and a minimum passing score in the class, which will also constitute 30 percent of the final grade. Sixth-grade students will also be required to pass the test before achieving promotion from middle school.

Obviously, while coursework is "on the books" in most states, assessments in civics and American government are sorely lacking, placing civics education (defined by David Campbell, political scientist at Harvard University, as "the knowledge, skills, attitudes, and experience to prepare someone to be an active, informed participant in democratic life" (1) on a type of back-burner. As a result, as the Center for Information and Research on Civic Learning and Engagement (CIRCLE) states, and as we learned in Chapter I, "current results are unacceptable, for only a quarter of young people reach 'proficient' on the NAEP Civics Assessment, and white, wealthy students are four to six times as likely as Hispanic or Black students from low-income households to exceed that level. Additionally, current policies do not have a significant effect and are not sufficient" (CIRCLE, Civics Education Quick Facts).

Due to the "unacceptable"—and, as we realized in earlier chapters, democracy-diminishing—nature of today's civics education, what are progressive experts recommending as solutions to circumvent a negative phenomenon, such as the *Wandervogel* movement

Political cartoon published in New York, 1883, captioned "An Appalling Attempt to Muzzle the Watch-Dog of Science," a statement about the First Amendment right to free speech (Friedrich Graetz, artist [1840–1913], Library of Congress).

in Germany? (Note: Historian Walter Laqueur explains that the *Wandervogel* movement among Germany's youth in 1898–1930 emphasized everything except civics: poetry, a return to nature, artistic productions, and German history; it failed to educate young people "toward participation in public affairs, and it is in this respect the *Wandervogel* completely failed. They did not prepare their members for active citizenship" [qtd. in Campbell 73]. Alarmingly, the *Wandervogel* movement eventually became the foundation of the Hitler Youth.)

First, a discussion of basic paradigms and infrastructure is in order. The mindset of all stakeholders must be figuratively reset, to remember the admonishments of our forefathers as provided in Chapter II. As E.D. Hirsch relates, "Cultivating an understanding of shared history, ideas and cultural norms is vital to ensuring that all Americans can participate fully in American life" (qtd. in Feith 91). We must also act upon the words of Reed Larson: "The economic and political world that youth are now entering demands strategic skills that are acquired when youth are given tactical challenges to solve and are supplied with adult support" (qtd. in Campbell 90). Such skills include the ability to actively participate in the political process. To quote Youniss, "Civic knowledge is not and should not be separated from democratic practices anymore than scientific knowledge needs to be separated from application to agriculture or industry. When political matters are integrated with classroom learning, students can develop identities as knowledgeable and capable citizens" (qtd. in Campbell 70). Accordingly, for educators to heed the call to "wake up" students to our current society of disparity (i.e., privacy and autonomy versus "war on terror" protocols, or equality versus the growing economic gap between the haves and the have-nots), they must become aware of and heed German educator Wolfgang Edelstein's admonition to create civics curricula that will "cultivate practices that evoke a sense of social responsibility, awaken a quest to understand policy, and develop a passion for equality" (qtd. in Campbell 72). In other words, as Saavedra notes, "To actually engage as citizens, students need to learn not only *about* citizenship, but also *how* to engage as citizens. That is, they need to learn and practice the skills necessary for citizenship" (qtd. in Campbell 111).

In summary, the paradigm shift must include a generalized societal reintroduction of the magnitude and significance of the American Revolution, the Constitution, and the Bill of Rights, as well as the *right and duty* of every citizen to speak freely, share ideas and viewpoints, debate issues, and advocate for justice, equality, and individual rights. Civics education must be recognized as the facilitator of such a productive and active citizenry, as well as the means by which we rebuild and maintain our republic and a working democracy. In accordance with this recognition, civics courses must be assessed in a manner similar to the progressive examples taking root in the states of Tennessee and Florida; in other words, they must be product/task/issue resolution based (active learning). With this end (the education of civically literate individuals) and these assessments in mind, as Peter Levine notes, curricula must contemplate standards "relevant to civil society as the main criterion of inclusion" (qtd. in Campbell 38), introducing standards that lend themselves to (1) experiential learning; (2) high levels of discussion and debate; (3) civic action; (4) teacher and student exploration; (5) liberal studies; and (6) mandatory as well as nonmandatory topics.

Prior to World War II, such civics learning was the norm, and courses were designed to support and facilitate student government, school newspapers, civics-oriented service projects, reading and debating current issues, and active engagement. As Levinson describes, "High quality civic education is dynamic, responsive to the present, committed to equity, capable of moving among virtual and offline worlds, attentive to identity and difference, and supportive of student action" (qtd. in Campbell 140). Such standards will, in turn, support an education that will help citizens to maintain the Republic and its associations, networks, viability and flexibility, and structure.

The approach to the standards should also focus on the Constitution and other founding documents, emphasizing the principles of self-government and governance rather than dry facts. Indeed, "without a solid grounding in the debates of the founding era, which represented the modern world's first major experiment in self-government, students are ill-prepared to understand the challenges of preserving individual liberty under the rule of law" (Ross, qtd. in Feith 122).

Research and scholarship confirm the need for this shift. Quigley, for example, found students who develop an interest in politics and a desire to participate in public affairs do so before reaching college age. Developmental and communication sciences research has shown the "efficacy of discussion for learning," defining the process by which deep understanding, obtained in open discussion, leads to informed views and appropriate civil discourse (feedback, meeting opposing viewpoints, correction or enrichment, reconsideration, expression, persuasion, debate). Campbell, Hess, McDevitt, and Kiousis revealed moderated discussions of current events increase student interest in both civic knowledge and public policy (politics). Levine points to evidence that education for civic empowerment leads to higher academic achievement, and Thomas and McFarland's studies determined that extracurricular activities (especially participation in drama and the performing arts) increase the likelihood of voting (Campbell 82). The 2010 NAEP scores also suggest that economically disadvantaged students' civic knowledge grows in open-discussion classrooms. Finally, according to a Harvard study, "The variables most closely related to current participation (political) are those that measure the activity of respondents as a high school student—in particular, involvement in high school government, but also involvement in other clubs and activities" (Campbell 87).

Based in such a reinstated and evolving paradigm, a supportive infrastructure must be rebuilt. First, scholars concur that at the federal level civic education must no longer be housed as a sub-office within the Department of Education's Office of Safe and Drug Free Schools, but rather must be afforded its own office and an empowered director who will cooperate with other federal and private agencies, such as the Corporation for National and Community Service, the Corporation for Public Broadcasting, and the National Park Service. Also, as Congress cut all funding for civics education in 2011, prior to reserving funding for "a program that provided the same set of textbooks to some students every year," federal funding needs to be reinstituted to "allocate funds on a highly competitive basis to school districts or organizations that propose to achieve substantial increases in students' civic skills, knowledge, and values through innovative approaches that could be rigorously tested and then widely imitated if they worked" (Levine, qtd. in Feith 211).

On the state and local levels, civic educators, curriculum specialists, and politicians must "think of themselves as the stewards of America's future civil society" (qtd. in Campbell 47). Civics education must become the province of all, "not a conversation only for the ivory tower or within the confines of the Washington Beltway. Civics education must be discussed in school board meetings and PTA luncheons, in living rooms and chat rooms" (Campbell 10).

Second, schools should once again be thought of as community centers, welcoming and facilitating civics education opportunities for the community as a whole. In fact, William Damon, author of *Making Good Citizens: Education and Civil Society,* wrote in 2001, "A positive emotional attachment to a particular community is a necessary condition for sustained civic engagement in that community" (qtd. in Feith 122). The *ethos* of the school environment (i.e., shared and encouraged norms) should also encourage an expectation of public engagement and personal contributions to our collective social and governmental capital. (In Campbell's *Why We Vote: How Schools and Communities Shape Our Civic Life,* details emerge as to how adolescents attending high schools with a strong civics *ethos* continued exhibiting high levels of civics engagement 15 years after graduation. As Campbell noted, "The school *ethos* ... has more long-term impact on civic engagement than an individual's personal sense of civic duty as an adolescent" [Campbell 300]).

Third, part of this *ethos* should consider students as "co-citizens," who are involved in school and student government associations as well as contributors and advocates for municipal policy. Students should be learning the governmental process via direct participation in the student government process—campaigning, assuming positions, fulfilling responsibilities of the position, and proposing and enacting new policies. (For example, at one high school in New Haven, Connecticut, contention and confrontational tactics are encouraged, for, as Alderman Justin Elicker notes, "These kids who cause problems are the ones who actually care. They should have input into their educational system" [qtd. in Campbell 91]. Another school in Hampton, Virginia, has a 20-year history of students being involved in the *actual construction* of municipal policy). Fourth, assessments should not only test a student's knowledge of civic principles and facts, but also demonstrate the student's ability for civic action (as noted in the Tennessee and Florida examples provided in Chapter II). Examples include community action projects; ongoing issue debates; civics-based theater; writing letters, essays, and opinion pieces to advocate for a cause; and computer simulations of community activism or legislative offices. Also, the National Assessment of Educational Progress in civics should be reinstituted, revamped, and, preferably, tied to English/language arts assessments for the purpose of receiving public recognition, awareness, and support.

Fifth, teachers themselves must be afforded professional development opportunities based in open and explorative classrooms, steeped in current events as they apply to a civics-rich knowledge base. In other words, teachers must understand America's founding era and the documents associated with it if they are to apply their principles and ideals to the discussion of current issue resolutions. As Jason Ross indicates, "We will continue to falter until educators can deepen their knowledge—and break free from teaching strategies, curriculum frameworks, and testing schemes that marginalize knowledge of the founding era and its principles" (qtd. in Feith 125). Damon reiterates, "For full participatory citizenship in a democratic society, a student needs to develop a love for the particular society, including its historical legacy and cultural traditions" (qtd. in Feith 122). Yet, blind faith in that legacy must not take hold, either, for our Founders would have encouraged constructive criticism and periodic improvements in our government structure. As Damon states, "The capacity for constructive criticism is an essential requirement for civic engagement in a democratic society, but in the course of intellectual development, this capacity must build upon a prior sympathetic understanding of that which is being criticized" (qtd.

It would be another 20 years from the time this poster for a New York drama, written by Charles Hale Hoyt, was displayed before women were allowed to "participate" and vote in general elections within the United States (U.S. Printing Office, 1898, Library of Congress).

in Feith 122). In summary, today's standards should foster deeply held understandings of the Constitution, the wisdom of our Founding Fathers, and ways to apply these precepts and concepts to daily events and current issues (via debate and an exchange of ideas).

Finally, materials must be closely examined. Textbook use should be minimal, being replaced by attention to the founding primary documents, online and print newspapers detailing current issues, engaging children's and young adult trade material, carefully researched opposing viewpoint articles such as are published by *Congressional Quarterly* or *Close Up*, foreign newspapers reporting news from the United States, C-SPAN materials, simulation sites (such as the League of Nations, Kids Voting USA, or Model UN), readings for mock trials (such as the Boston-based *Discovering Justice*), organized trips to state and national monuments and parks, and visits from community leaders and/or elected officials involved in government or civic advocacy. These materials can be acquired at one third to one half of the cost of traditional textbooks and have proved more effective in equipping students to practice civic skills and develop a propensity for civic action and participation. As Saavedra notes, "Textbook-based civics education on its own is not sufficient. Given the inherently static nature of hard-copy print, textbooks are not well equipped to help students practice their civic skills or to help them understand the value of civic participation in a meaningful way. Nor is textbook-based civic education an ideal way for students to learn to contextualize factual information about citizenship in current or local settings. Further, textbook-based civics education is the status quo, and current measurements of students' levels of civic knowledge and engagement indicate that the status quo has resulted in less-than-satisfactory civic outputs among U.S. youth" (qtd. in Campbell 110).

On a micro level, once infrastructure is established, how might 21st-century classroom practices improve? To teach the corrected standards mentioned previously, appropriate methods will include forays into experiential civics education: classroom discussion, student government participation, the development of intentional civics spaces, simulations (including mock elections and mock trials), group presentations, debates, letter and argumentative (persuasive) writing, journaling, gaming, digital civic media production, current events lessons, media literacy curricula, and service learning. Most scholars believe a rich civics curricula will develop not only exceptional readers, but also improve academic achievement. The entire process might be described within the 2011 Action Civics Declaration, which recommended "an authentic, experiential approach in which students address problems through real-world experiences that apply to their lives ... an iterative process comprised of issue identification, research, constituency building, action, and reflection" (Campbell 39). Basically, this listing might be narrowed to three broad practices: civics-based discussion and debate, action, and service.

First, regarding discussion, classrooms should be open to dialogue and an exchange of ideas relative to current issues, as applied to the rule of law, as well as the efficiency and soundness of America's original governmental structure, with students being free to agree or disagree about political and social issues. Students should also learn to ponder feedback, make connections with their own understandings and viewpoints, and, eventually, broaden their perspective and exhibit open-mindedness. Niemi notes, "Students should learn what issues are currently controversial, why they are controversial, what alternative proposals have been made for dealing with them, who is in favor and who is opposed to the various alternatives (including both individual and party positions), and so on. Having an eighth-grade (or ninth- or tenth-grade) civics class is not enough. What is required is a class in which students are asked to follow what is going on in the outside world. It means asking fourteen-year-olds to pay attention to what is happening in politics, to learn some of the language used in discussing political matters, and to get a grasp of the political actors and issues involved" (qtd. in Campbell 35).

Of course, engaging discussions lead to higher rates of participation among students and enhance their cognitive abilities, debate tactics, and conversational improvisation, while also helping the learners understand and internalize civil discourse (the resolution of disagreement, debate, viewpoints, and ideas within governmental and political forums). In fact, findings from the National Assessment of Educational Progress (NAEP) indicated classrooms bereft of discussion (never or rarely used) were not as successful as their counterparts, even in economically disadvantaged areas. Eighth-grade students in classes with no discussion scored 116, whereas their counterpart students in classes in which almost daily discussion occurred scored 146—a "highly significant" differential. Similarly, 12th-grade classes with no discussion scored 112 versus 138 for classes exposed to daily discussion. David Campbell's studies also report students in classrooms that encouraged expression "scored higher on tests of civic knowledge and appreciated conflict more than did students from less-open classrooms. Degree of openness contributed more to these measures than did sheer number of civics courses. And students from lower socioeconomic groups benefited from openness as much as their better-off peers" (Youniss, qtd. in Campbell 110).

"Rancorous debate," such as that engaged in by the creators of the U.S. Constitution (Madison, Mason, and Henry), in which differences are expressed and persuasion is utilized in public forums, no doubt helps students understand the reality of politics, encourages expression in a civil manner, raises civic awareness, confirms and substantiates ideas and critical thinking, and contributes to an intellectual exchange. Studies within communication sciences confirm debate encourages the cognitive process in which "the exchange of ideas leads to deeper understanding of one's own position and the sharing of perspectives" (Campbell 105). "Learning to act democratically, then, requires citizens not only to learn and apply deliberative decision making processes but also to navigate through the contradictions and tensions of democracy" (Kranich 79).

Civic action in today's schools may take many forms. One activity recommended by most of today's experts is participation in student government, allowing young people to "build experience with voting, campaigning, forming coalitions, negotiating, and dealing with institutional structure" (Youniss, qtd. in Campbell 120). Unfortunately, many socioeconomically challenged schools do not have student governments. Conversely, those who do brave challenges such as discipline, high-stakes testing, harassment, and inattentive administration in an adept and creative fashion, creating citizens who rise above their situation. These students, perhaps unconsciously, are contributing to equitable voting practices within our country. Indeed, as the Campaign for the Civic Mission of Schools relates, "We cannot be said to live in a true democracy if individuals or members of groups systematically possess unequal civic and political power, if some votes and voices count more or less than others, of if some stand either above or below the law.... Without civic knowledge, skills, identity, and propensity toward engagement, some students are essentially disenfranchised and disempowered. Civic learning opportunities are thus essential for promoting civic equity as a democratic ideal" (qtd. in Campbell 107).

Action may also be simulated with the use of mock trials, mock voting, or Congressional deliberation, as well as project citizen programs in which students learn how local and state governments operate by identifying a problem within the community, choosing one to study in depth, discussing the problem with peers, identifying experts, gathering reliable information, synthesizing findings, developing a public policy, and presenting the same to community stakeholders. An example is the Chicago Public School Mikva Challenge, in which policymaking, activism, and election prongs help students (1) create and enact policies, (2) learn how to vote as an educated citizen, and (3) ask questions of their local officials and require accountability. For example, one policymaking initiative by the program, the "Out-of-School Time" Council, worked with city government closely, to the extent that an out-of-school bill was passed in Chicago in 2010 which increased students' ability to find and obtain after-school and summer jobs.

Finally, service learning projects must find the connection to public policy. As Youniss explains, "Not just any service stimulates civic engagement. Rather the kind of service is what counts" (qtd. in Campbell 150). At this point in time, only 5 percent of service completed by students pertains to policy or political issues, though two thirds of high school seniors report having participated in service work in the past year. The activities are obviously apolitical, such as collecting clothes and food, cleaning parks, coaching, tutoring, and helping neighbors. These works are not adequate to civic education: "It is one thing to have students serve meals at a soup kitchen but a different matter to focus them on the causes of hunger and homelessness, which, in our own research, led students to question political priorities and policies regarding affordable housing, job training, drug rehabilitation, provision of mental health services, and the like" (Youniss, qtd. in Campbell 2102). The key to quality civic education service-oriented curricula is finding those governmental agencies, nonprofit organizations, and religious institutions that will expose the student to the sponsor's purpose (whether human dignity, basic human rights, or social justice), instituting service programming with these providers that will imbue the service with "a civic and political meaning at a time when young people are exploring their civic identities…. The identity process [is] probably helped along when students meet political controversy in the public arena" (Youniss, qtd. in Campbell 2125). Examples include science-in-public-policy projects, which might include, according to Youniss, promoting safety on rural roads, educating the public about mercury in cosmetics, or seeking to reduce water usage by agribusiness strawberry growers.

As we see, the 21st-century vision of standard civics education is simply adhering to Franklin's admonishment to "keep the Republic," and is a return to and revamping of 19th- and early 20th-century curriculum philosophies and practices. The road ahead will not be easy, as we have seen. To use a metaphor, a mountain of kudzu must be clear-cut or "bush-hogged." In civics education, these efforts must include elimination of the insistence upon dry, textbook-based curricula; inadequate assessments and Constitution-light standards; inactive, rather than active, learning; and negligence, defunding, and lack of understanding at the federal, state, and local levels. As Saavgard notes, "Structural support for dynamic civic education strategies is necessary if teachers are to overcome the coverage challenge. This focus will require multi-pronged, top-down efforts from teachers, administrators, parents, funding sources, and community organizations. It also requires that civic education providers … persist in building the sorts of political alliances that will strengthen their footholds in communities and schools" (qtd. in Campbell 2584). As Levine states, the reform will constitute a marathon, not a sprint, and "cannot be solved with a single intervention but requires constant attention to the quality of the curriculum, pedagogy, teacher preparation and assessment. Rather than expect any state or national reform to solve the civic education problem, *Americans* [emphasis added] should change the way that the government continuously addresses civics" (qtd. in Campbell 915).

Chapter IV

Traditional Role of School
and Public Libraries in
Civics Education

*"Libraries are ... essential to the functioning of a demo-
cratic society.... Libraries are the great symbols of the freedom of the mind."*—Franklin D. Roosevelt

The earliest example of a library that encouraged civic thought in America, "an individual's self-improvement and search for truth," was Benjamin Franklin's Junto (1728),
reopened as the Philadelphia Library Company (1731). Today considered the start of the
"social" library, the idea did not remain solely popular within circles of white male aristo-
crats, for "British Americans of the 1700s believed education should not be exclusively for
the wealthy or the clergy.... Later in the century, it was estimated that 90 percent of white
New England women and virtually all white males could read and write" (Murray 1754).
As the U.S. population began migrating westward, the idea became the province of all sorts
of groups and clubs: the YMCA, "ladies" clubs, mechanics, shop owners, and general interest
seekers. Known as organizations which appealed to one's "better angels," encouraging lively
discussions about the issues of the time and self-development, anyone who could pay the
moderate fee associated with purchasing and circulation could reap the benefits of these
emerging libraries. Outside of home and work, the social libraries became the "third place,"
one in which time was spent productively "conversing with friends, developing a sense of
community, and reading newspapers and magazines" (Arenson, qtd. in Rubin 48). As Rubin
notes, "By 1876, there were more than 10,000 libraries of over eighty different types: agricultural libraries, antiquarian society libraries, art society libraries, church libraries, county
libraries, government libraries, historical society libraries, hotel reading rooms, ladies'
libraries, law libraries, mechanics' libraries, medical libraries, prison libraries, public
libraries, railroad libraries, saloon reading rooms, scientific and engineering libraries,
sewing circle libraries, state libraries, university libraries, and YMCA libraries" (Rubin 46).
Within these libraries, titles on the "art of thinking" stood side by side with the works of
John Locke, the political philosopher. Consequently, as early as 1815, Jesse Torrey spoke for
"a cause consecrated by religion and enjoined by patriotism, the universal dissemination
of knowledge and virtue by means of free public libraries" (qtd. in Ditzion 58). (Torrey,

who established a free juvenile library in New Lebanon, New York, in 1804, wrote *The Intellectual Torch*, subtitled "Developing an Original, Economical, and Expeditious Plan for the Universal Dissemination of Knowledge and Virtue by Means of Free Public Libraries.") The movement to educate those moving into cities grew, with a focus on literacy and mandatory public education, and with the movement the idea that "democracy ... required educated, informed citizens" (Murray 2073).

Behind this trend came the advent of circulating (or rental) libraries, which loaned titles for a fee. They, too, contributed to the idea of equalitarianism: they were the first to serve women and to provide delivery to outlying areas. Numbers increased to the point America sported more libraries than England. Ditzion noted, "From the testimony presented in 1849 to the Select Committee (House of Commons) on Public Libraries, it would seem evident that our social libraries, school-district libraries, our mechanics' and mercantile institutions became far more integral a part of American popular culture than did their counterparts abroad. This difference in the reception given to the public library idea and its embodiment in a variety of agencies is obviously attributable to the advanced state of literacy and popular education in America. The American workingmen, in whose behalf public libraries were urged frequently and strongly, had always benefited from far more schooling than had their brethren abroad. Their political privileges and duties in most of our states demanded the existence of agencies of popular culture in a more compelling way than did the social position of the English artisan and mechanic" (Ditzion 1).

As readership grew among all social classes in America, the need for libraries increased year by year and decade by decade. Thus, several librarians heeded the civic call to create privately funded subscription libraries for the benefit of certain disadvantaged groups. As Murray notes, during this period, "everywhere, civic-minded citizens created public libraries with private gifts of books and funds from beneficiaries" (Murray 2193). For instance, the Hartford Young Men's Institute merged with the Hartford Library Company and moved into the famous Wadsworth Atheneum in 1844, with that building serving as the library's home for over a century. Henry M. Bailey, one of the librarians, helped to promote the profession even more with his essay *Thoughts in a Library* and the organization of the first Librarian's Conference, held in New York City in 1853.

Out of these social and subscription libraries grew Torrey's idea of a free public library, with unrestricted access to books, lectures, and exhibits—an institution that would "continue the educational process where the schools left off, and, by conducting a people's university, a wholesome capable citizenry would be fully schooled in the conduct of a democratic life" (Ditzion 74). The advent of school libraries, which supported the curriculum and which, in the later words of John Dewey, "provided a social experience that teaches children how to be self-directed" began in the state of New York in 1835, when the legislature allowed school districts to apply taxes received to the development of school libraries. By 1850, 1.5 million books were housed in New York's school system. These school libraries were eventually charged to serve only students and teachers, yet from the school-library concept grew the roots of America's public library systems.

One of the first proponents of Torrey's free public libraries was Francis Wayland, who, like Jefferson, believed in the intellectual and moral (virtuous) elite, a rising class structure developed by means of self-education and study. He felt society should provide not only necessary instruction to the individual, but also "instruction in the highest degree available" and the opportunity to participate in "all the reading which shall be necessary to prepare him for any situation for which his cultural endowments have rendered him capable." Thus, in Wayland's view, all started on equal footing, and "poverty here works no exclusion, and wealth furnishes no recommendation." Ditzion further paraphrases Wayland's contentions: "If the intention was to preserve our political democracy and to prevent our government from becoming a farce, the people as a whole must be intelligent, virtuous and, as a by-product of these, religious. The library is an important milestone toward reaching this goal" (Ditzion 13).

As the result of Wayland's admonitions and speeches, "free" tax-supported public libraries came to fruition in several townships in New England, culminating in the Boston Public Library in 1854, which is credited with being the first major public library. (Peterboro, New

Francis Wayland (1796–1865), proponent of free public libraries. His donation to the Wayland, Massachusetts, public library in 1851 was the catalyst for legislation in Massachusetts allowing towns to establish libraries.

Hampshire, founded the first wholly tax-supported public library in the United States—open to all and free of charge.) As Rubin notes, the developing public library system in America served at least four purposes, one being an intention "to produce more thoughtful people, individuals capable of making balanced and well-reasoned judgments in a democratic society that depended on their judgments at the voting booth. Such citizens would serve as a strong and stabilizing force to the democratic society" (Rubin 57).

The goal of the public librarian was to ensure the "greatest use for the greatest number." Thus the library was viewed as a true symbol of democracy, for it provided a commons, unobstructed by favoritism, to young and old, rich and poor, regardless of race or creed. In fact, Ditzion movingly describes this period: "The battle cry of freedom in New England and the promotion of libraries as weapons of the crusade.... The real ideological force which fostered the public libraries must be looked for in those islands of communal spirit which rose out of the political and religious backgrounds of democratic America and persisted amid the powerful currents of rugged individualism" (Ditzion 61). Emerson himself praised the growth of libraries: "Consider what you have in the smallest chosen library. A company of the wisest and wittiest men that could be picked out of all civil countries, in a thousand years, have set in best order the results of their learning and wisdom" (qtd. in Murray 2100).

Equality was also Boston Public Library proponent and financer Joshua Bates's dream. He stated, "Just in proportion to the degree of intellectual development to which the mass of people have attained, artificial distinctions have faded away (and) the people have become more and more homogeneous and more democratic.... The only aristocracy a free library could possibly help to create was one open to talent and toil ... the aristocracy of knowledge" (qtd. in Ditzion 60). Thus, librarians toiling at this time, around the mid–1800s, in a way became library missionaries, devoted to advancing the "people's philosophy" and believing that "The future of democracy, the very political and industrial future of the nation, depended upon a system of popular education" (Ditzion 72). They insisted that anyone contributing to the common defense must also contribute to the perpetuation of civilization, with the eradication of ignorance being seen as a type of defense bulwark for the Republic itself. Librarians argued the sectless, classless nature of a public library would supplement public school libraries and help adults to continue learning, educating both the owner and the worker, balancing intellect between the classes, and assisting in eradicating many of the ills of the society, such as railroad strikes and "city politicians." The "Madure Library Movement" exhibited the "missionary zeal" of the mid–1800 library establishment: "Light is always the one cure for darkness, and every book that the public library circulates helps to make Alderman O'Brien and railroad rioters impossible" (qtd. in Ditzion 73). (While not entering into politics personally, librarians stayed fully abreast of political issues and took full advantage of editorial possibilities.) One librarian at New York's Astor Library labeled

The main steps of the Boston Public Library, America's first major public library, built in 1854 (photograph by the author).

the possibility of the capitalist and the mechanic sitting together in the reading room "entirely fanciful." New York City clergyman Henry Ward Beecher heralded, "Among the earliest ambitions to be excited in clerks, workmen, journeymen, and, indeed among all that are struggling up from nothing to something, is that of owning, and constantly adding to a library of good books" (qtd. in Murray 2193).

Librarians also advocated for impartial reporting when the Hearsts and the Pulitzers began making newspaper reporting a capitalist venture. They realized (as we must today), as stated by ALA President Learned (1894), "that a clean, purposeful press was possible only under circumstances of disinterestedness which were not likely to exist" (qtd. in Ditzion 74). The slogan of "Loyalty to City and Country" became popular during the late 1800s, as the library profession saw itself as the penultimate promoter of citizenship, the vehicle whereby the people could learn their country's laws and thereby serve the country more effectively. To do so, libraries were expected to provide reading material rich in the history of our country's first strivings for independence, thus inculcating patriotic memories, "each of which is a pledge to the nation of unity, prosperity and peace" (Nourse, qtd. in Ditzion 74); build local history collections; educate foreign-born populations in cosmopolitan centers (to include collecting material in foreign tongues that helped the immigrant understand American history and government); and mitigate "divisive tendencies" among classes, labor and management, creeds, nationalities, and races.

Another contributor to the civic mission of the nation's emerging library system was steel magnate Andrew Carnegie. Born into poverty, he improved himself in a library organized by his father during Carnegie's youth in Scotland (for those in the weaving trade) as well as in the library of Colonel James Anderson of Allegheny, Pennsylvania, who opened his own personal collection to the working boys of the city. In gratitude, from 1870 to 1919, Carnegie donated $40 million to the construction of 1,670 public library buildings in 1,412 American communities. His action reflected his civic-minded belief that "It is only the feeling that the Library belongs to every citizen, richest and poorest alike, that gives it a soul" (qtd. in Murray 2250). Carnegie also wanted every working man or woman to enter the public library and think,

Andrew Carnegie (1835–1919), philanthropist who donated $40 million to the construction of 1,670 public library buildings in 1,412 American communities. "It is only the feeling that the Library belongs to every citizen, richest and poorest alike, that gives it a soul," he said (Theodore Marceau, photographer [1859–1922]).

"Behold, all this is mine. I support it, and am proud to support it. I am joint proprietor here" (qtd. in Murray 2269). The open stacks we enjoy in our country is another of Carnegie's contributions, for he believed stacks should be open so that readers could browse freely. Before Carnegie, many library collections were housed "in closed stacks and requests were fetched by staff as patrons waited outside a gate" (Murray 2281). As Martin notes, the reader-oriented library prevailed against the preservation-based library. Public libraries, one after the other, made the change, "a practice in keeping with the people's and community nature of the public library. Materials belonged to the people; they should have access to them.... It was to be responsive to all sections of the public, to the casual reader as well as the serious student, to the follower of ancient history as well as the person interested in yesterday's stock prices, to those who liked Shakespeare and to those who preferred Jack London" (Martin 26).

School libraries followed suit. As a report in 1892 by the National Education Association (NEA)—specifically, the subcommittee on history, civil government, and political economy—noted, the teaching of history required a "considerable school library," for it is "as impossible to teach history without reference books as it is to teach chemistry without glass and rubber tubing" (qtd. in NEA 193). Accordingly, the subcommittee's recommendations included (1) expanded school library collections so that students might compare materials against textbooks and (2) a large collection be acquired for each school, "suitable for use in connection with all the historical work done" (NEA 1892). Child labor laws allowed children to attend school on a more frequent basis and for longer periods; in turn, curricula mandated that students prepare to adopt a productive role in society, to be reflected in school library materials and offerings and the expansion of social studies offerings. The NEA Committee on Secondary Education (1918), in fact, listed one of the seven "Cardinal Principles of Secondary Education" as citizenship.

At the turn of the 20th century, to reach those outside of a public library's province, branch and traveling libraries continued the library movement's zeal to provide equal access to ethnic groups and rural dwellers. Melvil Dewey initiated the traveling library program as New York State Librarian, with his model subsequently being adopted and appearing in state after state. The branch libraries themselves reached special populations, such as industrial workers and English-as-a-second-language immigrant workers. In summary, "the major ideological currents of this period (1820–1900) were directed toward producing a unified nation based on the free informed choice of individuals rather than on measures of indoctrination in behalf of any particular group" (Ditzion 75).

The American Library Association, following Henry Bailey's example in the state of New York, was founded in 1876. With the establishment of a professional organization and the writings of educator John Dewey came the concept of the library as a learning community, bringing people face to face for the purpose of exchanging information and learning about and solving problems common to all. Martin believes Dewey's concept was institutionalized, stating, "By the new century, the democratic aims of popular education and wholesome recreation were in the saddle" (16). (Around this time Dewey also wrote, "Democracy needs to be reborn in each generation and education is its midwife" [22]. This rebirth will ideally reoccur during the 21st century, as will be seen in the next chapter, for as modern scholar Putnam extols, "Citizenship is not a spectator sport" [342].)

ALA President Learned followed this train of thought in 1924, popularizing the idea of libraries as informal education centers, leading the way for the establishment of the ALA's Board on Library and Adult Education. As Martin defines the library of the period, "The general public and the elected officials—then and now—pictured it as an educational agency, there to help people understand the world, to prepare them to function as citizens, and to gain information needed for their employment and their daily tasks" (17). He continues, "The concept of democracy, in all its ramifications, contributed to the growth of the library. Progress was in the air. Getting ahead was a shared goal. Government by the people flourished. The public library, it was felt, would help achieve each of these goals" (18).

With regard to school libraries, the progressive education movement of the 1930s, which promoted four objectives in secondary curricula—self-realization, human relationship, economic efficiency, and civic responsibility—allowed school librarians the opportunity to increase civics-based collections and support enhanced civics curricula. Additionally, in areas heavily inhabited by early 20th-century immigrants, libraries rose to the cause of helping "Americanize" newcomers, assisting millions with citizenship preparation and testing.

Archibald MacLeish, who served as Librarian of Congress in the 1940s, supported these progressive objectives, avowing, "Librarians must become active, not passive, agents of the democratic process" (388). The threat to democracy devised by the opposing forces during World War II also helped to perpetuate the civic mission of libraries. Libraries, as the quintessential symbol and "nest" of democracy, it was thought, would assuredly keep the human mind open and free from the brainwashing tactics of Hitler's SS. Indeed, Franklin Roosevelt equated libraries with democracy, speaking to the 64th annual conference (1942) of the American Library Association: "Libraries are directly and immediately involved in the conflict which divides our world, and for two reasons; first, because they are essential to the functioning of a democratic society; second, because the contemporary conflict touches the integrity of scholarship, the freedom of the mind, and even the survival of culture, and libraries are the great tools of scholarship, the great repositories of culture, and the great symbols of the freedom of the mind" (qtd. in Ditzion). Hence, as the war ended, and as the Universal Declaration of Human Rights was being adopted by the world, the American

Archibald MacLeish (1892–1982), librarian of Congress from 1939 to 1944 (National Library of Medicine).

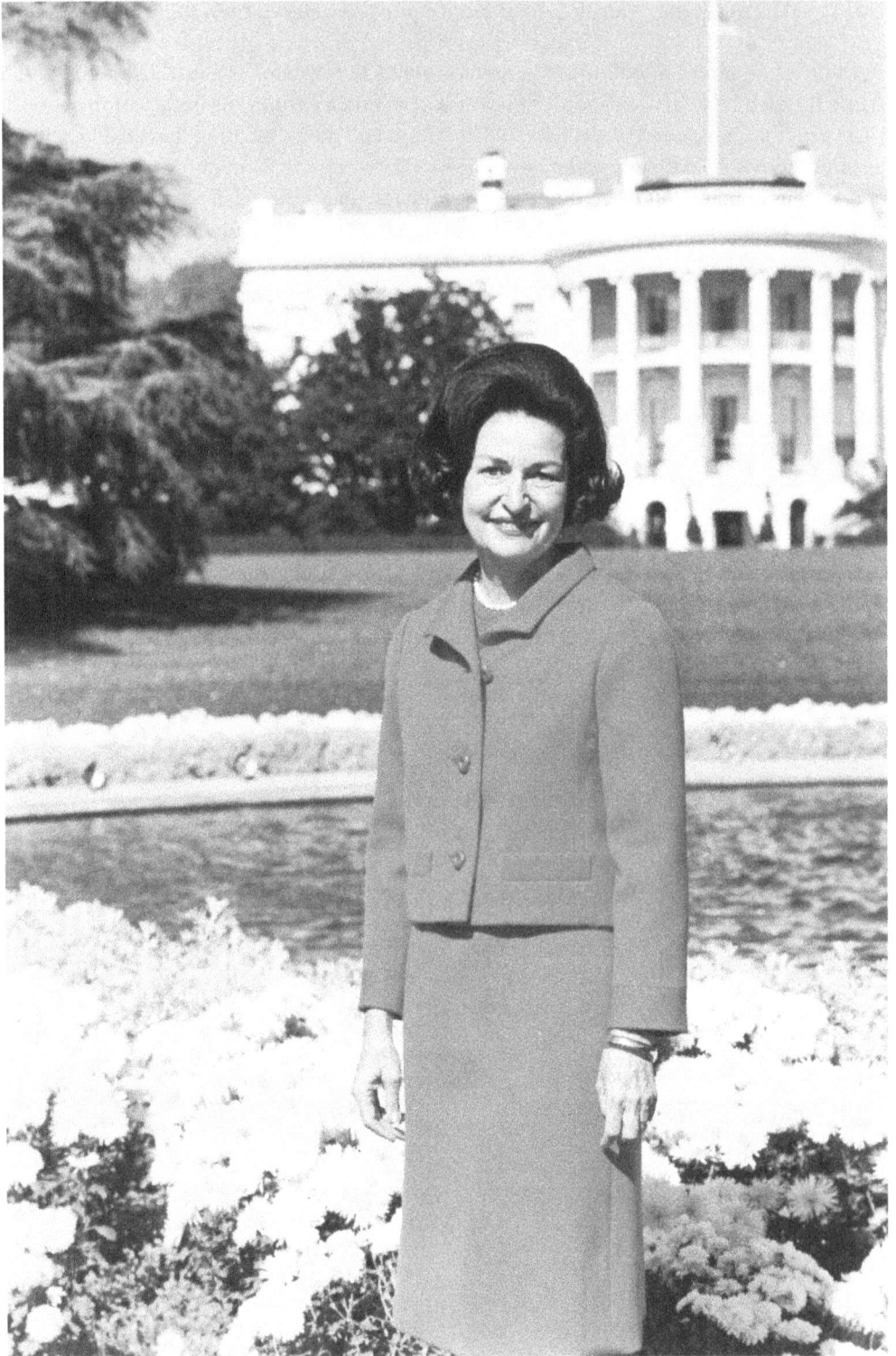

First Lady "Lady Bird" Johnson (1912–2007) at the White House, 1960s. "Perhaps no place in any community is so totally democratic as the town library. The only entrance requirement is interest" (Robert Knudsen, White House Press Office, photographer).

Library Association was busy amending and honing America's "Library Bill of Rights," a set of basic policies founded in equality of service and access, intellectual freedom, and free speech and expression. They read as follows:

> The American Library Association affirms that all libraries are forums for information and ideas, and that the following basic policies should guide their services.
>
> I. Books and other library resources should be provided for the interest, information, and enlightenment of all people of the community the library serves. Materials should not be excluded because of the origin, background, or views of those contributing to their creation.
>
> II. Libraries should provide materials and information presenting all points of view on current and historical issues. Materials should not be proscribed or removed because of partisan or doctrinal disapproval.
>
> III. Libraries should challenge censorship in the fulfillment of their responsibility to provide information and enlightenment.
>
> IV. Libraries should cooperate with all persons and groups concerned with resisting abridgment of free expression and free access to ideas.
>
> V. A person's right to use a library should not be denied or abridged because of origin, age, background, or views.
>
> VI. Libraries that make exhibit spaces and meeting rooms available to the public they serve should make such facilities available on an equitable basis, regardless of the beliefs or affiliations of individuals or groups requesting their use.

Carving at the entrance to the Boston Public Library: "Free to All" (photograph by the author).

In addition to this Bill of Rights, public libraries, with the New York Public Library at the lead, together with civic leaders, educators, and politicians, sponsored open discussions as to the meaning of the American democratic tradition, in an effort to rejuvenate a democratic spirit affected by a debilitating war. In 1948, in concert with the National Resources Planning Board, the ALA published a plan that included a listing of objectives for America's libraries, one of which was maintaining "the precious heritage of freedom." On its 75th anniversary in 1952, the organization launched the American Heritage Project, which enabled citizens to enter and participate in discussions related to issues of the day at their local library. Libraries were seen not only as agents of access, but also as facilitators of "engagement in a diversity of ideas" and the defenders of intellectual freedom. In the early 1960s, as the civil rights movement took hold in the country, and as President Lyndon Johnson instituted his idea of a "Great Society," the Library Services and Construction Act provided grants for the building of libraries in rural areas, for Johnson believed "our need for the storehouse of knowledge grows greater" (qtd. in Martin 143). Lady Bird Johnson's quote from the period summed up her husband's view of a library's role: "Perhaps no place in any community is so totally democratic as the town library. The only entrance requirement is interest" (Martin 134).

As noted in the introductory chapters, following the civil rights era, American citizens' participation in civic engagement plunged, largely due to factors such as the collective fatigue precipitated by social upheaval, the conservative politics of Presidents Nixon and Reagan, a new emphasis on the acquisition of information, the advent of multimedia and an upsurge in technology and the diversity of information formats, a shift in educational paradigms, and an emphasis on the well-being of corporations rather than individual enrichment. Such trends certainly affected the role of public and school libraries. Democratic discussion groups were suspended in local libraries, and public libraries drifted away from the democratic process. Information acquisition and access were emphasized to an extraordinary degree, rather than the active discussion of the ideas found within the provided library materials, or an active stance based therein.

This diminishment in purpose, as instituted by the Founding Fathers and developed up through the early 1970s, was finally recognized in the early years of the 21st century in a report by the Public Agenda (2006), which encouraged libraries to "look carefully at opportunities to strengthen their role in addressing serious problems in their own community" (13). Earlier, in 1998, the American Association of School Librarians had published *Information Power*, which defined the information-literate student as one who "understands that access to information is basic to the functioning of a democracy. That student seeks out information from a diversity of viewpoints, scholarly traditions, and cultural perspectives in an attempt to arrive at a reasoned and informed understanding of issues. The student realizes that equitable access to information from a range of sources and in all formats is a fundamental right in democracy" (Information Power). Now, in the second decade of the 21st century, as noted by former ALA President Nancy Kranich, "The challenge for libraries ... is to extend their reach well beyond educating and informing into a realm where they increase social capital, rekindle civil society, and expand public participation in democracy" (80). The next chapter highlights how this challenge is being answered.

Chapter V

21st Century Role of School and Public Libraries in Civics Education

"Where everyman is … participator in the government of affairs, not merely at an election one day in the year but every day … he will let the heart be torn out of his body sooner than his power be wrested from him by a Caesar or a Bonaparte."—Thomas Jefferson

As Jefferson noted, both education and engagement are required to create hearts laced in the love of freedom as well as minds focused upon a vigilant oversight of the "powers that be." As noted in the previous chapter, libraries traditionally adopted the role of providing both U.S. citizens and immigrants with the intrapersonal and interpersonal tools required for the development of civic-mindedness. Though libraries, along with the public education system, have struggled to fulfill this role as a result of the general

Franklin Delano Roosevelt (1882–1945), president of the United States, 1933–1945. "Libraries are the great tools of scholarship, the great repositories of culture, and the great symbols of the freedom of the mind" (Elias Goldensky [1868–1943], photographer).

apathetic, nonparticipatory trend found among American citizens (which began in the late 1970s), a "revival" of sorts is under way, both in public education (see Chapter III) and in school and public libraries. Nancy Kranich, former president of the American Library Association and author of the article "Libraries and Civic Engagement," notes, "The need to impart the skills to participate in a strong democracy provides ideal opportunities for libraries in schools, on campus, and in towns not only to inform, but also to educate and engage today's and tomorrow's citizens in a safe, neutral environment" (Kranich 79). Accordingly, school and public libraries, as well as institutes of higher learning and the American Library Association, are rising to meet this challenge.

Beginning with the school library, the American Association of School Librarians (AASL), a division of the American Library Association, has outlined the roles of the 21st-century school librarian in *Empowering Learners: Guidelines for School Library Programs.* As the AASL states, the guidelines were instituted for the purpose of "building a flexible learning environment with the goal of producing successful learners skilled in multiple literacies." The information and media literacies found in Guideline II, for example, lay out direct pathways to civic literacy: "The school library program provides instruction that addresses multiple literacies, including information literacy, media literacy, visual literacy, and technology literacy" (*Empowering Learners*). This media/information/technology/civic literacy connection is explained by Kranich: "Beyond redesigning facilities, collaborating with teachers, and developing resources, school library specialists can enhance civic participation by teaching students sophisticated information literacy skills to live, learn, and work in the digital age as well as to carry out the day-to-day activities of citizens in a developing, democratic society" (85).

Thus, the school librarian is charged with assisting students in shifting through, pick-and-choosing, and evaluating information and media—a most difficult task in a world of information (and propaganda) influx. For example, the school librarian may conduct lessons on the fact that "The Onion" is satirical or Fox News or MSNBC is slanted, rather than providing accurate news reporting; the librarian may instead point the student to such sources as World News (wn.com), a compilation of news from media sources around the world. In turn, the differing newscasts may be compared and contrasted and used for discussion purposes.

Of course, these types of lessons coalesce with National Civics Standards' essential question, "How can Americans participate in their government?," satisfying the mandate that "students should be able to identify ways people can monitor and influence the decisions and actions of their government by reading about public issues, watching television news programs, and discussing public issues" (Center for Civic Education, n.p.). The lessons also help develop civic dispositions associated with another National Civics Standards' essential question, "What dispositions or traits of character are important to the preservation and improvement of American democracy?," specifically promoting open-mindedness (willingness to consider other points of view) and critical-mindedness (the inclination to question the truth of various positions, including one's own). Finally, they advance instructional implementation associated with a third essential question, "What are important responsibilities of Americans?," especially two potential responsibilities associated with media/information literacy: (1) remaining informed and attentive to the needs of the community and (2) paying attention to how well elected leaders are serving the public. Both of these responsibilities may be met through careful selection, reading, and analysis of information sources. (Additional insight as to appropriate information sources is offered in Chapter VI.)

Turning back to AASL Guideline #2 from *Empowering Learners,* the school librarian is directed to be heavily involved in teaching for learning, most specifically collaboration: "The school library program promotes collaboration among members of the learning community, and encourages learners to be independent lifelong users and producers of ideas and information" (*Empowering Learners*). Thus, school librarians are, in essence, directed to engage with teachers in all subject areas (including civics) for the purpose of enhancing the learning experience, ensuring it is appropriate to the information-rich and format-diverse environment of the 21st century and founded in a meaningful purpose, and encouraging students to seek, find, and use information both inside and outside of the classroom (the cultivation of lifelong learning).

For example, if a school librarian were collaborating with a high school teacher in the state of Tennessee, and the civics standard being addressed was GC.32, "Cite textual evidence to defend a point of view about the meaning and importance of a free and responsible press," the librarian might introduce musings regarding the right of U.S. citizens to free speech and a free press as found in the writings of James Madison. Thereafter, the librarian and the teacher could create discussion questions to assist with student comprehension of Madison's contentions. If the teacher's resulting assignment included asking students to write letters to Congressional leaders lamenting the fact that Madison's principles are not being followed in the today's age, using Madison's writings to support such a contention, the librarian could assist in helping students synthesize Madison's quotes within the letters, while also directing a course in the nonplagiaristic, ethical usage of the Founder's writing (in-text citations and bibliographic references).

As is apparent from this discussion, the school librarian plays an important role in the delivery of civics education. Thus, the AASL writes and adopts not only guidelines, but also standards, which mirror the traditional role of librarians (discussed in Chapter IV), as a means of developing learners who can use skills, resources, and tools to "participate ethically and productively as members of our democratic society" (the same admonition found in both national and state civics standards). Such skill sets produce a civics-literate individual—one who is required to inquire, think critically, gain knowledge, and draw conclusions (civics discussion), share knowledge (advocacy and action), and pursue personal growth (service). In essence, "when librarians facilitate the development of critical thinking, creativity, and problem solving, students develop the necessary skills to exercise the requirements and responsibilities of citizenship" (Kranich 85).

AASL standards have actually evolved one step beyond the public school expert recommendations discussed in Chapter III, in that in addition to addressing discussion, action, and service, they consider student reflection. Indeed, civics-oriented "self-assessment strategies" are written into the standards that encourage the learner to reflect upon and determine whether his or her own "skills, dispositions, and responsibilities are effective," with the key question being, "Can the student recognize personal strengths and weaknesses over time and become a stronger, more independent learner (citizen)?" (AASL Standards for the 21st Century Learner).

AASL standard skill sets to be advanced via the individual and collaborative learning described earlier, which are necessary and conducive to the development of a 21st-century civically literate American, include the following:

> 1.1.4 Find, evaluate, and select appropriate sources to answer questions.
>
> 1.1.5 Evaluate information found in selected sources on the basis of accuracy, validity, appropriateness for needs, importance, and social and cultural context.
>
> 1.1.7 Make sense of information gathered from diverse sources by identifying misconceptions, main and supporting ideas, conflicting information, and point of view or bias.
>
> 2.1.4 Use technology and other information tools to analyze information.
>
> 3.1.5 Connect learning to community issues.
>
> 4.1.2 Read widely and fluently to make connections with self, the world, and previous reading.

Dispositions included in the AASL standards, which are also crucial to information/media/civic literacy, as developed from individual to individual, include the following:

> 1.2.1 Display initiative and engagement by posing questions and investigating the answers beyond the collection of superficial facts.
>
> 1.2.2 Demonstrate confidence and self-direction by making independent choices in the selection of resources and information.
>
> 1.2.4 Maintain a critical stance by questioning the validity and accuracy of all information.
>
> 1.2.7 Display persistence by continuing to pursue information to gain a broad perspective.
>
> 2.2.1 Demonstrate flexibility in the use of resources by … seeking additional resources when clear conclusions cannot be drawn.
>
> 2.2.3 Employ a critical stance in drawing conclusions by demonstrating that the pattern of evidence leads to a decision or conclusion.
>
> 4.2.3 Maintain openness to new ideas by considering divergent opinions, changing opinions or conclusions when evidence supports the change, and seeking information about new ideas encountered.

Similarly, standards that encourage responsible thinking patterns and actions among the citizenry include the following:

> 1.3.2 Seek divergent perspectives during information gathering and assessment.
>
> 2.3.1 Connect understanding to the real world.
>
> 2.3.2 Consider diverse and global perspectives in drawing conclusions.
>
> 2.3.3 Use valid information and reasoned conclusions to make ethical decisions.
>
> 3.3.1 Solicit and respect diverse perspectives while searching for information, collaborating with others, and participating as a member of the community.
>
> 3.3.2 Respect the differing interests and experiences of others, and seek a variety of viewpoints.
>
> 3.3.3 Use knowledge and information skills and dispositions to engage in public conversation and debate around issues of common concern.
>
> 3.3.5 Contribute to the exchange of ideas within and beyond the learning community.
>
> 3.3.6 Use information and knowledge in the service of democratic values.
>
> 4.3.1 Participate in the social exchange of ideas, both electronically and in person.

Finally, self-assessment strategies pertinent to civic-minded personal reflection (How are my contributions to society working?) are as follows:

> 1.4.2 Monitor gathered information, and assess for gaps or weaknesses.
>
> 2.4.1 Determine how to act on information (accept, reject, modify).

2.4.2 Assess for completeness of investigation.

2.4.4 Develop directions for future investigations.

3.4.2 Assess own ability to work with others in a group setting by evaluating varied roles, leadership, and demonstrations of respect for other viewpoints.

4.4.5 Develop own personal criteria for gauging how effectively own ideas are expressed.

The use of the scenarios provided to exemplify the AASL *guidelines* as found in *Empowering Learners* may also help describe how the *standards* might be incorporated into both individual and collaborative civics-based lesson planning and delivery in a public school library. The individual lesson comparing and contrasting inaccurate/biased/slanted news programming versus fact-based reporting fulfills the requirements of Standard Skills Set 1 (evaluating information resources for accuracy and validity), Standard Disposition Set 1 (demonstrating confidence in the independent selection of resources, pursuing additional information if accuracy is uncertain), and Standard Responsibility and Self-Assessment 1 (seeking divergent perspectives during information gathering while also assessing for gaps). The collaborative lesson plan in which Madison's views regarding free speech and the free press are used to strengthen an argument for the perpetuation of such rights in 21st-century news outlets satisfies AASL Standard Skills Set 3 (connecting learning to a community issues) as well as Standard Responsibility 3 (using knowledge to engage in public debate around issues of common concern, contributing to the exchange of ideas which serve democratic values). In total, AASL's adopted standards meet the Merrimack College's Center for Engaged Democracy public policy recommendations: "Crucial to democratic decision-making and active problem solving are skills used for inquiry, critical thinking, and the ability to communicate effectively across differences, which requires listening and negotiation skills. Such skills include the capacity to explain views that are different from one's own; understanding bias; identifying interdependencies within broader structures and systems; building inclusiveness and collaborative participation on community issues; coalition building on fundamental social values; and the identification of critical social issues" (Center 5).

A discussion of these AASL-driven collaborative civics education possibilities raises some questions: Which entity in the community will support the school library's efforts to engage civic learning? After grade 12, where is a citizen to turn to continue his or her course of civic engagement? Of course, the answer to both questions is the quintessential community-based preserver and protector of democratic values: public libraries, which are experiencing a surge—or we might say, a resurgence—in civic engagement practices and services, right alongside school libraries. A reading of the American Library Association's geomap highlighting libraries participating in the organization's Center for Civic Life projects indicates that public (as well as academic, special, and school) libraries across the country are hosting forums, discussion groups, film series, and institutes.

These activities echo the thoughts of Bill Ptacek, director of the King County Library System in Issaquah, Washington: "Public libraries are local, neutral, and respected for providing information that represents different viewpoints. Given its resources and community connections, it is the perfect arena to engage the community in civic discourse on important community issues. With the demise of local news sources, it would be reasonable to assume that local governments, service providers, and community leaders will turn to the library as a venue for discussion and feedback on issues that affect the public. At the same time, this role is consistent with the public's perception of libraries as a trusted source for information and meaningful community participation" (Ptacek, n.p.). For example, when King County acquired land from an outdated train line and needed to decide whether to use the land for a bike path, nature path, or light-rail track, the public library distributed comment forms at the physical locale, and hosted an online forum on the library website as well as virtual meetings. Instead of the very few people who would have attended a community meeting, over 700 voices were heard by county officials as a result of the library's outreach.

Civics-based programming targeting library youth services populations includes such examples as the Sacramento County Day School's "Lunch Leadership Series," in which students present on a variety of topics, such as diversity understandings; Napa Valley School Library Consortium's "Athletes as Readers and Leaders"; Berkeley (California) High School's library school-wide viewing and discussion of a presidential inauguration; Peabody Institute's (Maryland) Mayoral Forum, in which teens asked the two candidates about local flooding issues, public school funding, the environment, libraries, public safety, and jobs; and Dartmouth (Massachusetts) High School Library's Feeding the Hungry program (civic service). Other examples of programming initiated during the 2012 election season included the following activities:

- The LaCrosse (Wisconsin) Public Library asked young readers to vote for a shark or a train, as inspired by the children's book *Shark vs. Train*, by Chris Barton and Tom Lichtenheld. A space was created in which the book could be read, along with a polling booth. Children who voted also received a sticker, just the same as adult voters.

- The Kids Can Vote @ your library program sponsored by the Norwalk (Connecticut) Public Library asked children, on Election Day, to vote for a list of literary candidates, and a special Election Day story time and film screening (presidential subjects) was proffered.

- The Louisville (Kentucky) Public Library hosted meetings serving to remind teens that 2016 is not that far away, at which time the choice of America's leaders will fall to them. Teens had the opportunity to discuss issues of their choosing and participated in a mock election.

- As part of its Election Happening @ your library programs, the Garden City (Michigan) Library held an election where young readers voted for their favorite book. Picture books, children's fiction and nonfiction, and young adult books, whose subject was the democratic process, were also displayed and promoted.

A pilot project of mention is Chicago Public Library's Engage! Picturing America Through Civic Engagement. Targeted to young adult populations, the mission of this project is to "deepen participants' knowledge and appreciation of American art and its relation to American history and civic life, and to contribute to the development of informed and discerning voters." Program participants are encouraged to consider who they wish to become within a democratic society as well as what they choose to believe (i.e., what is the role of the military?). Using visual arts promptings, youth are asked to consider American civics life, as portrayed in substantial works of American art (such as World War II's Rosie the

Riveter), also participating in dynamic discussion and associated offerings, actions, and service work. Examples include creating individual, learning-responsive works of art, pairing a walking tour of Lincoln Square art exhibits with a service project of the participants' choosing, creating a mural to beautify the public library, and building garden totem poles from recycled products.

According to the Urban Libraries Council, public libraries are "no longer a passive repository of books and information or an outpost of culture, quiet and decorum in a noisy world." Instead, "the new library is an active and responsive part of the community and an agent for change" (Urban 2). Libraries are perfect candidates for change agents because they are accessible to all, are nonpartisan, hold reliable resources, understand what matters in

Statue at the steps of the Boston Public Library: "Art" (photograph by the author).

the community, and are trusted (both staff guidance and performance are accepted, almost unconditionally). The Council thus offers recommendations as to five civics-based roles which should be fulfilled by public libraries:

- *Civic Educator*: The library is charged with expanding awareness of civic knowledge and responsibility by maximizing access to resources crucial to civic engagement, creating civic awareness portals and databases; providing unbiased candidate fact sheets for voters; connecting with community organizations committed to civic engagement and outreach; and hosting civic education forums, classes, or institutes.

- *Library as Conversation Starter*: Many times communities do not address issues until a crisis point is reached. Libraries can prevent such crises by identifying issues requiring action, establishing opportunities for conversations (whether face to face or virtual), engaging community leaders and organizations in such conversations, and enhancing productive solutions.

- *Library as Community Bridge*: Because the library is seen as the "great equalizer" within a community, it shares the important role of bridging differences among peoples—for example, immigrants and citizens; community "natives" and "move-ins"; youth and elders. Thus, libraries are a perfect site for organizing immigrant education efforts (assistance in understanding the community, the naturalization process, and avenues of involvement) and may also contribute to digital learning labs designed to engage young people in learning, socializing, and participating in civics-based forums.

- *Library as Visionary*: Libraries should take an active role as to how the community may be shaped to the greatest effect, connecting with local government leaders, organizations, and businesses to establish an encompassing, broader wisdom base. For example, in Springfield, Massachusetts, the library, during an economic downturn, created plans to help reverse the city's downward economic spiral and build a brighter future for the city.

- *Library as Center for Democracy in Action*: As defined by the Council, this role requires "moving from events that support civic engagement to a coordinated strategy designed to achieve active and purposeful engagement that promotes civic health." Components of such a strategy might include hiring a civic engagement outreach librarian, providing paths to civic engagement, and displaying a willingness to tackle controversial issues that are important to community well-being.

Two recent nationwide projects that mirror these roles include Banned Books Week, held each September as a means of highlighting "the benefits of free and open access to information while drawing attention to the harms of censorship by spotlighting actual or attempted book banning incidences across the United States" (qtd. in Edwards 134). Local public and school libraries create displays of banned books, host activities in association with these books, promote reading of the books, hold discussion groups, hold forums on the right to read, invite guest authors or community members who have endured censorship efforts, and discuss the libraries' role in preventing attacks on First Amendment rights. In this way, a space is opened in which communities may enter into dialogues about "individual rights, community values, and the roles of the library in protecting freedom of access and inquiry" (Edwards 135).

The second effort, the September Project, was initially developed to discuss the ramifications of the September 11, 2001, terrorist attacks, but now focuses on broader issues—really any issue that affects citizens in a given community. The project is now worldwide, advertised with the tagline "Connecting the World, One Library at a Time." Associated events explore "freedom, justice, democracy and community and include book displays, community book readings, children's art projects, film screening, theatrical performances, civic deliberations, voter registrations, gardens, murals, panel discussions, and puppet shows" (Edwards 135). In a partisan world and a heated political climate, citizens are provided the means to discuss ideas, issues, problems, and resolutions within a comfortable and non-judgmental environment. Hence, citizens are more likely to become politically astute and engaged. As co-founder David Silver has noted, the events hold no political agenda, yet are civic in nature: "To talk about issues that matter—to talk about the war, to talk about human rights, to talk about the Earth—that's political. In our times, any idea that encourages us to be citizens rather than consumers is highly political" (qtd. in Edwards 135).

Public libraries are also beginning to engage citizens not only in these September activities, but year-round. For example, in 2012, the Chapel Hill, North Carolina, Public Library launched a series called "Civic Engagement and Social Justice: The Intersection of Rights and Responsibilities." The events, programs, and films presented in association with this series sought to engage citizens to "dig deeper" into social justice issues important to the community (Why do we have homelessness? Which energy sources are economical and sustainable within our community?). The program was founded in the belief that libraries are "boundary spanning advocates of intellectual freedom and trusted safe spaces for investigation and expression of diverse ideas" (Edwards 136).

"Socrates' Café" meetings are also taking root in libraries across the country. Organized to utilize the Socratic method—question, be questioned, and listen to others' questions to learn more—these meetings hope to "create a more vibrant and participatory democracy and empathetic society." Members decide on the issues to be discussed and questioned, abandon their assumptions, explore alternative viewpoints, and accept differences in opinion to reach an agreeable consensus. Some of the questions explored by the South Portland, Maine, Public Library included: What is free speech? What is community?

To summarize, both school and public libraries are charged by standards and best practice understandings to impart the skills necessary to promote civic literacy and deliberative democracy within communities of practice, as well as to foster the return of an American *ethos* conducive to open debate, participatory action, civic-oriented service, and meaningful reflection. As Aabo insists, "Even in the digital age, the purpose of public libraries, still, is to further democracy, equality, and social justice" (qtd. in Edwards 210). As former American Library Association President Nancy Kranich writes, "Around the country, libraries are poised to grasp this cause, build civic space, and reclaim their traditional role. If they are to fulfill their civic mission in the digital age, libraries must find active ways to engage community members in democratic discourse and community renewal. Working closely with a rich and diverse array of partners, libraries of all types can rekindle civic engagement, promote greater civic participation, and increase community problem solving and decision making" (89).

* * *

Professional Practice Tips for Chapters I–V

Chapter I

To stay abreast of statistics regarding civic literacy, visit the website for Tufts University's Center for Information and Research on Civic Learning and Engagement and sign up for Facebook or Twitter notifications. Especially visit the "Quick Facts" section, which condenses CIRCLE'S research and survey efforts in association with (1) youth voting; (2) civics education; (3) trends by race, ethnicity, and gender; (4) youth demographics; (5) noncollege youth; and (6) community service/volunteering.

Chapter II

To share the philosophies of civics education giants Rush, Webster, Mann, and Dewey with fellow professionals (in-service) or with patrons and/or students, internalize more of their theories, recommendations, and admonitions by reading and researching within the following resources:

> *Benjamin Rush, Patriot and Physician* by Alyn Brodsky (Truman Talley Books, 2004)
>
> *The Forgotten Founding Father: Noah Webster's Obsession and the Creation of an American Culture* by Joshua Kendall (Berkley Trade, 2012)
>
> *Horace Mann's Vision of the Public Schools* by William Hayes (R&L Education, 2006)
>
> *Horace Mann: A Biography* by Jonathon Messerli (Knopf, 1972)
>
> *Educating the Democratic Mind* by Walter C. Parker (State University of New York Press, 1995)

Chapter III

A dynamic, engaging, interactive civics laboratory will open in March 2015: the Edward M. Kennedy Institute for the United States Senate. The Institute will house a built-to-scale and model U.S. Senate Chamber in which student and general public visitors can simulate serving as a U.S. senator, learning the debate, negotiation, compromise, and advocacy skills required of our nation's senators. Teachers will be provided with packets of materials that assist in preparing students for a hands-on field-trip experience in which a bill is written, introduced before the Senate, researched and argued, and voted upon, passing "mock" legislation beneficial to the general welfare. Envisioned by Kennedy himself and spearheaded by his wife, Victoria, the Institute's mission is to "turn the tide on civic education, providing a portal into the legislative process and a training ground for active, responsible participation in democracy, community and country." As such, the Institute will provide interactive tablets allowing students to ponder and evaluate public policy, understand the workings of the legislative branch of government and its historical and day-to-day impact upon the American people (as well as people across the globe), discover the Senate's Constitutional authority, and, most of all, encourage civic participation. A Summer Senate program will welcome two students from each state (100 students per summer) to hold mock hearings and draft legislation. Interactive museum exhibits will outline the progression of legislation that spurred our country's political evolution and growth (e.g., immigration and civil rights). (Of note, the Institute will create an online digital library archiving U.S. Senate primary materials and resources. It will also offer programs for the general public and for newly elected senators.)

Chapter IV

Use the chapter itself as reading material for a civics lesson unit in which students in grades 9–12 reflect upon the advocacy associated with ensuring America's libraries were supported for the purpose of developing civic-mindedness amongst America's citizens. Specifically, students should recognize the contributions of Franklin, Torrey, Wayland, Dewey, Bates, Learned, Roosevelt, MacLeish, Carnegie, the Johnsons, and Kranich, determining the character traits, knowledge, and skills necessary for successful persuasion. After reflection and discussion, ask students to plan a library service project that contemplates a return to library-based civics discussion forums, based in current events and selected readings, as a means of preserving "the precious heritage of freedom." Approach other local librarians to organize community or statewide implementation. As a service project, qualify the impact of the discussion group by monitoring voter turnout, local political success stories, an increase in local political teamwork and efficient leadership, and public policy initiatives ensuring the declarations found in the ALA Library Bill of Rights are implemented.

Chapter V

Review and listen to the American Library Association's Center for Civic Life Deliberative Dialogue Training Tools at http://discuss.ala.org/civicengagement/training/. The most recent series, "The Conversation Continues at Your Library: The Place Where Democracy Happens," considers the following topics: "Naming and Framing Public Issues" and "Beyond Deadlock: A Better Way to Talk about Difficult Issues."

To learn more about putting the AASL Standards for the 21st Century Learner into action, consult the reference book *Standards for the 21st Century Learner in Action*, which provides benchmarks and action examples. The resource may be ordered online at http://www.ala.org/aasl/standards-guidelines/in-action.

Chapter VI

Collection Development for Civics Education Integration

"It is said that democracy is the worst form of government, except all the others that have been tried."
—Winston Churchill

The collection within a school or public library is, in essence, an intellectual infrastructure, the "bridge" which allows citizens to cross from ignorance to enlightenment. Collections conducive to civics education, therefore, must understand the prize, or product, which may be reached on yonder shore. In this instance, the end-in-sight is the perpetuation of our Republic, as described by Benjamin Franklin (and discussed in previous chapters). This large picture is made up of 300 million puzzle pieces, each of which must be carried over the body of water named civic illiteracy. What must each puzzle piece be cut from so that all fit together? That is, what is the common material, the common *ethos* in the United States regarding civics education for each individual, and how may this *ethos* be reflected in our school and public libraries?

The commonality which must support the civics collections (infrastructure) in civics and public libraries is a portrait of Lady Liberty—in other words, a civically literate individual living within the United States. To answer this question, librarians should not turn to standards or indicators, history or quotations, practices and recommendations, but rather to the end product which is the subject of all of the above, a portrayal of a quintessential American citizen whose life goal is to protect and defend the Republic in which he or she lives, works, and plays. One of the most thorough portrayals is found in the Campaign for the Civic Mission of Schools' report, "Guardian of Democracy." Relying on such a portrayal will, in effect, meet standards and assure recommendations are followed.

According to this report, first, such a citizen is informed and thoughtful, and "they have [*numbers added*] (1) a grasp and an appreciation of history and (2) the fundamental processes of American democracy, (3) an understanding and awareness of public and community issues and the ability to obtain information when needed, (4) a capacity to think critically, and a willingness to enter into dialogue with others about different points of view and to understand diverse perspectives. They are tolerant of ambiguity and resist simplistic answers to complex questions" (Campaign 11). Considering each of these headings, quality curricular and programming material, conducive to discussion and a catalyst for civic action and service, is presented here and annotated for collection development modeling purposes.

1. History of American Democracy

Grades 2–3 *Why Don't You Get a Horse, Sam Adams?* by Jean Fritz (Puffin, 2000)

Quintessential picture book biographer Jean Fritz addresses how the American Revolution may have started in the mind (and voice) of just one man, Samuel Adams. She presents the down-to-earth Sam as someone who walks from store to store and from tavern to tavern, making it his business to keep the people angry over the antics of the British crown. Along his walks, he, in a manner of speaking, fashions the American mind and kindles a revolution.

Grades 4–6 *King George, What Was His Problem: Everything Your School Books Didn't Tell You About the American Revolution* by Steve Sheinkin and illustrated by Tim Robinson (Square Fish, 2015)

A social studies teacher himself, Steve Sheinkin discovered all the juicy details of the American Revolution in an attempt to personalize and highlight its effect on the lives of those living through the War for Independence. Looking at the war on this level, Sheinkin reveals many of the absurdities contributing to the war, while also finding the humanity, and humor, within a serious subject. A thorough recounting of facts is laced with entertaining narrative, with chapter names themselves indicating the book's informative, yet engaging tone: How to Start a Revolution; A Sleepless Night before Revolution; George Washington, Meet Your Army; Declare Independence, Already; Losing and Retreating in '76; Showdown at Saratoga; Will We Ever Win This War?; The Great Race to Yorktown; and Whatever Happened to…?

Grades 7–12 *The Real Revolution* by Marc Aronson (Clarion, 2005)

In a book complete with endnotes, a bibliography, associated websites, and a timeline, Marc Aronson presents the true-to-life global scenarios which changed the world's mindset and set the American Revolution in motion, from Tom Paine's move to America, to the demand for Indian tea, to the courage of John Wilkes. Setting the scene as if in a play by including a listing of "players," Aronson uses art, maps, and documents of the period, in addition to a superb narrative flow, to engage even the most reluctant teen reader.

Website: America's Story— Revolutionary Period—Library of Congress

http://www.americaslibrary.gov/jb/revolut/jb_revolut_subj.html

The Library of Congress asks users to "jump back in time" and experience the American Revolution first-hand—virtually, of course! Short vignettes, complemented by art and maps from the period, contribute to differentiated learning and a myriad of reader response activity possibilities. Sample stories include "A Constitutional Army"; "Bluffing the British";

Inside the Library of Congress, Washington, D.C. (photograph by the author).

"Extra, Extra Read All about It"; "First in Freedom"; and "One of America's First Spies." Twenty-five such stories portray the events of the period, along with more than 50 visuals.

2. Fundamental Processes of American Democracy

Grades K–3 Woodrow Books (*Woodrow, the White House Mouse; House Mouse, Senate Mouse; Marshall, the Courthouse Mouse*) by Peter and Cheryl Barnes (Little Patriot Press, 2012)

Woodrow G. Washingtail, as well as various and asundry other mice politicians, are on-board to help kids understand the three branches of government in the United Mice of America. Explaining the roles of each branch in a kid-friendly style, these books immerse the reader in a presidential inauguration (the role of protecting and preserving), a bill passing through Congress (the duty to discuss, debate, and create law), and a Supreme Court decision-making scenario (the task of interpreting law). Filled with humor and wit, one reviewer notes: "Fun and worthwhile…. It should be required reading for all current members of Congress."

Grades 3–5 *Shhh! We're Writing the Constitution* by Jean Fritz and illustrated by Tomie de Paola (Puffin, 1997)

Jean Fritz uses humorous tidbits, such as Benjamin Franklin's belief that if term limits were not placed on the role of the president, he or she would never leave office, "short of a shooting." She reveals all the bickering and "horse trading" required for the ratification of the U.S. Constitution during the hot Philadelphia summer of 1787, all the while explaining the significance of the document and sharing endnotes which highlight meaning.

Grades 5–7 *In the Year of the Boar and Jackie Robinson* by Bette Bao Lord (Harper–Collins, 2003)

Changing her name to Shirley Temple Wong, "Bandit" immigrates to America to join her father. It is the year of Jackie Robinson, and baseball is the hit. As Shirley's teacher compares American democracy to the game of baseball, as a means of helping her understand the government under which she now lives, Shirley tries her best to understand and "fit in." When Jackie Robinson visits her classroom, Shirley knows the system works, despite the racism experienced by this superb athlete.

Grades 6 and up *A Kid's Guide to America's Bill of Rights: Curfews, Censorship, and the 100-Pound Giant* by Kathleen Krull (Avon Books, 1999)

Sharing fun anecdotes as well as the story of the 100-pound giant, James Madison, this book introduces secondary school students, in an unusually entertaining fashion, to the 492 words which constitute each American citizen's individual rights (Bill of Rights). Answering such questions as "What does it mean to take the Fifth," while also introducing the "Everything Else" nature of the Ninth Amendment, this book takes a thorough look, amendment by amendment, at the document which defines American society.

Website: Ben's Guide to the U.S. Government

http://bensguide.gpo.gov/

Engaging all ages in the process of learning about the U.S. government and its working processes, "Ben" (Benjamin Franklin), with the help of the Government Printing Office, guides students through the branches of government, how laws are made, historical documents of significance, how to become a citizen, and national versus state government. Along the way, he introduces print and interactive games and a glossary of terms. Pertinent U.S. government websites and a parents/teachers guide are also available.

3. Understanding and Awareness of Public and Community Issues

Grades K–3 *Library Lion* by Michelle Knudsen and illustrated by Kevin Hawkes (Candlewick, 2008)

When Lion enters the Library one day, quiet as paw pads on the floor, Miss Merriweather, the Library Director, allows him to stay, because he isn't "breaking any rules." Becoming sort of a fixture, licking the envelopes, and dusting with his tail, the lion remains quiet and doesn't roar, until one day when Miss Merriweather falls from her book stool. Saving the day, the lion reveals that for the most part rules should be followed, but, sometimes, when danger arises, it is time to break the rules and act.

All Ages *14 Cows for America* by Carmen Agra Deedy, Thomas Gonzalez, and Wilson Kimeli Naiyomah (Peachtree Publishers, 2009)

Warrior Kimeli returns to his Kenyan village to hear the news, nine months later, of the September 11 tragedy in New York City. He remembers a teaching from his youth: "To heal the pain in someone's heart, give them something close to your own." Kimeli takes this wisdom to heart and convinces tribal elders, by his own action of presenting a cow, precious to Kimeli's culture and economy, to America. When all is said and done, 14 cows are presented to the ambassador for the grieving nation. Worlds away, a foreign culture understands both the horror of evil and the saving grace of compassion.

Grades 4–9 *How I Became an American* by Karen Gundisch and James Skofield (Cricket Books, 2001)

Ten-year-old Johann ("Johnny" in America) lives a sort of "Pied Piper of Hamelin" existence when his father follows an Ohio steel mill propagandist to America. Life in America is not as easy as portrayed by the traveler, and Johnny must deal with cultural differences, deciding what to accept about his new homeland and what to keep from his German values. All along the way, the work is hard and ever enduring. The "squeak-by" existence of most immigrants, both then and now, is certainly revealed in this story, which weaves songs speaking to American immigration, both praising and condemning the move, within the plot trajectory.

The "Library Lion" at the Boston Public Library (photograph by the author).

Website: Labor by the Library of Congress

http://www.loc.gov/teachers/classroommaterials/themes/labor/

Replete with primary source material, this site contains not only lesson plans, but also "from the dawn of America" exhibitions and presentations, such as Virginia's Labor Problem 1617–1620, Rosie the Riveter (World War II), and Working in Paterson, New Jersey (1994). At the online student activity link, young "folk" will learn about the first Labor Day as well as the trials and sacrifices of millions in our country who fought for equal pay, equal rights, and humane working conditions, many times via community-based strikes and protests.

4. Willingness to Enter into Dialogue with Others About Different Points of View and Understand Diverse Perspectives

Grades 3–5 *Lilly and Miss Liberty*
by Carla Stevens and illustrated by Deborah Ray (Scholastic, 1992)

Lilly Lafferty comes face to face with the American value placed on individuality in point of view as she collects money for a gift from France which will soon be entering New York Harbor. Lilly is soliciting pennies in an effort to build a pedestal for the Statute of Liberty, but many believe she should instead be saving pennies for the poor. The history of the arrival of Lady Liberty is woven into this story touting free thought and expression.

Grades 4–7 *If America Were a Village*
by David J. Smith and illustrated by Shelagh Armstrong
(Kids Can Press, 2009)

Shrinking America down to a village of 100, the authors reveal the diverse ethnic, religious, and cultural groups comprising the American citizenry, also studying family patterns, jobs, wealth, and health. A microcosm of American society, this book allows students to "picture" the diversity found within our country.

Grades 9–12 *The Rifle*
by Gary Paulsen (Houghton–Mifflin, 2006)

Paulsen enters the ever-present debate over gun regulation in this poignant story tracing the history of an American Revolution flintlock to the present day, at which point the rifle, passed down through generations and eventually traded for an acrylic-on-velvet painting, is involved in the shooting death of Richard, a teenager who would have found a cure for the genetic causes of heart disease. Whether a killing machine is still a killing machine, no matter the art and engineering and family history involved, is the point of debate presented by Paulsen.

Website: Virtual Republic: The Idea of America

http://ideaofamerica.org/

Sponsored and written by the Colonial Williamsburg Foundation, Virtual Republic allows students to explore controversial issues and thus differing points of view. For example, one question explored is "What do we do with 52,000 child immigrants?" Children are introduced to the issue and how it affects local communities, the current policy, both past and present beliefs surrounding the issue, and news items highlighting the subject at hand. A "Proposed Policy Solution" opportunity allows student groups to create innovative policy solutions and post them for wide-reaching review by others. Finally, viewers are encouraged to take action surrounding the issue, posting their accomplishments. A listing of organizations which tackle or impact the issue are included as a starting point for additional action and service.

The second major characteristic of a model citizen is a tendency to participate in community improvement efforts. The habits exemplified are as follows, with materials conducive to the development of such habits being summarized:

1. Contributes to Groups in Civil Society Which Offer Venues for Americans to Participate in Public Service, Working with Others to Overcome Problems

Grades 2–3 *Scarlet Stockings Spy*
by Trinka Hakes Noble and illustrated by Robert Papp
(Sleeping Bear Press, 2011)

Maddie Rose is working for a rather impressive group in 1777 Philadelphia—George Washington's Continental Army. Using her petticoats and stockings as symbols of British war ships, she informs her enlisted brother as to the location of the man-o'-wars in the harbor, basically joining the Revolutionary spy network!

Grades 4–5 *One Nation*
by Devin Scillian and illustrated by Pam Carroll
(Sleeping Bear Press, 2011)

Short vignettes, written with numbers in mind, reveal how Americans work together as one to create a better union. For example, "seven pioneers, seven brave men … each knew our future lay beyond the blue," reveals the group effort of the astronauts chosen to first explore space. The number 15 vignette reveals the number of years required to build and erect the Statute of Liberty.

Grades 6–9 *Freedom's Children:*
Young Civil Rights Activists Tell Their Own Story
by Ellen Levine (Puffin, 2000)

Thirty individuals, who fought for their civil rights during their teen years in the 1950s and 1960s, offer first-person accounts of each struggle to acquire rights, including their action involving participating in sit-ins, refusing to go to the back of the bus, forcing the integration of public schools, or protesting on the streets for the right to vote. The courage and lack of fear of these youth drove them to tackle any challenge and make any sacrifice (including physical safety) for the cause of freedom.

Website: Your Commonwealth

http://www.yourcommonwealth.org/

Precisely because the issues faced by youth of the 21st century are extremely complex and global in nature, students may utilize this website to post, in a news-based format, articles or videos about issues in their own region which require international consideration, input, and resolution discussion. Considered a "hive of fresh ideas and creativity," youth may also comment or tweet about posts and enter posted competitions. Participants are asked to imagine themselves as citizens of the "Commonwealth," contributing to the eradication of poverty and injustice. (Note: The United States is not a member of this organization. Certainly, by using this website, however, students will be exposed to differing world viewpoints.)

2. Pursues an Array of Cultural, Social, Political, and Religious Interests and Beliefs

Grades K–3 *In America*
by Marisha Moss (Dutton, 1994)

As Walter and his Grandpa walk to the post office to mail his brother, Herschel, who still lives in Lithuania, a birthday present, Grandpa explains his reason for traversing the Atlantic at the tender age of ten: an opportunity to achieve the freedoms enjoyed by Jewish people, unheard of in his country during his early years. America, Grandpa explains, is a place where no one bothers you.

Grades 2–5 *Seeds of Change*
by Jen Cullerton Johnson and illustrated by Sonia Lynn Sadler
(Lee & Low, 2013)

Wangari Maathai, born in Kenya, wants to go to school just like her brother. When her parents finally decide to let her attend, due to the proficiency of her studies, she is awarded a scholarship in the United States, where she meets science professors who impact her life. Upon receiving her education in America, Wangari returns to Kenya to organize the planting of 30 million trees, saving her country's environment and achieving a Nobel Peace Prize.

Grades 6–10 *Forge*
by Laurie Halse Anderson (Atheneum, 2012)

Curzon is an escaped slave passing for free. He joins the safety net of the Continental Army, only to weather the horrific winter of 1777–1778 in Valley Forge. Attempting to remain free by posing as a soldier, Curzon must also inwardly wrestle with the hidden hypocrisy of the Revolutionary movement.

Website: Smithsonian Institute: Wonderful World

http://smithsonianeducation.org/mywonderfulworld/

To better understand the people and cultures found on the seven continents, students may click any continent and discover intriguing cultures from across the globe, past and present. Examples include, from North America, the Lakota winter count exhibit, which includes a documentary, archived images, and interviews; from South America, the Canela of Brazil exhibit, which features information on rituals, festivals, and body adornment; and from Europe, a photographic exhibition of the Life and Culture of the Sámi, Reindeer People of Norway.

Third, a civically trained American acts politically, as indicated in the major headings that follow (appropriate materials are highlighted).

Exemplifies the Skills, Knowledge and Commitment Necessary to Organize People, and...

1. Address Social Issues...

Grades 4–7 *Germy in Charge*
by Rebecca C. Jones (Dutton, 1993)

Sixth graders usually do not win the high school seat on the school board. But Germy is insistent, promising to fire teachers who give homework, improve cafeteria food, and call off school when it rains. When he wins the seat, what is "Germy Blew It" to do? Despite his inability to achieve as much as he hoped, Germy exhibits "stick-to-ive-ness" by actually reading the documents required for school board meetings and finding the players and shakers who will make things happen.

Grades 6–10 *With Courage and Cloth*
by Ann Bausam (National Geographic Press, 2004)

Two women organizations, from 1900 to 1920, advocated with "iron and steel" to ensure the passing of the 19th Amendment to the Constitution—that is, the amendment guaranteeing the right of women to vote. Bausam's well-researched creative nonfiction writing allows the movement to come to life, as she reveals the many colored pendants fashioned, designed, and sewed by women of the era to place on the streets, in buildings, in stores, and even in the jail houses to which they were sometimes sent. With never-before-seen photographs, Bausam reveals the incredible courage exhibited by women of the era as they fought for a social order which truly honored the mandates contained in the U.S. Constitution.

Grades 8–12 *The Bloody Country*
by James Lincoln Collier (Scholastic, 1980)

Set in an era just prior to the Revolutionary War, a state government's unchecked right to eminent domain is this book's subject. Ben and his family settle in Pennsylvania's Wyoming Valley, only to be told they cannot homestead the property or run their mill, as the property is owned by another. In reality, the land *is* available, and the Pennsylvania colonial (British) government is preventing settlers from finding land on which to earn a living, one of the contentions of the colonists. Not backing down in the face of both government opposition and a harsh winter, Ben and his family learn to persevere, developing the staunch freedom and independence indicative of those who fought the War of Independence.

Website: United Nations Cyber School Bus

http://www.un.org/pubs/cyberschoolbus/

Discussions about social issues in America are encouraged in Colonial Williamsburg's *The Idea of America*, but to introduce students to world issues, visit the UN's Cyber School Bus. Issues addressed include poverty, rights of indigenous peoples, women's rights, and saving tomorrow's world. Children may play a simulation game in which they learn how to respond during a disaster, play quizzes and games whose subject is the world's water supply, and walk in the shoes of a refugee via an interactive online tour.

2. Speak in Public...

Grades 1–4 *A Very Important Day*
by Maggie Harold (HarperCollins, 1995)

In this book, hear immigrant voices from such countries as Scotland, Ghana, India, and El Salvador speak about the pride they feel while traveling into New York City to take their oath of citizenship. Despite a heavy snow, the families are cheerful and proud, trudging through the harsh weather with willing hearts. As the judge swears the families in, he notes they are experiencing a very important day. Over and over again, among the crowd, a proud father determines, "This has become our country on a very important day."

Grades 2–5 *Colonial Voices*
by Kay Winters (Dutton, 2008)

Ethan, the printer's errand boy, is running through the city to deliver his employer's message. An urgent meeting is to be held; the colonists are determined not to pay the British tea tax, and the Sons of Liberty must gather. Along the way, Ethan hears the voices of Boston's tradesmen and seamstresses, bakers and shoemakers, basket makers and tavern owners, all of whom talk about how the tax affects their earnings.

Website: American Rhetoric

http://www.americanrhetoric.com/

At this site, students may listen to audio speeches of famous American leaders, from Abraham Lincoln to Martin Luther King, Jr. A Top 100 page links viewers to the most significant political speeches in American history, those that changed the course of American history and inspired a course of action true to American principles and ideals. Speeches from our current president are archived at a prominent link/page.

5. Petition and Protest to Influence Public Policy

Grades K–3 *I Have the Right to Be a Child*
by Alain Serres (Groundwood Books, 2012)

A young child narrator speaks to his rights as a child in a simplistic way, though one which mirrors the UN's Convention on the Rights of a Child, adopted in 1989. The book is meant to elicit discussion, with even the back cover asking questions: "I am a child. But, do I have rights? What about the right to know, express, and talk about my rights?"

Grades 9–12 *The Weirdo*
by Theodore Taylor (HMH Books for Young Readers, 2006)

When Chip and his father move to the North Carolina swamplands, Chip becomes friends with a graduate student working to safeguard the indigenous bears from poachers and hunters. When Chip's friend disappears, he and his girlfriend elicit the help of the media to advance their environmental cause and solve a murder!

Website: First Amendment Center:
Educating for Freedom and Responsibility

http://www.firstamendmentschools.org/freedoms/speechfaqs.aspx

At this website, students may learn about the interpretations of their right to free speech and peaceful protest by browsing frequently asked questions, including "What are the free expression rights of students in public schools under the First Amendment?" Students also become familiar with major court cases qualifying the right to expression. Helpful website resources are provided, and students may even petition school administrative personnel to apply as a project or affiliate member of the Center.

6. Vote

Grades Pre-K–3 *Duck for President*
by Doreen Cronin (Atheneum, 2004)

Duck and the cattle do not like the way Farmer Brown is running the farm, so Duck runs for farmer. He wins, but it is too much work. He runs for governor—still too much work. He runs for president and learns a lot about campaigning along the way—still too hard. A want ad is in the paper for a job as duck on a farm. He takes it and begins his memoirs!

Grades 4–6 *Off and Running*
by Gary Soto (Yearling, 1997)

Miata Ramirez is running for school president on a platform of school beautification while her opponent promises free ice cream, every day. Miata finds a way to pull through and win, even though she is asking classmates to plant flowers and clean up. Her answer: get her opponent interested in soccer!

Website: Double-Click Democracy: Kids Voting USA

http://kidsvotingusa.org/vote/

At this site, students may replicate the issues and contests being held at the local, state, or national level or may simply use the site to host school elections, book or poster contests, or other contests. The goal of the site, however it is used, is to "foster the habit of voting."

Fourth, and most importantly, a good citizen is:

1. Concerned for the Rights and Welfare of Others

Grades 1–4 *A Is for America* by Devin Scillion (Sleeping Bear Press, 2001)

Americans working hard to improve the plight of their fellow Americans are highlighted in this alphabet book. For example, K is for King and Kamehameha; F is for Ford; and P is for Rosa Parks. Fun juxtapositions (Rockwell painting a picture of Armstrong, while both are on the moon) engage the reader and lead to biographical discussion points.

Grades 7–12 *Americans Who Speak the Truth* by Robert Shetterly (Puffin, 2008)

From Mark Twain to John Muir, Shetterly creates portraits of 50 significant Americans, all of whom withstood trials and tribulations to speak the truth as a means of empowering others, all expounding upon and calling attention to the heart and soul of American freedoms and values. For example, a mystical portrait of Walt Whitman is accompanied by his quote: "Hate tyrants, argue not concerning God, have patience and indulgence toward the people."

Website: Do Something

https://www.dosomething.org/

Do Something provides a multitude of options allowing students to either (1) fight for the rights of others, (2) join a good cause, or (3) help others. For example, a student may host a "bye-bye bullies" night as a means of discussing, customizing, and contributing to the school anti-bullying policy; host a voter registration booth at school; participate in Red, White, and Soup on July 4 (helping at a soup kitchen); or start a petition to demand accessible spaces on campus. Once students join a campaign, they will have the support of students from around the globe working to make the "world suck less."

2. Socially Responsible

Grades 4–8 *Who Cares? Millions Do* by Milton Meltzer (Walker, 1994)

Meltzer not only highlights nonprofit organizations working to improve humanity's lot and share means of improvement on an international basis (CARE, Peace Corps, Habitat for Humanity), but also captures the stories of altruistic individuals, such as Oskar Schindler and Jean-Henri Dunant (founder of the Red Cross). Through his portrayals of obscure individuals who have unselfishly, willingly, and inexhaustibly sacrificed for the benefit of others, readers will realize the extent of altruistic action on a worldwide basis.

Grades 9–12 *The Last Safe Place on Earth* by Richard Peck (Laurel Leaf, 2007)

Todd Tobin's family moves to the suburbs in an attempt to find tranquility. Unfortunately, they find only superstition, censorship, and closed-mindedness. To secure his own rights and freedoms, as well as those of his family and friends, Todd fights book censorship and religious brainwashing tactics.

Website: MTV Act

http://act.mtv.com/

At this site, high schoolers may read about celebrities making a difference through social action, enter contests offering ideas on how they would (or can) make the world a better place, read interviews about prominent youth making responsible decisions, and learn means of volunteering, donating to important causes, influencing decision makers, creating a video for change, and registering to vote.

3. Confident in Their Capacity to Make a Difference

Grades K–3 *My Grandma's the Mayor* by Marjorie Pelligrino (Magination Press, 2000)

Annie's grandma doesn't have much time for playing with her grandchildren after she is elected mayor. At first, Annie is sad, but when she realizes the impact of her grandmother's role and the manner in which the town counted on Grandma when a fire broke out in the community, Annie decides to quit sulking and discover ways to help, too.

Grades 4–7 *We Are the Ship: The Story of Negro League Baseball* by Kadir Nelson (Jump at the Sun, 2008)

Lauded with several ALA award designations, Nelson, in nine innings (chapters), introduces the struggles of the Negro League baseball players in the first half of the 20th century. Never giving up on either their love of the game or their fight to be accepted for their accomplishments, the sports figures featured in this book exhibit confidence in a governmental system which may be influenced via sheer willpower and talent.

Grades 3–8 *Our White House: Looking In, Looking Out* edited by NCBLA (Candlewick, 2008)

In this collection of vignettes about life in the White House, written by award-winning children's authors, readers are introduced to the significant obstacles our country's presidents have experienced as residents, which they have overcome due to talent, fortitude, and proactive decisions based in self-confidence. Scattered among these poignant tales, humorous and tender moments expose the joys and sorrows of everyday life in the White House.

Website: Civics Action Project: Civics Action Toolkit

http://www.crfcap.org/mod/resource/view.php?id=142

Establishing confidence prior to the initiation of a project, this site provides step-by-step instruction, a how-to guide for civic action. Recommendations to get started (visiting the library or conducting an interview), move forward (letters to the editor, social media), and succeed (using the media, linking to policy) are defined, exemplified, and modeled.

The types of books presented here lend themselves to the development of the quintessential American citizen versed in civic literacy, as defined in "Guardian of Democracy." Such a definition considers an individual versed in the history and processes of our nation and government who is also willing to contribute to, advocate for, and participate in his or her country's well-being, thereby exhibiting a sense of social responsibility and concern for the general welfare. To educate such an individual, the standards and practices discussed in Chapters III and IV are required; however, an exemplary collection must start with "the end in mind."

A listing of additional collection resources follows. These websites indicate other resources important to civic education efforts. Also, *do not forget to collect the resources contained in the thematic integration and reading promotion chapters to follow!*

Civic Bookshelf: http://www.lawanddemocracy.org/bookshelf.html
Teaching through Children's Literature: http://teachingcivics.org/lesson/teaching-civics-through-childrens-literature/
Patriotic Books for Children: http://blog.biguniverse.com/tag/civics-books-for-children/
Civics Literature: http://www.pabar.org/public/lre/2009/civicsliterature.PDF
Social Studies Themes: http://www.udel.edu/dssep/literature.html
NCSS Listings: http://www.socialstudies.org/resources/notable
Fiction and the Bill of Rights: http://www.ala.org/offices/publishing/booklist/booklinks/resources/billrights
Connecting Social Studies and Children's Literature: http://blog.richmond.edu/openwide-lookinside/archives/22
Patriotism and the United States: http://www.thereadingnook.com/usa/
U.S. Senate Listing: http://www.senate.gov/reference/bibliography/kids/kids.shtml
Center for Civic Education—Conflict and Peace Resolution: http://www.civiced.org/resources/publications/resource-materials/391-literature-for-children-and-young-adults
Youth Leadership Initiative: http://208.81.226.245/civics-resources/
PBS Social Studies Civics: http://www.pbs.org/teachers/socialstudies/inventory/civicsunitedstatesgovernment-912.html

In addition to using these quality resources, as you begin or improve a civics collection, consider the following evaluation criteria. The resources should:

- Provide information about the influence of government and law on historical events and on economic and social systems (also acquire examples from multiple government systems for purposes of comparison).

- Balance information about government structure with discussion on how to be an active and considerate citizen.

- Reflect age-appropriate activities and materials which mirror real-life situations, highlight vocabulary, and include focused and uncluttered graphics, illustrations, maps, primary source documents, and case studies that build active citizens.

- Give fair and objective presentations of civics issues.

- Elicit civics analysis and discussion and critical thinking.

- Balance objective presentations of contemporary civics issues with global perspectives that are balanced, pertinent, accurate, and current.

- Provide examples of citizens who have effected change within our Republic and the democratic system.

- Include characters who portray the responsibilities, actions, and perspective of a model citizen.

- Include high-interest materials and activities that are focused, engaging, and uncluttered.

- Include multiple perspectives of America's historical beginnings, historical events, and pertinent issues.

- Present a fresh perspective or original theme on a traditional topic.

- Be easily readable, yet of high literary quality.

- Appeal to a wide range of sophistication and reading abilities.

- Exhibit intriguing cover art and engaging titles.

Grants

Turning to acquisition (and therefore funding), several grants, if awarded, are conducive to the development of a strong civics-based collection:

- *Bookapalooza Program*: Sponsored by the Association for Library Service for Children (ALA division), this grant cycles each February 1 and is specifically geared toward transforming a library's collection. Criteria examine the creative and innovative means by which the books will be shared with children of the community. http://www.ala.org/awardsgrants/awards/247/apply

- *NEH Challenge Grant*: Intended to support long-term efforts to enhance humanities programs and resources, the National Endowment for the Humanities Challenge Grant may provide capital to support the acquisition of collections needed for humanities-related activities (such as civics education). http://www.neh.gov /grants/challenge/challenge-grants

- *Laura Bush Foundation for America's Libraries*: Specifically targeted to school libraries, each year this foundation awards $5,000 to successful applicants for the purpose of expanding, updating, and diversifying collections. http://www.laurabush foundation.com/index.html

- *R.R. Donnelley Foundation*: Supporting both public schools and public libraries, this foundation strives to support youth, education, inclusion, and diversity efforts. http://www.rrdonn-elley.com/about/external-affairs/community-relations. aspx

- *Snapdragon Book Foundation*: For school libraries serving disadvantaged children, this foundation may provide funding for civics-related books. http://www.snapdragonbookfoundation.org/

First Lady Laura Bush, who initiated the National Book Festival and the Laura Bush Foundation for America's Libraries.

- *Union Pacific Community-Based Grant Program*: For those public libraries located in areas served by the Union Pacific railroad, this program's mission is to fund a variety of civics programs in any given community that seek to improve the general quality of life. http://www.up.com/aboutup/community/foundation/grants/index.htm

- *Starbucks Foundation*: This foundation is interested in supporting organizations equipping 15- to 24-year-olds to develop an interest in long-term civic engagement in their community. Letters of inquiry are accepted only between November 1 and December 15. http://www.starbucks.com/responsibility/community/youth-action/grant

- *Barnes and Noble Donation Program*: If a school or public library can partner with a local Barnes and Noble bookstore for civics education purposes (providing the donor visibility by means of planned in-store events which reach a wide audience), donations of civics-oriented materials may be possible. http://www.barnesandnobleinc.com/our_company/sponsorship/sponsorship_local/donations_local.html

- *Ford Foundation*: This foundation supports those organizations that promote democratic values, free expression, and human achievement. This grant would be ideal for large civics-based school or public library efforts which require collection building in association with a particular project. http://www.fordfoundation.org/pdfs/grants/ grant-application-guide.pdf

- *Robert R. McCormick Civics Program*: If the reader's school or public library is located in the Chicago area, luck has knocked at the door! The perfect grant program for developing a schoolwide civics education initiative, to include an exemplary library collection, the McCormick Foundation supports programming which strives to engage young people in lifelong civic participation. http://www.mccormickfoundation.org/page.aspx? pid=575

- *Braitmayer Foundation*: For those strengthening a civics curriculum in general (to include resources), this foundation offers grants nationwide to schools interested in curricular and school reform initiatives. http://www.braitmayerfoundation.org/guidelines/

- *Ben and Jerry Foundation*: For public libraries hoping to begin a community civic engagement program, complete with necessary resources, this foundation's guidelines might require a second look. The purpose of its grant awards is to support activities and strategies contributing to social change. http://benandjerrysfoundation.org/the- grassroots-organizing-for-social-change-program/

- *Brinker International Foundation* (owner of Chili's Grill & Bar, Romano's Macaroni Grill, On the Border Mexican Grill & Cantina, Maggiano's Little Italy, Cozymel's Coastal Mexican Grill, Corner Bakery Café, and Big Bowl restaurants): If your school or public library is located in an area in which one of these restaurants is found, you may apply for a grant which supports programs and projects that are affiliated with children/family-and civics-related educational programs. http://www.brinker.com/contac- t/charitable_requests.asp

- *New Schools Venture Fund*: Does your school have a new idea about promoting and expanding civics education? If so, use this grant to advance your idea. This fund wishes to invest in the most promising, scalable education ventures in the country, creating a nationwide network of those committed to improving the public education system. http://www.newschools.org/entrepreneurs/submit

- *Safeway Foundation*: Funding general projects in education and human services, both school and public libraries are eligible for this grant. http://www.safewayfoundation. org/get-funded/what-we-fund.html

- *McCarthey Dressman Education Foundation*: K–12 librarians may apply for this grant, which seeks applicants who have facilities, expertise, and community endorsement, but need additional resources for materials, time, and transportation. Specifically targeted to develop in-class and extracurricular programs that improve student learning, the Foundation considers proposals that foster understanding, deepen students' knowledge, and provide opportunities to expand awareness of the world. http://mccarthey dressman.org/academic-enrichment-grants/

- *Awesome Foundation*: This grassroots grant, funded by people in all walks of life, considers funding for any and all projects of worth—hence the name. http://www.awe somefoundation.org/en/faq

In addition to these nationally based grants (minus the McCormick grant), do not forget to research local- and state-based grant funding opportunities. Also, consider cooperative efforts among libraries in your school district or regional area (if a public library), as well as gift-giving groups such as the PTA, church charities, grassroots civics organizations, and local philanthropists.

Grantwriting Tips

As you may apply for grants annually or biannually, maintain an electronic folder that preserves—and allows library personnel to periodically update—a mission statement, an organizational history, a strategic plan, the library's structure (board members, bylaws, financial statement, and federal tax ID number), service population demographics, and levels of patron usage of resources and services, backed by statistical reports. Read guidelines two to three times before preparing the narrative or completing the application, calling grant personnel to ask questions if need be. Participate in webinars and online grant-information offerings that explain the grant goals, requirements, and mandates in detail and that introduce grant-funding players. Preview sample grant applications provided by the grantor with a keen eye.

Incorrect grammar, punctuation, syntax, and style will significantly inhibit the granting of an award. Thus, you should proofread documents and applications at least twice, asking one or more peers to review all papers as well. Answer the queries presented within the grant guidelines in a clear, concise, straightforward, creative, and truthful manner, ensuring the narrative describes both the library's individuality and its creative and innovative service and resource delivery methods, meetings and discussion groups, community-based offerings, and/or building improvements. Do not exceed the number of pages suggested by the guidelines.

Watch for detail indicators, such as signing grant applications in blue ink. Make sure supporting documentation is accurate and statistically valid. Double-check budgetary calculations for accuracy. Before submitting the grant, set it aside for a few days after peer review and corrections. Then, with a fresh eye, double-check the document one more time before clicking the submit button. Do not forget to make a copy for your records before submitting the application; print copies of all narrative statements, budget requests, statistics and supporting documentation, and completed applications. If the application is mailed via the postal service, utilize tracking and return-receipt services to ensure the grant package is received by the grantor. Wait graciously for a reply from the funding organization.

Promote the Collection

In addition to the reading promotion plans found in Chapter XII, promote a newly acquired civics-based materials collection within the school or local community. Use the collection to plan events for such high-profile times as Constitution Day, the Fourth of July, Veterans Day, Memorial Day, Martin Luther King, Jr. Day, President's Day, Election Day, and Thanksgiving. Provide handouts and brochures during such events that explain civic education efforts within your school or public library, and highlight the importance of such education, as explained in Chapters I and II. Provide a form in the brochure that will allow participants to donate to the collection. Also, reference an online page on your library's website at which donors may make contributions.

Challenges

Finally, remember censorship is a reality. Be prepared to defend the choices found in your civics-based collection at all costs. For school libraries, each book selected should fulfill the goals of state-based civics standards. Public library employees should be familiar with court cases protecting First Amendment rights within public venues, such as *Sund v. City of Wichita Falls, Texas*, 121 F. Supp. 2d 530 (N.D. Texas, 2000), and *Right to Read Defense Committee v. School Committee of the City of Chelsea*, 454 F. Supp. 703 (D. Mass. 1978). School librarians should be aware of the following cases: *Board of Education, Island Trees Union Free School District No. 26 v. Pico*, 457 U.S. 853, 102 S.Ct. 2799, 73 L.Ed.2d 435 (1982), and *Tinker v. Des Moines Independent Community School District*, 393 U.S. 503, 89 S.Ct. 733, 21 L.Ed.2d. 731 (1969). For additional information, support, and resources, refer to the American Library Association's page on censorship and First Amendment issues: http://www.ala.org/advocacy/intfreedom/censorshipfirstamendmentissues.

Chapter VII

Thematic Integration

Introduction and Activities and Resources, Pre-K to Grade 1

"Teach the children so it will not be necessary to teach the adults."—Abraham Lincoln

Introduction to Thematic Integration: K–12

This chapter, and the four which follow, introduce school and public librarians to activities which strive to build civic literacy among young students and patrons, while also introducing additional resource material for expanded lessons and/or enrichment, as well as student self-learning opportunities. These integrative plans are divided into the following grade/reading levels: pre-K to 1, 2–4, 5–7, 8–10, and 11–12. Reference is sometimes made to graphic organizers found in Appendix A. Both print and web-based multimedia resources are summarized and thereafter used to spur activities which mirror the scholarly recommendations found in Chapters III and V. In other words, the resources serve as educational material which foster (1) discussion opportunities, with questions included for each resource; (2) civic action, with ideas presented as part of each guide; and (3) civic service, again with possibilities provided for the librarian educator offering civic education lessons/programming. The American Association of School Librarian standards conducive to the activities are listed. Finally, at points throughout the chapters, preeminent educational websites and multimedia tools are evaluated and reviewed for the benefit of librarian professionals.

Activities and Resources: Pre-K to Grade 1

At the introductory grade levels, students and young patrons need to understand the concept of community; group interactions and decision making; governance; civic virtues such as freedom, justice, and liberty; balancing the needs of individuals versus the group; and examining experiences in relation to ideals, democratic practices, and citizenship as exemplified in stories. Concrete activities should be utilized, as children at this age cannot think abstractly. Activities should mirror what children have experienced in their own lives.

The three books featured for discussion, action, and service-based purposes at this level are *Red, White, and Blue Good-Bye* by Sarah Wones Tomp, *Death of the Iron Horse* by Paul Goble, and *Now and Ben: The Modern Inventions of Benjamin Franklin* by Gene Barretta.

Red, White, and Blue Good-bye
by Sarah Wones Tomp

Daddy is a Navy man, about to sail away for too many days! With the help of a red mailbox flag, white clouds, and the blue ocean, as well as the good old red, white, and blue, a young girl comes to accept her temporary loss and sacrifice.

Discussion

Read this book in association with *F Is for Flag* by Wendy Lewison.
Ask students:

1. Has your mother or father ever had to leave home for a period of time to work and provide for the family? How did his or her absence make you feel? How did your mother or father make you feel better?
2. Why did the girl's father use the colors of red, white, and blue to help ease the daughter's sad feelings associated with her Daddy's Naval deployment? Why is the flag important to the father? Why is he using the flag to help his daughter understand the reasons he must leave to serve America's Navy?
3. Why do fathers (and mothers) serve in the American Navy? What is special about our country that needs protecting? How will Daddy's protection help his daughter and others just like her? How is Daddy helping his country?
4. How does serving at sea protect our country? What is the role of the Navy? Who is the person in Washington, D.C., who is the commander of America's military? Where does he or she get the authority to be the commander?
5. Which principles and values does the flag stand for? What do the stars and stripes and colors mean? Draw a picture within or beside the flag included as Exhibit 1 in Appendix A, showing people enjoying what the flag stands for.
6. Do you know who started the postal service that mailed the daughter's letters to her dad? Why was the postal service important in early America?

Additional Resources

U.S. Consulate: Flag as Symbol, http://www.usconsulate.org.hk/pas/kids/sym_flag.htm

PBS Resource: The American Flag, http://www.pbs.org/americaresponds/theamericanflag.html

History of U.S. Flag: http://www.hellokids.com/c_6764/reading-online/stories-for-children/the-history-of-the-united-states-flag

Ben's Guide on Flag: http://bensguide.gpo.gov/k-2/symbols/flag.html

The American flag, Alexandria, Virginia, 2012 (photograph by the author).

AASL Standards

1.1.6 Read, view, and listen for information presented in any format (e.g., textual, visual, media, digital) to make inferences and gather meaning.

4.1.8 Use creative and artistic formats to express personal learning.

Civic Action

The flag stands for the men and women who sacrifice their lives for liberty, freedom, and justice, every day of the week. Plan a library field trip to downtown local, state, or federal office buildings. Do most of the buildings have a flag out front? Is the flag in good shape? Eliciting student opinion, write down the location of any flag which is torn or ragged. Once back at school or the public library, during library class, in association with the art teacher (or with a local artist if a public library), ask students to draw a picture of someone using the flag in a way which helps others. Place your pictures in the school's main office or local art gallery, charging a small entry fee. Use the monies from the fees to replace the torn or ragged flags encountered on the field trip. On a second field trip or public library community walk to present the flag, ask students to explain to the person in charge of the community facility why it is important to keep the flag in good shape, as it stands for the values others have fought for and the freedoms we all hold.

AASL Standards

4.1.6 Organize knowledge in a way that can be called upon easily.

4.3.3 Pursue opportunities for improving personal and aesthetic growth.

Civic Service

Host a program in the library which allows the spouses and children of those serving out of state or overseas to visit one another via Skype or Facetime. (Many times families do not have appropriate Internet service at home.) Ask pre-K–1 students to honor these families by serving as volunteers during allotted visitation times, distributing tissues, headphones, schedules, water, needed hugs, or other small treats, and gathering as a group following visitation to sing songs about America or talk about other books which show the importance of freedom (the children and spouses may need to smile after signing off from speaking with their parent or spouse).

AASL Standards

3.1.5 Connect learning to community issues.

3.2.2 Show social responsibility by participating actively with others in learning situations.

Death of the Iron Horse by Paul Goble

Goble's story reveals the dire cultural and lifestyle disruption imposed upon Native Americans during the age of the railroad. This story depicts one brave group of Cheyenne young men who disrupted the destructive pattern, if only on one occasion.

Discussion

In association with this discussion, also read *Brother Eagle, Sister Sky* by Susan Jeffers. Discuss the Constitution (see the book *We the Kids* by David Catrow) and our Bill of Rights.

1. Based on Jeffers's book and Sweet Medicine's prophecy, why would the Cheyenne be distraught about the Iron Horse traveling through their lands (other than the fact it looked and sounded like a monster)? How did the train affect Cheyenne beliefs about the Earth? How did it affect their right to human dignity and liberty? Were the Cheyenne being denied basic rights to life, liberty, and the pursuit of happiness?
2. Based on your answers to question 1, do you feel the Cheyenne had a right to derail the Iron Horse? Why or why not?
3. Does the rule of law (the Constitution and the Bill of Rights) encourage Native Americans to believe as they want to believe about the value of the Earth? In what way?
4. Do all individuals in America have a right to say what is on their mind, including Native Americans? If so, how is this right protected?
5. Do Native Americans have the right to warn others about harm to the environment? Would you join in this discussion if you could? What would you say?

Additional Resources

Ben's Guide: Constitution, http://bensguide.gpo.gov/6–8/documents/constitution/index.html

Celebrating Constitution Day: http://v7.k12.com/constitutionday/lessons/K-1/lesson_holder.htm?preloader.swf?Title=Preview%20-%20CH_K-01_01&userType=1000&lesson-File=content_lesson_39166.txt&previewMode=1&subjectID=4&uiType=33&target-Type=1&stateAbbrev=PA&envID=1%27

Ben's Guide: Bill of Rights, http://bensguide.gpo.gov/6–8/citizenship/billofrights.html

AASL Standards

3.3.3 Use knowledge and information skills and dispositions to engage in public conversation and debate around issues of common concerns.

4.2.3 Maintain openness to new ideas by considering divergent opinions, changing opinions or conclusions when evidence supports the change, and seeking information about new ideas encountered through academic or personal experiences.

Civic Action

In library class, after reading these books, discuss how Native Americans are faring in the 21st century. Invite a Native American speaker or knowledgeable citizen into the library to discuss the plight of Native Americans on our Indian reservations. Read some of the statistics found as Exhibit 1 in Appendix B. Listen to stories about Native American experiences in the 21st century found at http://www.nbcnews.com/id/21134540/vp/52096500#52096500.

Next, as a class or group, choose one fact about modern-day Native American life that is of highest concern to you. Ask students to think about what they would include in a letter to a member of Congress describing these problems and asking for reform efforts.

Write and send the letter on behalf of the class and inform students you will ask the representative to write back describing why this situation still exists, in light of the rule of law, Bill of Rights, and modern conveniences, and how he or she plans to rectify the situation. Have first graders write one sentence each that might be included in the letter.

Additional Resources

K–12 Cheyenne Resource: http://www.sd84.k12.id.us/farmstid/Native%20American%20Web/cheyenne.htm

Omaha Public Library Cheyenne Resource: http://www.omahapubliclibrary.org/transmiss/congress/cheyenne.html

AASL Standards

2.3.1 Connect understanding to the real world.

2.4.1 Determine how to act upon information.

Civic Service

Did you know that only 2 percent of clothing and fabric is now made in the United States—certainly a different scenario than when the Cheyenne played with the cloth being delivered via the Iron Horse. Read books to students about the history of textile and clothing manufacturing in America. Ask students to bring in clothing discarded by their parents and help sort through the clothing, finding articles made in the United States. Use the scraps from the U.S.A.-made items to create a butterfly collage with the slogan "You Were Beautifully Made in the U.S.A." Read books about the Cheyenne and their respect for elders, and then donate the collage, framed if possible, to the local nursing home.

Caveat: If you would like to share this book and idea for service with older students, utilize the following "Textile Day" idea: As a means of promoting local companies which manufacture or sell clothing or any sort of accessory using fabric (e.g., placemats, curtains), discover, along with older students, such companies or independent businesses within the county served by the school or public library (or the nearest county if one exists). Host a "Do You Know Where Your Fabric Comes From?" Day in which representatives from such local companies or independent businesses (can be a home business) visit the library, speaking with students and visiting parents about the manufacturing or distribution process (invite all school or public library stakeholders) and showcasing samples (so that local, American businesses may be served). Also, invite a state or federal representative to visit the event to explain, after hearing the business owner's talk, how such "mom and pop" businesses are supported. Prior to the event, introduce students to the Library World Online Patron Access (OPAC) and how to find books which highlight America's textile manufacturing history, as well as the diversity of America's clothing styles throughout history. Also speak to the diversity of clothing worn by America's cultural or ethnic subgroups. Prior to Fabric Day, ask students to choose which books should be displayed at the event and how best to make guests "feel at home" during their visit.

AASL Standards

4.1.8 Use artistic and creative formats to express personal learning.

Now and Ben: The Modern Inventions of Benjamin Franklin by Gene Barretta

This bright, humorously illustrated book applauds the inventions contributed to the common good of our country by Benjamin Franklin. Most are still in use in today's age, though highly improved upon. They include the Franklin stove, the lightning rod, and, most importantly, swimming flippers!

Discussion

Also read *A Picture Book of Benjamin Franklin* by David Adler.

1. What is a statesman? How did Benjamin Franklin meet the definition of a statesman?
2. The author of *Now and Ben* says Benjamin Franklin helped write government documents that we still use today. What are those documents? Why are they important? Why are government documents important? What is a rule of law?
3. How would you define the word *community*? Why is it important for people to work together to help and improve upon a community?
4. How did Benjamin Franklin improve your community? How are others helping and improving your community? Who works to help and improve your community every day? How might you help your community?

Associated Resources

Biographical sources on Benjamin Franklin include:

http://www.biography.com/people/benjamin-franklin-9301234
http://www.history.com/topics/american-revolution/benjamin-franklin
http://www.libertyskids.com/arch_who_bfranklin.html

AASL Standards

4.4.4 Interpret new information based on social and cultural context.
4.3.1 Participate in the social exchange of ideas.

Civic Action

After reading *Now and Ben*, ask each student/patron to consider this fact: when Benjamin Franklin saw something that needed doing, he did it! Skype in local community workers who can explain why the agency represented is so important to the community (or public libraries could invite local workers to story hour). Have each student pick one action completed by Franklin which remains the most important to the life of his or her community (e.g., development of a library, hospital, post office, fire department, or sanitation department). Conduct a vote to see which agency carries the most weight in the minds of your readers (based on the visits and discussions).

Reading Room of the Boston Public Library, 2014 (photograph by the author).

AASL Standards

1.3.2 Seek divergent perspectives during information gathering and assessment.

3.3.6 Use information and knowledge in the service of democratic values.

Civic Service

Ask students or patrons to observe the places they visit in the community for a period of two weeks, thinking about something that might need changing or improved upon. Come back together as a group and ask students to discuss anything they want changed or improved in their community. Ask students to think of one small action they might take to help. Super-shy students at this age might wish to digitally record their observations instead, with the help of the library assistant.

AASL Standards

2.1.3 Use strategies to draw conclusions from information and apply knowledge to curricular areas, real-world situations, and further investigation.

2.3.1 Connect understanding to the real world.

Chapter VIII

Thematic Integration
Activities and Resources, Grades 2–4

"The people themselves must be the ultimate makers of their own Constitution."—Theodore Roosevelt

In this stage of development, students begin thinking logically about tangible objects and events within their world and may focus on multiple parts of a problem. They also understand the concept of perception and ownership of perspective in others.

Revolutionary Friends: General George Washington and the Marquis de Lafayette by Selene Castrovilla

As the American Revolution raged, George Washington did not have a son or male confidant to whom to turn for comfort. A brave 19-year-old youth from France supplied the answer, Marquis de Lafayette. Having defied the King of France to sail to America and volunteer for the Revolutionary cause, Lafayette would take any risk to help the beleaguered Continentals, all the while earning the respect and admiration of one of the world's most honored military leaders.

Discussion

1. Why was Lafayette so enchanted with America? Which values did he admire? (Look at his quotes, especially.) What did he mean when he said his "heart was enlisted"? What are some other instances in which other countries or other people became enamored with the ideals of America?

2. How did Lafayette's behavior reflect his idea that liberty must win at all costs (see quote)? Which sort of bravery was required to defy the King of France, and, once in America, charge into battle? To leave for France to ask for additional assistance?

3. Why did Lafayette remain at Washington's side, even when others were questioning his leadership? Read Thomas Paine's poem "Liberty Tree" (Appendix A, Exhibit 2).

Based on this poem, what do you believe the green branches in the Patriots' hats represented?

4. Why were Lafayette's and Washington's portraits placed side by side in the House of Representatives? What do the portraits tell us about the civic character of these men? What does the placement mean for both America and France today?

http://history.house.gov/Exhibitions-and-Publications/House-Chamber/Lafayette-Washington/

Additional Resources

Lafayette at the New York Historical Society: http://www.nyhistory.org/exhibit/marquis-de-lafayette-1757–1834–0

Marquis de Lafayette: http://www.mountvernon.org/research-collections/digital-encyclopedia/article/marquis-de-lafayette/

AASL Standards

2.1.3 Use strategies to draw conclusions from information and apply knowledge to curricular areas, real-world situations, and further investigations.

Civic Action

Assign each student or library patron a different country. Help the child navigate Time for Kids' Around the World website: http://www.time-forkids.com/around-the-world. Question children about their assigned country to make sure they understand the people and their lifestyles, challenges, and culture. In round-robin style, ask each child to go around the room and meet their "international" classmates. The children are to pretend they are meeting a dignitary from another country, one who will be a friend to the United States and its people (children will rotate between being the international friend and the dignitary). Ask children to consider the manner in which they will "charm" the dignitary. How will the students let the dignitaries know they are working for the cause of liberty, freedom, and democracy? How will each member of the pair learn to admire the other's

Portrait of Gilbert Motier, the Marquis de la Fayette (1757–1834), as a lieutenant general (Artist Joseph Désiré Court [1797–1865]).

"noble spirit?" Come back together as a class after the meetings and discuss how American citizens can best respect and honor citizens of other nations. How can Americans make other citizens honor and respect them? How might nations more easily become friends?

AASL Standards

1.2.1 Display initiative and engagement by posing questions and investigating the answers beyond the collection of superficial facts.

1.3.4 Contribute to the exchange of ideas within the learning community.

Civic Service

During the War for Independence, fife and drum units participated in July 4 parades. On their tricorner hats, they placed green twigs as decoration—most likely as a symbol of a bright new world, freedom from tyranny, and the celebration of a nation born from revolution. Liberty trees were also a leading symbol during the Revolution, and a sprig from one, worn in the hat or on clothing, signaled a Continental. Find a nursery in your area that might be willing to donate seedlings that could be planted around the school or public library grounds in remembrance of prominent local military heroes who have served the military overseas. Ask the honorees to visit the library on the day of the planting and speak to their sacrifice for liberty. Have students present a readers theater for the heroes, portraying the story of Lafayette and/or the meaning of liberty trees, basing the drama in the poem written for Lafayette when he visited the United States in 1824 (rewrite it for the modern ear if needed—see Appendix C, Exhibit 1).

AASL Standards

2.2.4 Demonstrate personal productivity by completing products to express learning.

4.2.3 Respond to literature and creative expressions of ideas in various formats.

Eyewitness Books: American Revolution
by Stuart Murray

Written in association with the Smithsonian Institution, this book examines the events that precipitated the American Revolution, as well as the movers and shakers, commanders, battles, symbols, life behind the war front, and famous art and objects from the Revolutionary period, now housed at the Smithsonian.

Discussion

1. Before reading this book, were you aware as to the extent of bravery exhibited by our forefathers and first commanders during the American Revolution? What, in your opinion, was the bravest moment, as found in the book? How did living in the colonial era make early Americans a brave and independent people? Does anything about our current lifestyle create a degree of bravery within modern-day Americans? Are we brave in the 21st century? In which ways?

2. Based on what you learned in this book, do you believe the American Revolution was necessary? Why or why not? Did the colonists have a good argument? What were

their most persuasive points? Did they make their points known in the best possible way?

3. What did Thomas Paine mean when he wrote, "A government of our own is our natural right"? Why is this right "natural"? Do all peoples have such a right? Read the Universal Declaration of Rights (abridged for youth—Appendix A, Exhibit 3) as a classroom and compare it to the Declaration of Independence (Appendix A, Exhibit 4).

4. What are the symbols of American freedom in the 21st century? Do they carry the same meaning as the symbols of the American Revolution? Why do we need such symbols? What do they help us remember? How do they inspire democratic action?

5. Which battle or historical place mentioned in the book carried the most meaning for you and why? How did each part of the 13 colonies work together for the benefit of the whole?

AASL Standards

4.4.3 Recognize how to focus efforts in personal learning.

4.2.1 Display curiosity by pursuing interests through multiple formats.

4.1.2 Read widely and fluently to make connections with self, the world, and previous reading.

Civic Action

Listen to an actor's reenactment of Patrick Henry's "Give Me Liberty or Give Me Death" speech: http://www.history.org/almanack/life/politics/giveme.cfm Make props that will make your library seem like the Richmond church in which Patrick Henry delivered his speech. Then, with the assistance of the art teacher or a local art council member, make paper costumes to dress up like the gentlemen (and ladies outside) who actually heard Henry's speech. Hold a reenactment in which students/patrons dressed in costume and in character react as the people who heard the speech may have (ask students to use their best theatrical voices). Before holding the reenactment, ask students to vote as to which student (or students, if the speech is divided into parts) will play the role of Patrick Henry (you might have students exhibit "best voices" before voting). Then, ask students to pretend they are walking back to their homes after hearing the speech. What will some of their comments be? As time allows, read other famous speeches in American history and hold the same sort of reenactments.

Other Famous Speeches in American History

America Rhetoric: http://www.americanrhetoric.com/top100speechesall.html

Time's Top 10: http://content.time.com/time/specials/packages/completelist/0,29569,1841 228,00.html

AASL Standards

4.3.3 Seek opportunities for pursuing personal and aesthetic growth.

3.3.2 Respect the differing interests and experiences of others, and seek a variety of viewpoints.

Washington and Lafayette inspecting the suffering men at Valley Forge, 1777 (painted and drawn by A. Gibert; lithograph and publication by P. Haas, Washington City; Library of Congress).

Civic Service

As a class or library group, write a "Did You Know Soldiers Needed Shoes at Valley Forge?" pamphlet about the American Revolution, creating bullet points of interesting facts about the soldiers' travails during the winter of 1778–1779, especially pointing out that many of the soldiers did not own shoes. Be sure to include the fact these same soldiers, in the spring, would stand against British regulars at the Battle of Monmouth. Make the story and listing short enough that it might be made into the shape of a shoe sole. Find shoe size pattern molds, and cut the story and listing to fit different sizes of shoe soles. Find a local agency providing shoes to needy children in the community. Ask the agency personnel if they might place the story inset in shoes they give away during the winter months for children to read for purposes of encouragement and the building of self-esteem. Talk about why some people in today's world still do not own adequate shoes. Think about how your group or class might contribute shoes to the needy.

Associated Sources

Mount Vernon: Valley Forge, http://www.mountvernon.org/research-collections/digital-encyclopedia/article/valley-forge/
Liberty's Kids: Valley Forge, http://www.libertyskids.com/arch_where_valleyf.html
Monmouth: http://lcweb2.loc.gov/diglib/legacies/NJ/200003296.html

AASL Standards

3.2.2 Show social responsibility by participating actively with others in learning situations and by contributing questions and ideas during group discussions.

3.3.5 Contribute to the exchange of ideas within and beyond the learning community.

Thomas Jefferson: A Picture Book Biography by James Cross Giblin

Following Thomas Jefferson from his first remembrance, riding high atop a horse, to reminiscences 50 years after he wrote the Declaration of Independence, to his death at his cherished home, Monticello, this book highlights Jefferson's major accomplishments as a statesman and president. It also introduces his beliefs and values, trials and triumphs, sorrows and joys. An appendix, "The Words of Thomas Jefferson," adeptly follows Giblin's narrative.

Discussion

1. Does it take people with all sorts of talents to effect change, especially a governmental revolution? Which talents did Jefferson use to help build America? Did he use just one talent or all of his talents? Should we ever limit our talents to just one subject or interest? When someone makes fun of another individual, does the person being made fun of work harder to strengthen his or her talents? Does that apply to nations as well? Did such a turnabout apply to the budding United States?
2. The Declaration of Independence is only 1,137 words. Why did it take Jefferson so long to write the Declaration? Which values and beliefs was Jefferson trying to convey, define, and describe within the document?
3. Jefferson wrote in the Declaration of Independence, "We hold these truths to be self-evident." Which truths was he talking about ? How would you explain them to someone who had never heard of such truths? Why had these truths not been evident in the general populace prior to 1776 (or had they)? How might we keep these truths in the forefront of the thoughts of America's citizens in today's age?
4. How did Jefferson sacrifice for his country? Which actions did he take? Do we sometimes have to take action and make sacrifices for our country today? In which ways?
5. What was significant about the way Jefferson dressed for his inauguration? Or the way he arranged the White House table or changed dinners from formal affairs to private events? How did his actions and lifestyle mirror the causes for which he wrote?
6. What is the difference between the method by which Americans came to be in charge of their own land as a result of the American Revolution versus the way land was acquired through the Louisiana Purchase? What did Napoleon understand that King George III did not?
7. Thomas believed a good citizen had to be educated. Why? How does education help an American citizen understand his or her country ? How does it make him or her a better citizen?
8. Thomas Jefferson wanted to be remembered for writing the Declaration of Independence, establishing religious freedom as a basic right, and developing the University

of Virginia. Why were these three actions preeminent in his mind? Why were these actions so important to the development and evolution of our governmental system and country as a whole?

9. Is a democracy always improving? If not, should it be? Did Jefferson's words set the ball of liberty in motion? Did his words eventually help eliminate the horror of slavery?

Associated Resources

Thomas Jefferson: http://www.chesapeake.edu/Library/EDU_101/eduhist.asp

Science and the Declaration of Independence: http://nautil.us/blog/how-science-helped-write-the-declaration-of-independence

Education in Colonial America: http://www.ushistoryscene.com/uncategorized/riseofpubliceducation/

Louisiana Purchase:

http://www.librarypoint.org/louisiana_purchase

http://www.ushistory.org/us/20c.asp

Great Hall. View of grand staircase and bronze statue of female figure on newel post holding a torch of electric light, with bust of Thomas Jefferson at right. Library of Congress, Thomas Jefferson Building, Washington, D.C. (Carol Highsmith [1946–], photographer; Library of Congress).

AASL Standards

3.3.3 Use knowledge and information skills and dispositions to engage in public conversation and debate around issues of common concern.

2.1.5 Collaborate with others to exchange ideas, develop new understandings, make decisions, and solve problems.

Civic Action

Think about Jefferson's words regarding the importance of newspapers. Discuss the term *"slanted" news*. Find newspapers published in our country that are not slanted. Follow them every day for two weeks to help students form a habit of reading newspapers. Create a brochure that describes the newspaper and explains why it is appropriate for a democratic citizen. Distribute the brochures on the playground, at lunch, on the bus, and at assemblies.

AASL Standards

2.4.1 Determine how to act on information (accept, reject, modify).

2.4.3 Recognize new knowledge and understanding.

2.3.1 Connect understanding to the real world.

3.3.6 Respect the principles of intellectual freedom.

4.1.8 Use creative and artistic formats to express personal learning.

Civic Service

Consider Jefferson's quotes about the importance of libraries. Join the efforts of Friends of the Library or the Parent–Teacher Association. Ask how you might volunteer at fundraising events so that more civics-related books can be purchased by your school or public library. If you can use class or group discussion time to help with small projects, make arts and crafts or stories about our forefathers, or create book reviews to sell, do so.

AASL Standards

4.1.5 Connect ideas to own interests and previous knowledge and experience.

3.2.3 Demonstrate teamwork by working productively with others.

Chapter IX

Thematic Integration
Activities and Resources, Grades 5–6

"Never doubt that a small group of thoughtful, committed citizens can change the world. Indeed, it is the only thing that ever has."—Margaret Mead

As this concrete operational developmental stage continues, children can imagine differing scenarios and envisage "what if" outcomes. Readers can infer meaning from surrounding text and can identify details that support a conclusion and/or judgment.

Only one book, *Our White House, Looking In, Looking Out*, is used here for this grade level. This book is a compilation of stories and covers a plethora of civics standards.

Our White House: Looking In, Looking Out by the National Children's Book Literacy Alliance

This collection of stories, poetry, jest, and remarkable illustration brings the White House and its inhabitants, both people and pets, to life! Did you know President Harrison had a milk cow delivered to the White House? Or that Teddy Roosevelt's children brought a pony inside? All joking aside, the collection also reveals the poignant, intense moments experienced by our country's leaders, such as Lincoln's charge to unify the country and Roosevelt's worldwide fight to preserve democracy.

Discussion: Part I

1. Why is it important to remember those who constructed or fashioned the White House? How does such remembrance promote our country's values and beliefs?
2. How did the work crew mirror the nature of the country at its beginning? How might that mirror have shown a more appropriate image?
3. How could Jefferson have "stood still" in the face of slavery after writing the Declaration of Independence, the document that eventually helped to free slaves? Why is it important to show the very human sides of our presidents?

4. Why is science important to governmental leaders? How did it help the country in Jefferson's time? In our time?

AASL Standards

1.1.6 Read, view, and listen for information presented in any format (e.g., textual, visual, media, digital) to make inferences and gather meaning.

Civic Action: Part I

Speaking to Jefferson's interest in science, join a nationwide scientific debate, and one very much in the forefront of energy and environmental policy decisions: is fracking a good idea? Follow the example of the *US News & World Report*'s Debate Club, "a meeting of the sharpest minds on today's most important topics" (http://www.usnews.com/debate-club/is-fracking-a-good-idea). You might participate in the national debate as a class or public library discussion group after appropriate research, debate among students, a classroom/group vote, and the development of a logical, written reply. Alternatively, you might create a personalized debate club on a web-building site or start a classroom blog for such purposes. Either way, point out resources that will allow students and their parents to personally write their representatives: http://www.house.gov/representatives/find/; http://www.senate.gov/reference/common/faq/How_to_contact_senators.htm; http://usgovinfo.about.com/od/uscongress/a/letterscongress.htm; and http://www.senate.gov/general/contact_information/senators_cfm.cfm.

AASL Standards

2.3.3 Use valid information and reasoned conclusions to make ethical decisions.

2.1.6 Use the writing process, media and visual literacy, and technology skills to create products that express new understandings.

Civic Service: Part I

To further reveal the human aspects of our presidents and the manner in which those governed may ask presidents to evaluate their actions, during a book fair or Friends of the Library sale, ask students to brainstorm ways to promote the fact that part of the proceeds will be used to buy a copy of the book *So You Think You Want to Be President?* for children staying in local homeless shelters. Ask students to write a one-page publicity flyer to be inserted within the front pages of the book: "The Meaning of the Declaration of Independence." If possible, take a field trip to visit the homeless shelter and distribute the book, with children explaining to other children why the book should be read.

Additional Activities

http://www.trumpetclub.com/intermediate/activities/president.htm
PBS Homeless Facts: http://www.pbs.org/now/shows/526/homeless-facts.html

AASL Standards

3.1.3 Use writing and speaking skills to communicate new understandings effectively.

Discussion: Part II

1. Why is it important to save and preserve our "national treasures," such as the painting of George Washington? What are some other national treasures of which you are aware, and what meaning do they hold for you?
2. How have Native Americans contributed to the continuation of our nation's freedom? During the American Revolution? In other wars? Today? Based in many of their traditions, would Native American tribes also promote a "Great Mother," if a woman were elected president?
3. How might we ensure more politicians are in office to serve the people of our country rather than to promote themselves, similar to the reason John Quincy Adams served? Have you heard a news story of a representative accomplishing great work for his or her constituents? How will we let such representatives understand our gratitude?
4. How might we encourage forward-thinking governmental leaders, such as John Quincy Adams? What are some modern-day examples of forward thinking?

The Washington Monument, on the banks of the Potomac River, cherry blossom season, April 2014 (photograph by the author).

Additional Resources

Great Paintings: http://www.complex.com/style/2012/05/the-50-greatest-american-paint-
ings/1

Native American Contributions:

http://www.scholastic.com/teachers/article/native-american-contributions

http://www.nrcs.usda.gov/Internet/FSE_DOCUMENTS/nrcs141p2_024206.pdf

AASL Standards

3.1.2 Participate and collaborate as members of a social and intellectual network of learners.

3.1.5 Connect learning to community issues.

Civic Action: Part II

Complete a "10-Minute Guide to the Constitution of the State of ____." Fill in the blank with the name of your state. Help students or patrons find resources which allow them to understand the Constitution of the state in which they live. After sharing research and holding brainstorming sessions, complete a listing similar to that found at http://www.upworthy.com/whats-223-years-old-4543-words-long-and-routinely-ignored-by-both-par-ties: "A 10-Minute Guide to the U.S. Constitution" (See Appendix B, Exhibit 2). Compare and contrast the rule of law of your state to the rule of law of the land. Share the state and U.S. brochure with all classrooms in your school or at the brochure/public papers display.

Additional Resources

State Constitutions: http://www.usconstitution.net/stateconst.html

http://www.landofthebrave.info/state-constitutions.htm

U.S. Constitutions:

http://www.usconstitution.net/constkids4.html

http://www.historyforkids.org/learn/northamerica/after1500/government/constitution.htm

AASL Standards

3.2.1 Demonstrate leadership and confidence by presenting ideas to others in both formal and informal situations.

4.2.1 Display curiosity by pursuing interests through multiple resources.

Civic Service: Part II

Create a "Constitutional Lawyer" booth in the library, which will be open at certain specified hours for the school as a whole or, in the case of a public library, during youth-related events or discussions. Make sure students or public library young group participants are well versed in the common, elementary precepts of the U.S. Constitution. Ask students from different classrooms to file by during specified times and ask general questions of rotat-ing student or group discussion volunteers. Hand out the "10-Minute Guide" brochures pre-pared for the civic action portion of Part II of *Our White House*. If a question is too complex, tell the inquiring student or patron that the "Supreme Constitutional Lawyer" will be in at

___, and provide the appropriate times and dates. Ask lawyers in the community to volunteer to periodically (maybe once a month) man the "Supreme Constitutional Lawyer" booth and answer questions about both the state and national rules of law.

AASL Standards

4.3.1 Participate in the social exchange of ideas, both electronically and in person.

4.4.2 Recognize the limits of own personal knowledge.

Discussion: Part III

1. Charles Dickens was a British author. Why would he have been welcome in the White House? Based on the summary of his works, as provided by your teacher or discussion leader, do you believe he was an American at heart? Why?
2. Why was Dickens amazed that all was in order (and all were safe) in the White House without police presence? Why was he amazed at the "decorum and propriety of behavior," even though guests included plainclothes men?
3. How might every American citizen, the same as Elizabeth Keckly, use wise words to further a cause? Calm a hostile fellow citizen with a different point of view? Hostile country? Does being an exemplary citizen require the use of patience? In what way?
4. Did Lincoln have a dream for America? What was his dream? What is the American Dream? How can each citizen help make that dream come true?

Associated Resources

Dickens: http://www.bbc.co.uk/schools/primaryhistory/famouspeople/charles_dickens/
Lincoln: https://www.teachervision.com/presidents-day/video/73208.html
http://www.ducksters.com/biography/uspresidents/abrahamlincoln.php

AASL Standards

1.2.1 Display initiative and engagement by posing questions and investigating the answers beyond the collection of superficial facts.

1.2.7 Display persistence by continuing to pursue information to gain a broad perspective.

Civic Action: Part III

Just like the butterflies fluttering from Lincoln's hat (in his dream), find a Lincoln-sized-and-shaped hat on which to place butterflies that contain citizen action prompts. Refer to http://www.goodcitizen.org/100%20Citizen%20Actions/Actions%20Main%20Page.htm for ideas. Use readings from *Our White House* and the discussion prompts to facilitate interest in citizenship, also reading "Introduction to Citizenship" (http://congress-forkids.net/citizenship_intro.htm).

Then, ask students to pick an action out of the hat to complete. If they do not like the action, let them have one other choice. Allow the student or patron one to two weeks to complete the action. Thereafter, come back together as a group to discuss how action makes one a better citizen. Ask students to comment on how they may continue seeking action projects or expand upon the action project just completed.

AASL Standards

2.1.5 Collaborate with others to exchange ideas, develop new understandings, make decisions, and solve problems.

2.4.4 Develop directions for future investigations.

Civic Service: Part III

As a class or public library group, plant a butterfly garden near the building. Before planting, determine which veteran or public servant (living or deceased) within the community or county will be honored by the planting (one plant per honoree). Prepare a wall of names to be placed on a plague near the garden. Example: Butterfly bush planted in honor of Lieutenant Greene, veteran of the Iraq War (2008–2010) and community alderman (2011–2013). Hold a garden opening in which the service of the honorees is noted and acknowledged, along with the plant or bush planted in their honor.

Associated Resources

Butterfly Gardens: http://m.almanac.com/content/plants-attract-butterflies
http://www.nwf.org/How-to-Help/Garden-for-Wildlife/Gardening-Tips/How-to-Attract-
    Butterflies-to-Your-Garden.aspx

AASL Standards

2.1.2 Organize knowledge so that it is useful.

2.2.4 Demonstrate personal productivity by completing products to express learning.

Civic Discussion: Part IV

1. How do news reporters play a part in our governmental system of checks and balances? Should all reporters be as diligent as Ms. Thomas? Do today's reporters "probe enough" to protect American citizens from potential political evils? Support your answer.
2. Have you ever visited a national park, recreation area, or forest? How was the visit to your benefit? To the benefit of all American citizens? Who is in charge of protecting these lands today? How do your representatives vote in association with National Park Service concerns? How can and will you ensure these lands are protected during your lifetime and for generations to come?
3. The song played over and over by President Taft, *Alexander's Ragtime Band*, includes these lyrics:

> Come on and hear, come on and hear,
> Alexander's Ragtime Band.
> Come on and hear, come on and hear,
> It's the best band in the land.
> They can play a bugle call like you never heard before,
> So natural that you wanna go to war.

Is it a good idea to associate music with war? Why or why not? Does the answer depend on the time or the reason for war?

Associated Resources

Checks and Balances:
http://congressforkids.net/Constitution_checksandbalances.htm
http://www.socialstudieshelp.com/lesson_13_notes.htm
    National Park Service:
http://www.nps.gov/aboutus/index.htm
http://www.nationalparks.org/about-us

AASL Standards

2.1.4 Use technology and other information tools to analyze and organize information.

2.2.3 Employ a critical stance in drawing conclusions by demonstrating that the pattern of evidence leads to a decision or conclusion.

Civic Action: Part IV

Listen to *America the Beautiful*, which speaks to the beauty of our nation's topography: https://www.youtube.com/watch?v=5s6lcG7rjuI. Which national parks fit the lyrics to this song: http://www.nps.gov. As a class or group, adopt one of the parks as identified in your discussions. Discover the needs of your adopted national park. Discuss as a group how you will strive to help meet those needs, such as by contacting your representatives, holding fund-raisers to contribute to the park's foundation, volunteering (having a field experience or holding class or group meetings at a local park, if the one chosen is nearby), joining Park Service youth programming, staying abreast of conservation efforts and/or environmental issues, or helping educate the community on how best to preserve the park and its flora, fauna, and wildlife. (As a science-based project, research the flora, fauna, and wildlife and discover the most endangered species in the park. Discuss ways to protect the species.) If the park chosen is not local, hold an event at a favorite local park which highlights the national park, travel opportunities there, ways that voters might encourage representatives to protect the park, and ways that the Park's ecosystem is essential to our collective sustainable future.

Associated Resources

Get Involved NPS: http://www.nps.gov/gettinginvolved/index.htm

AASL Standards

4.1.1 Determine how to act on information (accept, reject, modify).

2.4.2 Reflect on systematic process, and assess for completeness of investigation.

Civic Service: Part IV

John F. Kennedy said in his inaugural speech, "Ask not what your country can do for you, ask what you can do for your country." In that spirit, while reading this text, ask what you might give back to your local, state, and national representatives. What might you offer to help make their job easier or thank them for their efforts on your behalf? Brainstorm ideas as a class or group, and complete a service project for the chosen representatives. Might you send them a picture of how educational funding has helped the class or group learn a certain concept or enjoy certain literature? Might you write a collective thank-you letter or card? Might you complete a work of art for the representative's office? Take a nice photograph and blow it up to place on an office wall? Collect and send unusual, but necessary office supplies? Or even send Epsom salts for sore feet after a day of speeches or constituency visits?

AASL Standards

4.3.3 Seek opportunities for improving personal and aesthetic growth.

Discussion: Part V

1. Did you realize women did not obtain the right to vote in the United States until 1920? How did the Bill of Rights, Constitution, and Declaration of Independence help the suffragists champion an amendment allowing women to the right to vote? Can you

Statute of Franklin Roosevelt and his dog, Fala, on the National Mall, Washington, D.C. (photograph by the author).

find stories within your family of the first woman to vote? How did that vote affect and improve the life of the women in your family?

2. Are there issues being debated in our country today in which the answer will seem certain in 50 to 100 years? What are these issues, and how might we as American citizens belie the fear of necessary change? How might the disgruntled man and woman interviewed in Stephanie Tolan's *Eyewitness to History* have been convinced of the positive aspects of a woman's right to vote?

3. Compare the four freedoms discussed by President Roosevelt to President Eisenhower's Prayer for Peace. How do they match? From which historical documents did these presidents receive their ideas for the speech and the prayer, respectively? How far have we come in our goal to achieve world peace? Is the world a more peaceful place today? What are several methods of spreading peace across the globe, based in the illustrations provided (four freedoms)? How do these illustrations speak to you? How do they help you understand the means to worldwide peace?

Associated Resources

Women's Suffrage:
http://www.timeforkids.com/news/fight-vote/81911
http://teacher.scholastic.com/activities/suffrage/history.htm
Constitution:
http://www.scholastic.com/teachers/article/explaining-bill-rights
http://www.studyzone.org/testprep/ss5/c/usconbillofl.cfm
http://www.usconstitution.net/constkids4.html
http://www.scholastic.com/browse/article.jsp?id=3750120

AASL Standards

2.3.1 Consider diverse and global perspectives in drawing conclusions.

3.3.3 Use knowledge and information skills and dispositions to engage in public conversation and debate around issues of common concern.

Civic Action: Part V

As a class or group, discover the plight of the homeless or the jobless in your community or county. Brainstorm how to write and illustrate a two-page spread cartoon that depicts the manner in which this population is suffering (see examples under "Hoover's One Term" in *Our White House*). Complete the spread with the assistance of an art teacher or community artist.

Of course, such extremes always require action. Research means of assisting those without homes or jobs in your community. Ask local officials to Skype your classroom or group and discuss the problems and issues causing the social ill. Which action might be taken to alleviate or remedy the existent suffering? Also speak with professionals at the local Employment Security Commission, homeless shelters, church-based relief organizations, Department of Social Services, Chamber of Commerce leaders, county commissioners, town council members, and nonprofit charity groups. Brainstorm a two-page spread cartoon in which citizens are taking the appropriate actions necessary to reduce or eliminate homelessness and joblessness. Again, complete the spread, seeking the expertise of local artists.

Combine the two cartoon spreads, make color copies, and distribute them in conspicuous public places, such as the library, courthouse, tax office, Chamber of Commerce, town hall, and post office.

Associated Resources

Cartoon Drawing:
http://www.my-how-to-draw.com/how-to-draw-cartoon-characters.html
http://kidsfront.com/how_to_draw/bird_drawing_20.html

AASL Standards

3.2.2 Show social responsibility by participating actively with others in learning situations and by contributing questions and ideas during group discussions.

2.1.1 Continue an inquiry-based research process by applying critical-thinking skills (analysis, synthesis, evaluation, organization) to information and knowledge to construct new understandings, draw conclusions, and create new knowledge.

Civic Service: Part V

Ask local soup kitchens how your class or group may sign up to assist their operations on differing dates. Get to know some of the community members who visit the soup kitchen. Ask several if they would like to share the story of why they must visit the soup kitchen for food. Record the stories of those who volunteer. Place the records at a specified site on the library's webpage, creating a type of oral history project. Make sure local officials responsible for assisting these individuals or writing policy that affects this population are forwarded the link, along with the class's or group's ideas about how policies and procedures might be improved for the better (ideas spawned as a result of the oral collection).

AASL Standards

2.1.4 Use technology and other information tools to analyze and organize information.

3.1.4 Use technology and other information tools to organize and display knowledge and understanding in ways that others can view, use, and assess.

Discussion: Part VI

1. Do you believe the children of today are as aware of international affairs as the children of the Cold War era? Are you? Why might they not be as aware of the news? Should they be? How might you find accurate, reliable news sources today?
2. Many of the presidents' pets were eccentric. Were the owners eccentric as well? Does a president need to be eccentric? Which qualities or traits do you believe are essential to the man or woman holding office? If you were voting, which president might receive "best in show" and why? (Don't forget Washington, who is not on the spread provided in the book, but rather placed all to himself.) What are presidents expected to give of themselves for the benefit of the people?

3. What might you give of yourself for the benefit of your country? Where do you think your traits and talents and qualities could best be used—in one of the three branches of government, in an administrative agency, in a campaign, as an advocate, or as an organizer, ambassador, or diplomat?

Associated Resources

Character Traits: http://quizlet.com/16723714/sample-character-traits-definition-flash-cards/

AASL Standards

3.3.1 Solicit and respect diverse perspectives while searching for information, collaborating with others, and participating as a member of the community.

Civic Action: Part VI

Watch local broadcast news programs with student or youth patron groups. Choose a story to compare against newspaper reports and editorials as well as radio reports. Conduct a thorough investigation of the event by inviting local officials to speak with your classroom or group over Skype or Adobe Connect or in person. Upon completing the investigation, determine which report (TV, newspaper, or radio) was most accurate. Attempt the same type of investigation and comparison with a national news report. Were any of the reports inaccurate? Incomplete? Sensationalized? If so, write the managing editors of the news sources and explain your findings. Ask the editor what he or she will do to ensure a return to accurate, reliable, unbiased, fact-based (rather than emotion-driven) reporting? Monitor the actions supplied by the managed editor if he or she replies. If no reply is received, point out the inconsistencies in a community-based forum, such as a school-based newspaper, local newspaper editorial, "report the news accurately" library event, or blog (you might start a blog that holds newscasters accountable to both a democratic society and the people).

Associated Resources

World News: http://www.wn.com
Guardian: http://www.theguardian.com/us

AASL Standards

3.3.1 Conclude an inquiry-based research process by sharing new understandings and reflecting on the learning.

3.3.6 Use information and knowledge in the service of democratic values.

Civic Service: Part VI

Hold a diversity fair in the library whose purpose is to "make gentle the life of this world." Highlight the accomplishments and contributions of all the diverse groups important to your community. Point out how each group has contributed to the welfare and evolution of our country (e.g., working groups, inventions, cultural or artistic legacies, leaders, activists) with booths, reenactments or character portrayals, guest speakers, music and dancing, storytelling, crafts, video or film presentations, and/or book displays and book talks.

Associated Resources

Immigrant Contributions: White House, http://www.whitehouse.gov/blog/2012/07/12/ten-ways-immigrants-help-build-and-strengthen-our-economy

PBS: http://www.pbs.org/independentlens/newamericans/foreducators_lesson_plan_05.html

AASL Standards

    3.3.2 Respect the differing interests and experiences of others, and seek a variety of viewpoints.

Discussion: Part VII

1. Are the doors to America open to everyone? How might we best instill a love for America and its true beliefs and values in the heart of immigrants? Look at the requirements associated with becoming an American citizen. Do these requirements instill a love for America in the heart of immigrants? A respect? How might you model exemplary citizenship to an immigrant hoping to become naturalized? Is the White House a good symbol of America's values for those hoping to attain citizenship? Why or why not?
2. What are the roles of the president and vice-president according to the Constitution? Did Vice-President Cheney overstep his limits of authority while at the White House just after the September 11, 2001, attacks and before President Bush returned to the White House?
3. How do we keep abreast of the character and conduct of our rulers? Do we accomplish this necessary task adequately in our country? How might we improve accountability standards and transparency for leaders in all branches of our government? Which type of behavior exemplifies true presidential conduct and character?
4. Why is willpower necessary to productive citizenship? Is our work as a model citizen ever complete? Provide examples of why citizenship requires vigilance, as exemplified by so many presidents during our country's history.

Associated Resources

Citizenship: http://congressforkids.net/citizenship_1_whatdoesittake.htm

AASL Standards

    1.2.1 Display initiative and engagement by posing questions and investigating the answers beyond the collection of superficial facts.

    1.2.4 Maintain a critical stance by questioning the validity and accuracy of all information.

Civic Action: Part VI

Hold a book festival highlighting books that portray civic virtues or put them in a historical context. Apply the books to national and state standards, and prepare curriculum guides for teacher use. Invite corresponding authors, either local or national, or play author interviews or presentations by streaming video. Ask students to assist in the selection of featured books; hold book talks during the festival; build booths that speak to the importance of civics-based books (fiction and nonfiction); create book dioramas; put on skits portraying scenes from specific books; hold debates or forums in association with books that introduce an important issue; record and/or video presentations to share on the school's social media or to place on a disk and distribute to elderly, blind, or disabled members of the community; conduct readings; share artwork; or speak to the meaning of symbols (e.g., flags throughout American history, eagles) that portray civic values. Play songs that express our values in the background at the event and feature books that describe the songs' history and meaning.

AASL Standards

1.1.5 Evaluate information found in selected sources on the basis of accuracy, validity, appropriateness for needs, importance, and social and cultural context.

1.3.5 Use information technology responsibly.

Civic Service: Part VII

Ask the physical education teacher or a Parks and Recreation employee to help plan a "president's baseball game," in which players dress up like presidents and their wives (minus long dresses). Prior to the game, have each player provide a short history of the president or first lady they represent for the audience, highlighting major historical contributions as well as their association with softball/baseball. Introverted students could introduce artwork, write scripts for other students, pantomime, or prepare a sideline booth for visitors. Also ask students to prepare booths that highlight books whose subject is softball/baseball, such as Kadir Nelson's *We Are the Ship*. Charge a small admission fee for parents and community members. Use the proceeds from the event to support civics education professional development within the school or public library or to buy books that support a civics education curriculum.

Associated Resources

Baseball:
http://www.ducksters.com/sports/major_league_baseball.php
http://www.factmonster.com/ipka/A0875086.html

AASL Standards

3.1.1 Conclude an inquiry-based research process by sharing new understandings and reflecting on the learning.

3.1.4 Use technology and other information tools to organize and display knowledge and understanding in ways that others can view, use, and assess.

Chapter X

*

Thematic Integration
Activities and Resources, Grades 7–8

> *"There is but one method of rendering a republican form of government durable, and that is by disseminating the seeds of virtue and knowledge through every part of the state by means of proper places and modes of education and this can be done effectively only by the aid of the legislature."*—Benjamin Rush

Resources based in civics education are abundant at these grade levels, for good reason. As Piaget noted, the increase in cognitive abilities at this age is significant, allowing librarians to present engaging challenges to their students/patrons. Three books will be featured for discussion, action, and service-based purposes: *The Midnight Ride of Paul Revere* by Henry Wadsworth Longfellow, illustrated by Ted Rand; *Sophia's War: A Tale of the Revolution* by Avi; and *Lafayette in the American Revolution* by Russell Freedman. One teaching website, Lafayette at Valley Forge, and one interactive website, iCivics, will also be highlighted. Also, in this chapter, only the AASL Standard number is included, as the goal is to portray the manner in which many of these standards are associated with any one of the discussion, action, and service prompts contained in these chapters on civics integration in the library.

The Midnight Ride of Paul Revere by Henry Wadsworth Longfellow, illustrated by Ted Rand

After introducing students to the disgruntlement associated with the Stamp Act, the Boston Tea Party, and the Boston Massacre (http://www.masshist.org/revolution/teaparty. php), read *The Midnight Ride of Paul Revere* aloud to a class or book discussion group. Play the NPR audio about the true story behind the lanterns, starting at minute 6:03 and running to 7:49:

http://www.npr.org/player/v2/mediaPlayer.html?action=1&t=1&islist=false&id=1231017&m =1231018.

Take a virtual ride at http://www.paulreverehouse.org/ride/virtual.html.

Paul Revere on his charger, Brown Beauty, Boston, Massachusetts (photograph by the author).

Discussion

1. Why are the folk in the countryside outside Boston weary of British regulators coming into town? Why are Paul Revere, Samuel Hawes, and Dr. Prescott running so fast and out past midnight? Why are John Hancock's and Samuel Adams' lives in danger? Why must they hide from the British?
2. Did you know that a federal income tax was not instituted until 1913 (World War I)? Should American citizens be required to pay tax to the federal government, in your opinion? Should someone have stepped up to voice their opinion about paying money into the federal government in 1913, as is seen in this video: http://ideaofamerica.org/content/nutshell-history-series-rebels-cause?
3. Who might be running from our own government in today's age? See http://ideao-famerica.org/current-event/traitors-or-saviors-whistleblowers-surveillance-security. Who is Edward Snowden? Why can he not come back into the United States? What is he running from? Do you believe he is a patriot or a traitor?
4. Do you have a cause you are passionate about? How would you serve the public as a rebel with a cause?

Additional Resources

Inside the Mind of Edward Snowden: http://www.nbcnews.com/feature/edward-snowden-interview/exclusive-edward-snowden-tells-brian-williams-i-was-trained-spy-n115746
Understanding Taxes: http://apps.irs.gov/app/understandingTaxes/student/index.jsp
Taxation and the Colonies: https://history.state.gov/milestones/1750–1775/parliamentary-taxation

AASL Standards

1.1.6, 1.3.2, 1.3.4, 2.1.5, 2.2.2, 2.3.1, 2.3.3, 2.4.1, 2.4.3, 2.4.4, 3.1.2, 3.1.3, 3.1.5, 3.2.1, 3.2.2, 3.2.3, 3.3.1, 3.3.2, 3.3.3, 3.3.5, 3.3.6, 3.3.7, 3.4.3, 4.1.2, 4.1.5, 4.2.3, 4.3.1, 4.4.4, 4.4.5

Civic Action

Explain the concept of federal income tax. (You might refer to https://kids.usa.gov/teachers/lesson-plans/money/explaining-taxes-to-kids/index.shtml.) Ask students or patrons to evaluate how federal tax monies are spent (http://cdn.billmoyers.com/wp-content/uploads/2014/04/TAXIMAGE1.jpg). Discuss the pros and cons of the tax expenditures chart. Have students/patrons reach a consensus as to how the chart should read and create an alternative class chart based on their research (see Budget Explorer at http://www.kowaldesign.com/budget/index.html). Create a flyer that displays the two charts, contrasts them, and supports the alternative contention. Place flyers in a conspicuous place in the school or public library.

Additional Resources

National Priorities Project Statistics: https://www.nationalpriorities.org/budget-basics/federal-budget-101/spending/
National Priorities Project Video: https://www.nationalpriorities.org/budget-basics/peoples-guide/

White House Receipt: http://www.whitehouse.gov/2013-taxreceipt
http://diglib.library.vanderbilt.edu/ginfo-ubpol.pl?searchtext=FederalBudgetSpending&
 Type=LTR&Resource=DB&Website=GOVTINFO

AASL Standards

1.1.9, 1.3.2, 2.1.1, 2.1.2, 2.1.3, 2.1.5, 2.1.6, 2.2.2, 2.2.4, 2.3.1, 2.4.1, 3.1.2, 3.1.3, 3.1.4, 3.1.5, 3.2.1, 3.3.1, 3.3.3, 3.3.4, 3.3.5, 3.3.6, 4.1.2, 4.1.7, 4.2.3, 4.3.1, 4.4.4

Civic Service

Ask students to identify, through the local Project on Aging, elderly citizens who might need assistance. Collect pennies to help cover the tax money associated with the elderly citizens' grocery purchases. (Students/patrons will need to ask for and keep receipts, calculate costs on a weekly or monthly basis, and reimburse the elderly citizen the appropriate amount from the penny fund on a reoccurring basis.) Take a field trip to a local County Commission meeting to present ideas based on the findings and reflections associated with this program, with students or grades 7–8 public library citizens emphasizing how these taxes might be altered to become less burdensome for the community's elders, if so proved. Ask the students/patrons to explain to the commissioners how they are imitating Paul Revere's friends, having traversed "through alley and street, wandering and watching with eager ears," and how these eager ears are excited about the commissioners' actions and comments.

Additional Resources

Least and Most Tax-Friendly States for Retirees: http://www.today.com/money/taxes-most-least-friendly-states-retirees-8C10990277

Retirement Living: Taxes by State, http://www.retirementliving.com/taxes-new-york-wyoming

AASL Standards

1.1.1, 1.1.3, 2.1.1, 2.1.2, 2.1.3, 2.3.1, 2.3.3, 2.4.1, 2.4.4, 3.1.2, 3.1.3, 3.1.4, 3.1.5, 3.2.1, 3.2.2, 3.2.3, 3.3.3, 3.3.5, 3.3.6, 3.4.3, 4.3.1, 4.4.5

Sophia's War: A Tale of the Revolution by Avi

While John André is quartered in her parents' home, Sophia comes to like the British spy. But things change when her brother is held as a prisoner-of-war on a disease-ridden ship.

Discussion

After reading the book and introducing the beginnings of the Revolutionary War, the imprisonment and hanging of Nathan Hale, and the British seizure of New York City, discuss the following points:

1. What was happening in the colonies that forced Nathan Hale to put his life on the line at such a young age? Would you have acted the same way as Nathan Hale did?

Why or why not? Is there any cause in our country today for which citizens should be putting their lives on the line?

2. Both Nathan Hale and Sophia were spies. Which agencies control espionage (intelligence) on behalf of the United States in today's age? See http://www.nsa.gov/kids/home.shtml and https://www.cia.gov/kids-page/6–12th-grade/who-we-are-what-we-do/index.html. How are both the agencies *and* the employees of these agencies protected as Sophia and Mr. Townsend were protected by the Colonial Army? Look up the Whistleblower Protection Act and the Espionage Act of 1917 to answer this last question.

3. Do the CIA and the NSA go "overboard" in today's age and time? Read https://www.aclu.org/protecting-civil-liberties-digital-age before answering this question.

4. In the digital age, what is your opinion about how and when the NSA and CIA should obtain information?

5. In today's world, when is it appropriate to report or "turn in" a government official, just as Sophia turned in John André and Benedict Arnold?

Additional Resources

American Revolution: Nathan Hale, http://goose.ycp.edu/~tgibson/knowlton/knowlton46/
Hazardous Tales: One Dead Spy by Nathan Hale
Idea of America: The Current Policy, http://ideaofamerica.org/current-event/traitors-or-saviors-whistleblowers-surveillance-security
Whistleblower Protection Act: http://www.dni.gov/index.php/about-this-site/contact-the-ig/whistleblower-protection-act
    Espionage and Sedition Acts:
http://home.comcast.net/~mruland/StuGallery/ushist/reform/2007/46.html
Government Tracking: https://www.aclu.org/how-government-tracking-your-movements

AASL Standards

1.1.3, 1.1.9, 1.3.2, 1.3.4, 2.1.3, 2.3.1, 2.3.3, 2.4.1, 2.4.3, 3.1.3, 3.1.5, 3.2.2, 3.3.3, 4.1.2, 4.2.3, 4.3.1

Civic Action

Ask students/patrons to invite a local judge to the school or public library. Ask the judge to address questions about what can be searched (on your body, at your home, or on your electronics) and the procedures that must be followed for legal searches. Get the judge's opinion about protecting Fourth Amendment rights (right to privacy) and which constraints, if any, should be placed on the NSA and CIA. Then, based on your research, discussion, and interview of an expert, ask the local bar to volunteer for the purpose of coordinating and conducting a mock debate in which students/patrons argue whether the NSA and/or CIA should have access to the phone and Internet records of American citizens, with the debate points to be supported by the rule of law and associated case law. Hint: ask the local bar to pair up with teams to provide counsel, research, and argument/counterargument tips.

Additional Resources

American Bar Association: http://www.americanbar.org/aba.html
Intelligence Squared: http://www.intelligencesquared.com/video-search/
How to Debate: http://www.sfu.ca/cmns/130d1/HOWTODEBATE.htm
The Art of Debate: http://www.youtube.com/watch?v=LesGw274Kjo

AASL Standards

1.3.4, 2.1.1, 2.1.3, 2.2.2, 2.3.1, 2.3.3, 2.4.1, 3.1.3, 3.1.5, 3.2.1, 3.2.2, 3.2.3, 3.3.3, 3.3.5, 3.4.3, 4.1.2, 4.1.5, 4.2.3, 4.3.1, 4.4.5

Civic Service

Sophia's brother was a veteran. Many of today's veterans (of the Iraq and Afghanistan Wars) are suffering as William did. Read http://nchv.org/index.php/news/media/background_and_statistics/. As a school or public library discussion group, find a needy veteran in your community. Determine why the veteran has reached this point of need. Contact a local Department of Veterans Affairs (VA) office to meet with a case manager and attempt to expedite assistance for the veteran. As time allows, meet with local officials to address creating a veterans' outreach service program within your community.

Colin Powell speaking to veterans gathered on the National Mall, November 11, 2010 (photograph by the author).

Additional Resources

Department of Veterans Affairs: http://www.va.gov/
    Lack of Services to Veterans:
http://archive.sctimes.com/VideoNetwork/3583951938001/Amidst-VA-scandal-this-veteran-pleads-for-treatment
Veterans' Outreach: http://wgrw.org/what-i-do/

AASL Standards

1.1.6, 1.3.4, 2.1.3, 2.1.5, 2.3.1, 2.4.1, 2.4.4, 3.1.2, 3.1.5, 3.2.1, 3.3.3, 3.3.6, 4.1.2,

Lafayette in the American Revolution by Russell Freedman

Who knew the great French hero, the Marquis de Lafayette, defied the king of France to join the Revolutionary cause, and swam to shore in shark-infested waters to avoid British warships? Read Freedman's account to learn all the details!

Discussion

1. Have you ever heard any news concerning your country which "enlisted your heart," in the same way as when Lafayette heard news of the American revolutionaries? Did you take action of any sort or do you plan to one day?
2. How do you see the value of liberty, which Lafayette fought for, reflected in today's American society? Other international societies?
3. If you added a seal to your family crest that said "Why not? (similar to Lafayette's action), what would you be fighting for, taking into consideration Lafayette's traits— "proud, determined, and adamant"?
4. Lafayette entered battle due to his values: liberty, freedom, and justice for all human beings. For what other causes (if any) is military intervention applicable, in your opinion? Under which circumstances may our country *officially* enter war?

Associated Resources

Bill of Rights: http://www.archives.gov/exhibits/charters/bill_of_rights.html
Universal Declaration of Human Rights: http://www.un.org/en/documents/udhr/
Declaring War: http://thepeoplesguidetotheusconstitution.com/blog/articles/congressional-power-to-declare-war/ and http://www.loc.gov/law/help/war-powers.php

AASL Standards

1.1.3, 1.1.6, 1.1.9, 1.3.2, 1.3.4, 2.1.3, 2.1.5, 2.2.2, 2.3.1, 2.3.3, 2.4.1, 2.4.3, 3.1.2, 3.1.5, 3.2.1, 3.2.2, 3.3.1, 3.3.2, 3.3.3, 3.3.6, 4.1.2, 4.1.5, 4.2.3, 4.3.1, 4.4.4

Civic Action

If you were advocating for a special interest for your country, as Lafayette advocated for funding of the Revolutionary War effort from Louis XVI, what would your cause entail?

As a classroom or public library book discussion group, form a mock caucus that plans to travel to Washington, D.C., to support this cause (advocacy group). Plan your argument; identify the representative whom you will target and/or write to; and develop your speech, arrangements, organization, and contacts. If asked to testify, what will each witness say?

Associated Resources

How Congress Works: http://www.congressforkids.net/Legislativebranch_makinglaws.htm
How a Bill Becomes Law: http://kids.clerk.house.gov/grade-school/lesson.html?intID=17
Activate: https://www.icivics.org/games/activate
Play, Fight, Repeat: http://playfightrepeat.com/2011/02/kids-civic-engagement/
Citizens Lobbying Guide: https://movetoamend.org/toolkit/citizens-lobbying-guide

AASL Standards

1.1.6, 1.1.9, 1.3.2, 1.3.4, 2.1.2, 2.1.3, 2.1.5, 2.2.2, 2.3.1, 2.3.3, 2.4.1, 2.4.3, 2.4.4, 3.1.2, 3.1.3, 3.1.5, 3.2.1, 3.2.2, 3.2.3, 3.3.1, 3.3.2, 3.3.3, 3.3.5, 3.3.6, 3.4.3, 4.1.2, 4.2.3, 4.3.1, 4.4.4, 4.4.5

Civic Service

Lafayette noted that America was (and would and will be) "a respected and safe asylum of virtue, integrity, tolerance, equality, and a peaceful liberty." Organize and initiate a club in your school, or a public library group, which discusses, defines, and invites others (from the community and beyond) to discuss how these virtues will be preserved in our community, state, and federal governments (a Lafayette club).

Additional Resources

Franklin's Junto: http://www.pbs.org/benfranklin/l3_citizen_networker.html
Junto Club Questions: http://nationalhumanitiescenter.org/pds/becomingamer/ideas/
   text4/juntolibrary.pdf
Kids Care Clubs: http://generationon.org/service-clubs/join/about

AASL Standards

1.1.6, 1.1.9, 1.3.4, 2.1.3, 2.1.5, 2.2.2, 2.3.1, 2.3.3, 2.4.1, 2.4.3, 3.1.2, 3.1.3, 3.1.5, 3.2.1, 3.2.2, 3.3.1, 3.3.2, 3.3.3, 3.3.5, 3.3.6, 4.1.2, 4.1.5, 4.2.3, 4.3.1, 4.4.4

Website

The Marquis de Lafayette at Valley Forge: http://www.mountvernon.org/educational-resources/encyclopedia/lafayette-valleyforge

Discussion

After having read the article on the website as a class or discussion group, answer the following questions:

1. How did Lafayette display an egalitarian spirit of justice at Valley Forge? If a member of France's National Assembly (a government organization equivalent to our Congress)

George Washington's writing desk at Valley Forge, Valley Forge National Park, Pennsylvania (photograph by the author).

were to visit your classroom, would you treat him or her formally or informally, and why? Would you think it proper if he or she "lived among you"?

2. How did Lafayette provide service to the cause of the American Revolution while stationed at Valley Forge? Referring to the website article, why was he loyal to Washington instead of Congress? Is service not only an act, but also a stance or belief?

3. Read more about the Conway Cabal at http://www.mountvernon.org/educational-resources/encyclopedia/conway-cabal. Then discuss with middle schoolers a moment in recent history in which a political faction created a "stir," without just cause and to no effect. How was a representative's service to the country affected by the political intrigue? In what way might we support public servants who have the good of the country at heart, when they are attacked by political bands?

4. Why did Lafayette continue to advance to Canada, despite his own and Washington's misgivings? Did you ever have to complete a task you did not want to do, knowing that in the end you would be proven correct? How did it work out for both yourself and the instructor? Did both parties learn from the "mistake"? Is this type of "trial-and-error" of benefit to the balance of powers between the three branches of government? Why or why not?

Associated Resources

French National Assembly: http://www.assemblee-nationale.fr/english/
Obama's Birth Certificate Intrigue as Example: http://www.cnn.com/interactive/2011/04/politics/interactive.obama.birth.certificate/index.html?hpt=C1
Three Branches of Government: http://bensguide.gpo.gov/3–5/government/branches.html
Balance of Powers: http://kids.usa.gov/three-branches-of-government/

AASL Standards

1.1.3, 1.1.6, 1.1.9, 1.3.2, 1.3.4, 2.1.3, 2.1.5, 2.2.2, 2.3.1, 3.1.2, 3.1.3, 3.1.5, 3.2.2, 3.2.3, 3.3.1, 3.3.3, 3.3.5, 4.1.2, 4.1.5, 4.3.1, 4.4.4

Civic Action

Using drama and theater techniques, with your students or patrons write, create, and produce a play depicting an imagined discourse Lafayette has with the Continental Congress about the delivery of his conditions in association with his agreeing to attempt the trip to Canada. Relate it to the actual powers provided in the Constitution eventually ratified (executive branch given the power to direct war; Congress given the power to declare war only). Pretend General Washington is considered the executive power and the Continental Congress is the legislative body (Senate and House—Congress) eventually formed. Thus, Lafayette's discourse will inform the Continental Congress about his belief as to the separation of these powers (allowing Washington to direct the war and Congress to support it).

Associated Resources

Guideline on Informal Classroom Drama: http://www.ncte.org/positions/statements/informalclassdrama

Playwriting for Students: http://www.youngplaywrightstheater.org/Programs/InSchool/
index_E.html (scroll down to Resources for a script example)

Declaring War: http://thepeoplesguidetotheusconstitution.com/blog/articles/congressional-
power-to-declare-war/ and http://www.loc.gov/law/help/war-powers.php

AASL Standards

1.1.3, 1.1.6, 2.1.2, 2.1.6, 2.2.4, 2.3.1, 3.1.3, 3.2.1, 3.2.2, 3.2.3, 3.3.4, 3.3.5, 3.4.3, 4.1.2, 4.3.1, 4.4.4, 4.4.5

Civic Service

Discuss political propaganda. As the librarian, work with your students or patrons to find resources which are valid and reliable and which explain the pros and cons of political issues in a frank, fact-filled, and investigative manner (such as CQ Researcher). Prepare a roster of these sources, in an attractive format, and place the "Who Do You Believe" flyers/brochures in a conspicuous place in the library for students/patrons/stakeholders' benefit. Be sure to share the list on the library's website as well.

Associated Resources

Propaganda: What's the Message?, https://www.icivics.org/teachers/lesson-plans/propa-
ganda-whats-message

CQ Researcher: http://library.cqpress.com/cqresearcher/?PHPSESSID=i4crdk4hf2nrgvqv
cc49q3lrm3

World News: http://wn.com/

AASL Standards

1.1.6, 2.1.2, 2.2.4, 2.4.4, 3.1.4, 3.3.4, 3.3.5, 3.3.7, 4.1.2, 4.1.7, 4.3.1

Interactive Website Discussion

http://www.icivics.org

Named one of the "Best Websites for Teaching and Learning" by the American Association of School Librarians, former U.S. Supreme Court Justice Sandra Day O'Connor's conceptualization, iCivics, envisions "a nation where all young Americans are prepared for active and intelligent citizenship. To support this vision, iCivics provides engaging and effective on-line educational games and curricular materials for students and teachers." Divided into two sections, "Play" for students and "Teach" for civics educators, the site has a growing base: 40,000 educators and 3 million students, representing half of our country's middle-grade students.

The "Play" section introduces games which promote knowledge, action, and service. For example, "Branches of Power" allows the student to function, as a member of one of the three branches of government, in a capacity in which "issues become full-fledged laws." Students will gain insight as to how all three branches, working at the same time in their own capacity, pass laws. To do so, students will answer questions at a press conference to reveal the public relations role of the executive branch, gather citizen support while a member of the legislative branch, and decide the constitutionality of a passed law at the judicial branch. Next, students may spring into action with the "Activate" game, raising awareness of the plight of national parks, for example. Other games include "Bill of Rights," "Supreme Decision," and "Argument Wars." Students earn badges and can monitor their progress nationwide on the "Leaderboard." As a means of teaching service, students may donate game points earned to one of ten service projects organized by Ashoka Youth Projects. The iCivics Foundation awards $1,000 to the project receiving the most points within a four-month time frame.

For the educator, the "Teach" portion of iCivics provides objective-based curriculum units highlighting our country's beginnings, the rule of law, and the three branches of government. Activities include the use of skits, debates, graphic organizers, and, of course, gaming. A drafting board allows students to build an argumentative essay founded in civics principles. Finally, webquests allow teachers to introduce resources that tie civics learning to real-world issues. Justice Sandra Day O'Connor's video messages inspire the teacher, and updates remind him or her of the importance of this learning tool through highlighting of research findings and personal success stories.

Chapter XI

Thematic Integration
Activities and Resources, Grades 9–10

> *"Liberty cannot be preserved without a general knowledge among the people, who have a right ... and a desire to know."*—John Adams

According to Piaget, at this stage, adolescents enter the formal operational stage at which they may deduce a specific outcome from a general principle and participate in creating hypotheses. They may also participate in and contribute to simulated scenarios which require problem resolution (possible outcomes and consequences of action). Readers at this level may interpret and/or compare text, make connections, and draw conclusions (and support their reasoning).

One nonfiction source published by National Geographic will be shared for purposes of civics education integration, *The Revolutionary John Adams* by Cheryl Harness, as well as two fiction award-winners, *The Notorious Benedict Arnold* by Steve Sheinkin, and *Johnny Tremain* by Esther Forbes.

The Revolutionary John Adams by Cheryl Harness

In the words of the author, this book is a portrayal of John Adams, the "stout, stubborn, New Englander" who left a legacy of a checks-and-balances–based government, our emphasis on a strong, efficient Navy, and a tendency toward diplomacy. Though a monument has never been erected for this Founding Father, as Ms. Harness indicates, the "United States is a proper, living monument to intense, cranky, warm, heart-on-his-sleeve John Adams—America's champion" (Harness 1).

Discussion

1. How might Adams's early childhood experiences and hard farm work have contributed to his ability to withstand so many political hardships? What might nature teach us about citizenship? How does time spent in nature contribute to the development of a

115

civically engaged American? Why did Adams also need a formal education? Do today's leaders need to have experienced hardship before entering or running for office?

2. In association with this book, read Adams's 1776 pamphlet, "Thoughts on Government." How did Adams model the type of politician imagined in this writing, one exhibiting "the great political virtues of humility, patience, and moderation"? What would be included in Adams's writings if he were witness to elections in 21st-century America? How would he say we should create and nourish virtuous politicians and governmental leaders? Would Adams say the 21st century is an age of "tryal … the consequences I know not."

3. Adams spoke to the happiness of as many citizens as possible. Would he say it is possible for 300 million people to form and establish a wise and happy government? What are the costs we must endure today to preserve freedom for our own posterity and progeny? What are the sacrifices each of us must make today? What do our politicians need to sacrifice? What are the actions which need to occur today to preserve the freedoms and government established by Adams and the other Founding Fathers?

4. How did Abigail Adams contribute to her husband's political success? Might women be at the forefront of the change required to preserve our freedoms (freedom from the political vices mentioned in Adams's "Thoughts on Government")? How might a feminine take advance the cause of liberty in the 21st century? How will you ensure that women have an equal say in the government of our land?

Associated Resources

John Adams's pamphlet "Thoughts on Government": http://www.heritage.org/initiatives/first-principles/primary-sources/john-adams-thoughts-on-government
　　Women's Rights:
http://history.house.gov/Exhibitions-and-Publications/WIC/Historical-Essays/No-Lady/Womens-Rights/
http://www.history.com/topics/womens-history/the-fight-for-womens-suffrage

AASL Standards

3.2.1 Demonstrate leadership and confidence by presenting ideas to others in both formal and informal situations.

3.3.7 Respect the principles of intellectual freedom.

Civic Action

The author points out that Adams was the heart and "voice" of the Revolution, while Jefferson was the mind and "pen." Adams himself believed our system of government, as provided within the rule of law—that is, the Constitution—was itself "the result of good heads prompted by good hearts." How might you ensure future generations are provided with both strong civics and character education programs within public and private school and public library service offerings? First, examine your own school or public library with your students/patrons. Research the school curriculum and/or examine library services. How does the institution currently engage in civics learning and character development? Research the professional standards that either the public school library or the public library should be reaching with regard to these two subjects. Are the offerings at least adequate? If not, what must be taught or offered by the school or library to meet these standards? Ask students to create persuasive argument essays, with associated charts, diagrams, statistics, and other elements that highlight inadequacies. Present these arguments, in written or oral format, or both, to local administrators, school board members, and/or state legislators. Follow up with each official contacted to ensure they are taking action so that these two subjects will not be ignored within our educational and informational infrastructure.

Additional Resources

Should Character Be Taught?: http://learning.blogs.nytimes.com/2011/10/18/should-character-be-taught-students-weigh-in/?_php=true&_type=blogs&_r=0
    Character:
http://www.presspublications.com/opinionscolumns/146-dare-to-live-without-limits/3359-facing-adversity-builds-character-
http://www.merriam-webster.com/dictionary/civil%20servant

AASL Standards

3.3.3 Use knowledge and information skills and dispositions to engage in public conversation and debate around issues of common concern.

3.3.5 Contribute to the exchange of ideas within and beyond the learning community.

3.3.6 Use information and knowledge in the service of democratic values.

Civic Service

John Adams believed American citizens must be "fellow laborers in the same cause … acting together like a band of brothers" (and sisters)! He also believed the cause should have an end in mind. As a class or group, help students/patrons decide on a subject of inquiry in which one brother or sister reflects on a work or philosophy and/or explains values and belief systems. Begin with letters written to another member of the classroom or group. Hold a discussion about the *John Adams* book, leading to other books with civics-based themes: revolution, education, work, war, politics, issues of the day, and so on. Next, expand the "explain ourselves to each other" letter-writing service to others within the community; for example, consider a fellow classroom or discussion group exchange of "brother/brother, brother/sister, sister/sister" letters, teacher/student letters, or student/administrator letters. After a bit of time, expand the writing to members of the community in need of a brother or sister—for example, residents of nursing homes, those in relief shelters or safe houses, or hospital patients who choose to participate in the program. Then expand the letter-writing adventure to local leaders and political candidates. Finally, ask students to initiate such a campaign with national leaders. Make sure the initial causes, issues, or subjects are delineated before the start of each phase of this letter-writing exchange.

Associated Resources

Jefferson/Adams Writings:
http://www.monticello.org/site/jefferson/john-adams

http://nationalhumanitiescenter.org/pds/livingrev/religion/text3/adamsjeffersoncor.pdf
http://www.ushistory.org/Declaration/related/sons.htm

AASL Standards

3.1.3 Use writing and speaking skills to communicate new understandings effectively.

3.1.2 Participate and collaborate as members of a social and intellectual network of learners.

Johnny Tremain by Esther Forbes

The illustrious John Hancock asks Johnny Tremain's master to make a silver set within a week. Johnny, trying to appease the respected merchant, destroys his hand in an accident, becoming a cripple of sorts. This injury does not prevent him from riding the spirited steed, Goblin, in service for the Sons of Liberty! At the same time, Johnny finds, and rejects, his family and legacy.

Discussion

1. Many of the Sons of Liberty were pious men who referred to God in their conversations about liberty and equality. In fact, they believed they were protected by God. Nevertheless, they fought for personal religious freedoms. Does this point of view seem strange or conflicting in today's age? Why were they adamant about religious freedom? What was the history of religious persecution in England? Were these men aware of this history? Do we have as much religious freedom today as Americans experienced right after the Bill of Rights was written? Why or why not? What are some court cases in the 21st century that consider religious freedoms? (See the *Hobby Lobby* case as an example.) What is your opinion of this decision—should this business entity be considered a "person" for the purpose of interpreting religious freedoms?

2. Are there periods in history in which peace just cannot be maintained? In your opinion, was the American Revolution such a period? Were the Sons of Liberty correct in beginning the war according to the reasoning given in their speeches, literature, sketches, and meetings, and in inciting support for their cause? Which other periods in our country's history required a declaration of war? Which periods did not, yet war occurred anyway? How may each individual citizen ensure our leaders do not unnecessarily begin conflicts or wars? How may citizens contribute to "necessary" war efforts, or are wars ever "necessary"?

3. Do today's newspapers "slant" the news, just the same as occurred with the reports about the Sons of Liberty? In what way? Find examples of slanted news reporting and discuss (1) what the publishers hope to gain, (2) the degree of truth in the article, (3) whether the propaganda may have a positive effect, and (4) what might become the negative connotations of the report and how such consequences may be overridden.

4. Who were the Sons of Liberty's role models? Whose writings did they read and discuss to form their opinions, beliefs, and viewpoints? What were their role models' viewpoints on government and rebellion, and how did they translate into the viewpoints of those living during the American Revolution? Do the philosophies and viewpoints of these models (both those read by the Sons of Liberty and those espoused by the

Sons of Liberty themselves) pertain to the issues and human rights questions of our day? In which ways? How may these philosophies contribute to the resolution of these problems/issues?

5. How will you "stand up like a man" (and woman) for your country today? In five years? Ten? Twenty?

Associated Resources

http://www.ushistory.org/Declaration/related/sons.htm
http://www.bostonteapartyship.com/sons-of-liberty
http://www.iep.utm.edu/home/about/

AASL Standards

4.3.1 Participate in the social exchange of ideas, both electronically and in person.

4.3.3 Recognize that resources are created for a variety of purposes.

Civic Action

As a class or group, discover the contributions made by each of the historical figures who are part of the montage found in this book. Next, assign each student or patron an individual citizen. The student or patron should carefully research the contributor assigned, becoming aware of that individual's belief system, values, and stance on important issues. Hold an "Ask Your Founding Citizens" Day in the library, in which students, book group members, or patrons may file past their student or students or choice, with the prompt: "If you could ask anyone of the Revolutionary War generation just one question, what would it be and who would you ask?" Allow each member of the Revolutionary generation time, one by one in turn, to be excused to ask their question as well.

Associated Resources

List of Important People: http://www.theamericanrevolution.org/peopledetails.aspx

AASL Standards

4.1.6 Organize personal knowledge in a way that can be called upon easily.

4.3.1 Participate in the social exchange of ideas, both electronically and in person.

Civic Service

In the library, sponsor a weekly/biweekly broadcast/streaming event that airs one of the following weekly civics-oriented programs (choose one or alternate between them):

The Thomas Jefferson Hour: http://www.jeffersonhour.com/what_would_tj_do.html
Colonial Williamsburg's Electronic Field Trips (HERO): http://www.history.org/history/teaching/eft/index.cfm
Williamsburg Connect: http://connect.history.org/archived-webcasts
Colonial Williamsburg Media: http://www.history.org/media/

You might plan for the broadcasts to be shown in association with PTA or library board meetings, book fairs, fall festivals, or other special events, or you might hold them

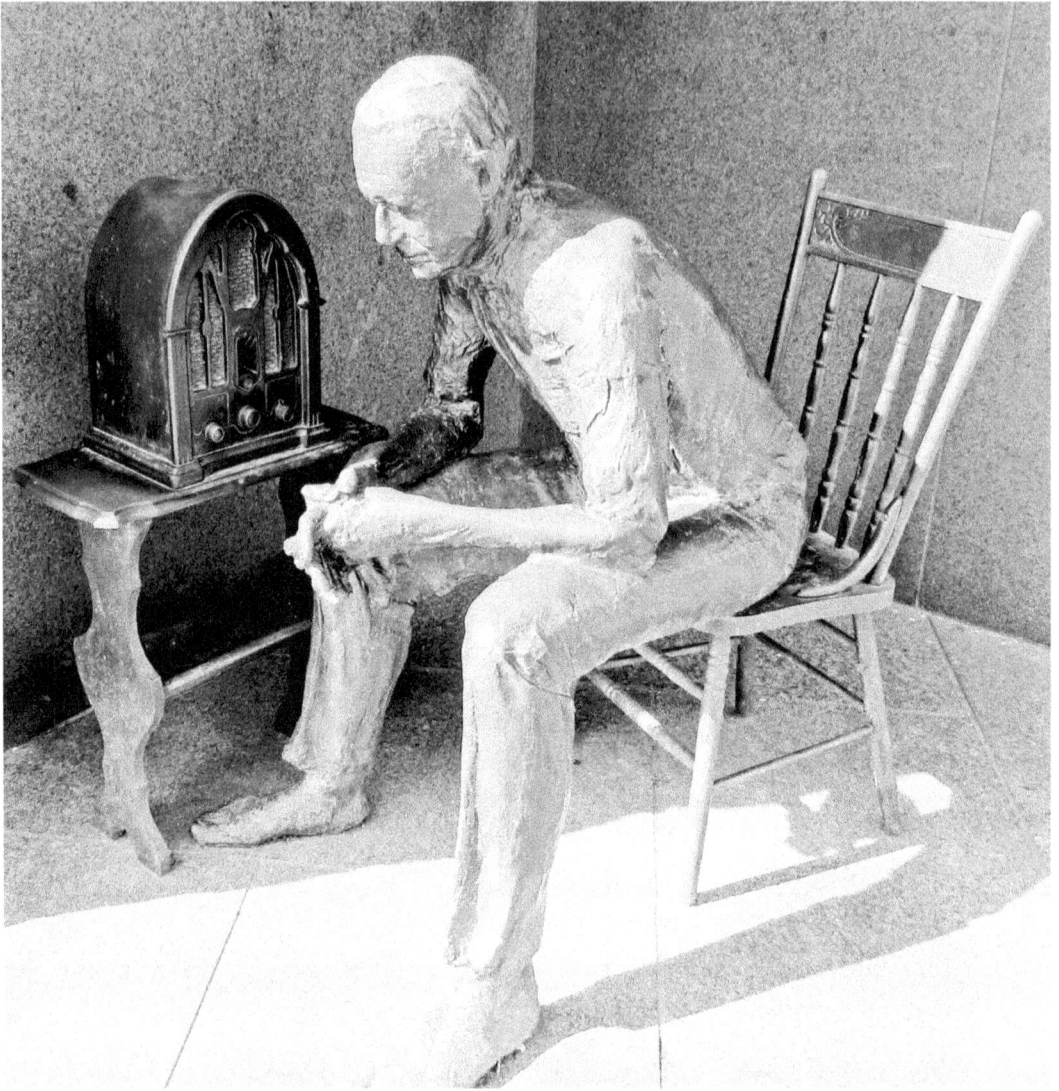

An American citizen listening to a radio hour during World War II, Franklin Roosevelt Memorial, Washington, D.C. (photograph by the author).

solely in designated classrooms and/or for discussion groups. Ask students or patrons to create or order bookmarks highlighting the website address of the chosen broadcasts (obtain permission from the broadcast owner). Sell the bookmarks for a small fee at the major events to either (1) donate to and sponsor the civics-oriented broadcast service or (2) pay the minimal subscription fee charged by the service. Be sure to allow time for discussion following the broadcast, preparing the discussion prompts ahead of time.

AASL Standards

1.1.8 Demonstrate mastery of technology tools for accessing information and pursuing inquiry.

1.2.3 Demonstrate creativity by using multiple resources and formats.

The Notorious Benedict Arnold
by Steve Sheinkin

Benedict Arnold was a traitor, yet also a human being. This story reveals the adventurous, brave spirit of a man who was at first "on fire" for his country's cause, only to find that fire extinguished by all-too-human circumstances and decision-making choices.

Discussion

1. The author of this book says, "There's more than one side to every good story." Even though he betrayed our country, what debt of gratitude do we owe Benedict Arnold? Was his course of action inevitable? Did he undergo too much trauma on the campaign to Quebec? How can we prevent soldiers from enduring too much trauma in action? Are multiple deployments ethical? Should the military have guidelines about the degree of service it can impose upon members of the military? Should drugs ever be used to ensure lengthy periods of service, rather than rest and recreation (R&R), as has been the case in previous times of war?

2. Benedict Arnold at one point stated he could no longer serve his country with honor. Was it honorable for Arnold to enjoy the pleasures of Boston while his country was still at war, taking into consideration the trials he had just passed through? How do we balance our country's needs against our own personal needs as human beings?

3. What inspires you most about your country? Does that inspiration make you want to share your talents in service to the country? If you have not yet found the "spark" which motivates service to your country, how will you go about trying to find it?

4. Should one's passion for civic action and advocacy ever be tempered? In which instances? Are the passions of our present leaders overboard? Underdeveloped? Inappropriate? On target?

5. Why did Benjamin Franklin believe moderation was the key to a successful government? How can we moderate our passions for action and make them effective and productive? How might our leaders do the same? In the book, which leader displayed the most productive course of action, based upon his passions?

6. Is there any instance in which our leaders must make rash decisions? If so, what might those instances entail? Who oversees high-ranking military generals? Should the decisions of these generals be reported, monitored, and more heavily scrutinized?

7. Was John Adams correct in his argument on page 147 about military heroes? How do we control idolization of either our military or officially elected leaders? How do we ensure our leaders do not take attention away from where it should rightfully be directed, in effect "ending America's experiment with democracy"?

8. Benedict Arnold was a man of action. After the Boston Massacre, he asked of the city's citizens, "Why are they not out in the streets?" Does our civic duty call us to action? Are such men as Benedict Arnold necessary to the perpetuation of a republic? In which instances are they necessary? How are such men controlled by our system of government (how is their power checked—remember, Arnold noted at one point, "I will be second in command to no person whatsoever")? Do you know of any leaders today whose personality is similar to that of Benedict Arnold?

Associated Resources

Benedict and Benjamin:
http://www.history.com/topics/american-revolution/battle-of-quebec-1775
http://www.ushistory.org/valleyforge/served/arnold.html
http://www.pbs.org/benfranklin/pop_virtues_list.html

AASL Standards

2.3.3 Use valid information and reasoned conclusions to make ethical decisions.

2.2.3 Employ a critical stance in drawing conclusions by demonstrating that the pattern of evidence leads to a decision or conclusion.

Civic Action

As a class or discussion group, find a voice! Find an instance in local, state, or national government in which money is negatively affecting the manner in which policy or laws are written. In other words, how are certain policies or laws serving the buck instead of the people? Hold an event in a public area in which freedom of speech may be exercised in a lawful, peaceful manner. Ask students to produce brochures or pamphlets explaining the cause or issue which needs to be addressed and possible remedies. Construct signs, develop further reading book lists (or website lists), sign up to staff "join the cause tables," and so on. Hold the gatherings as many times as needed. Conduct follow-up research which determines how the peaceful protest affected the law or policy. Who became involved? What further steps need to be taken to protect the interest of the people?

Associated Resources

http://www.truth-out.org/
http://www.alternet.org/

AASL Standards

2.1.3 Use strategies to draw conclusions from information and apply knowledge to curricular areas, real-world situations, and further investigations.

2.1.5 Collaborate with others to exchange ideas, develop new understandings, make decisions, and solve problems.

Civic Service

As a discussion group or class, and to mirror the boot statute which reminds Americans of Arnold and Saratoga, put on a pair of working boots and volunteer to clean up the military memorials, parks, battlegrounds, statutes, veterans office buildings or hospital grounds, or museum/library grounds nearest your community. Place public relations notices in local news media to inform the public about the volunteer service and each citizen's duty to make those grounds, which were set aside in honor of those who have unselfishly served to protect our individual rights and liberties, welcoming, clean, and inviting.

Associated Resources

Memorial List: http://www.npca.org/news/media-center/fact-sheets/2013-Antiquities-Act-monument-list-updated.pdf

AASL Standards

1.3.5 Use information technology responsibility.

3.3.6 Use information and knowledge in the service of democratic values.

Chapter XII

Thematic Integration
Activities and Resources, Grades 11–12

> *"Democracy is never a final achievement. It is a call to an untiring effort."*—John F. Kennedy

Almost adults, students in grades 11 and 12 think about moral, philosophical, ethical, social, and political issues that require theoretical and abstract reasoning. They can read across multiple texts for a variety of purposes, analyzing and evaluating titles both independently and as a set. They can analyze meaning and synthesize support for their opinion to provide complete, explicit, and precise substantiation of an idea or argument.

Two books will be highlighted in this section: one nonfiction compilation of words from the Founding Fathers and one fiction book that challenges our belief systems and assists in the continuing improvement of human rights for all American (and world) citizens.

Our Country's Founders: A Book of Advice for Young People, edited by William J. Bennett

Sharing poignant excerpts from letters, documents, essays, legalese, and addresses penned by the Founding Fathers, this collection provides young adults with timely advice on how to cultivate the virtues of patriotism and courage, education, and industry, also offering wisdom about how to promote justice and solidify morality.

Discussion: Part I—Patriotism and Courage (pages 7–54)

1. Discuss the causes of the American Revolution by previewing and investigating the following timeline: http://www.pbs.org/ktca/liberty/chronicle_timeline.html. Was Thomas Paine correct in saying, within the pages of *The American Crisis*, that the British were "binding me (and the colonies) in all cases whatsoever." In your opinion, how was the Revolution a matter of self-protection? What can we suffer today? Are there instances of tyranny within our 21st-century laws? Are tax breaks for the wealthy and corporations as people examples of tyranny? Do we have cause to rebel? If so,

how should we proceed now that we have our Founders' gifts of a Constitution, a Bill of Rights, elections, and federal and state laws—rights not afforded, yet won by, the colonists? Do the Universal Declaration of Human Rights and the existence of the United Nations help in any way?

2. Alexander Hamilton believed America could become "one great respectable and flourishing empire … which it is incumbent upon successors to improve and perpetuate." You (we) are the successors of whom he spoke. How should we improve upon our government in the 21st century? Which actions will you take to implement such improvements? In your opinion, is the perpetuation of our government in peril? Support your answers with reasons. If you believe the U.S. government is in peril, what must you (we) do to negate and extinguish the danger?

3. In regard to the American system of government, Washington believed a citizen should show "respect for its authority, compliance with its laws, and acquiescence in its measures," as "duties enjoined by the fundamental maxims of true Liberty." Yet, he continued, "The basis of our political systems is the right of the people to make and to alter their Constitutions of Government…. The Constitution which at any time exists, 'till changed by an explicit and authentic act of the whole People, is sacredly obligatory upon all." Amendments to the Constitution have served as improvements to the original Constitution. How have "the people" ensured the passage of these amendments? Why is this history important to know and understand? Which amendments to the Constitution might our country require in the present age? How will we ensure the amendments are presented and ratified?

Associated Resources

Rights:

http://constitutioncenter.org/constitution#amendment-list

https://www.aclu.org/united-states-bill-rights

http://www.un.org/en/documents/udhr/

https://www.humanrights.gov.au/publications/what-universal-declaration-human-rightsts—

AASL Standards

2.2.2 Use both divergent and convergent thinking to formulate alternative conclusions and test them against the evidence.

2.3.2 Consider diverse and global perspectives in drawing conclusions.

Civic Action: Part I—Patriotism and Courage

Benjamin Franklin believed governmental leaders should argue and debate, come to a reasonable meeting of minds, and "well administer" or wisely uphold precepts established, both at home and abroad. He spoke against partisanship, noting the importance of "unanimity" among governing bodies and their leaders. Allow students a virtual opportunity to become such a leader. Participate in the University of Virginia's E-Congress as a class or discussion group: http://208.81.226.245/learning-programs/econgress/.

Next, as a class or discussion group, apply your learning to a rule, principle, policy,

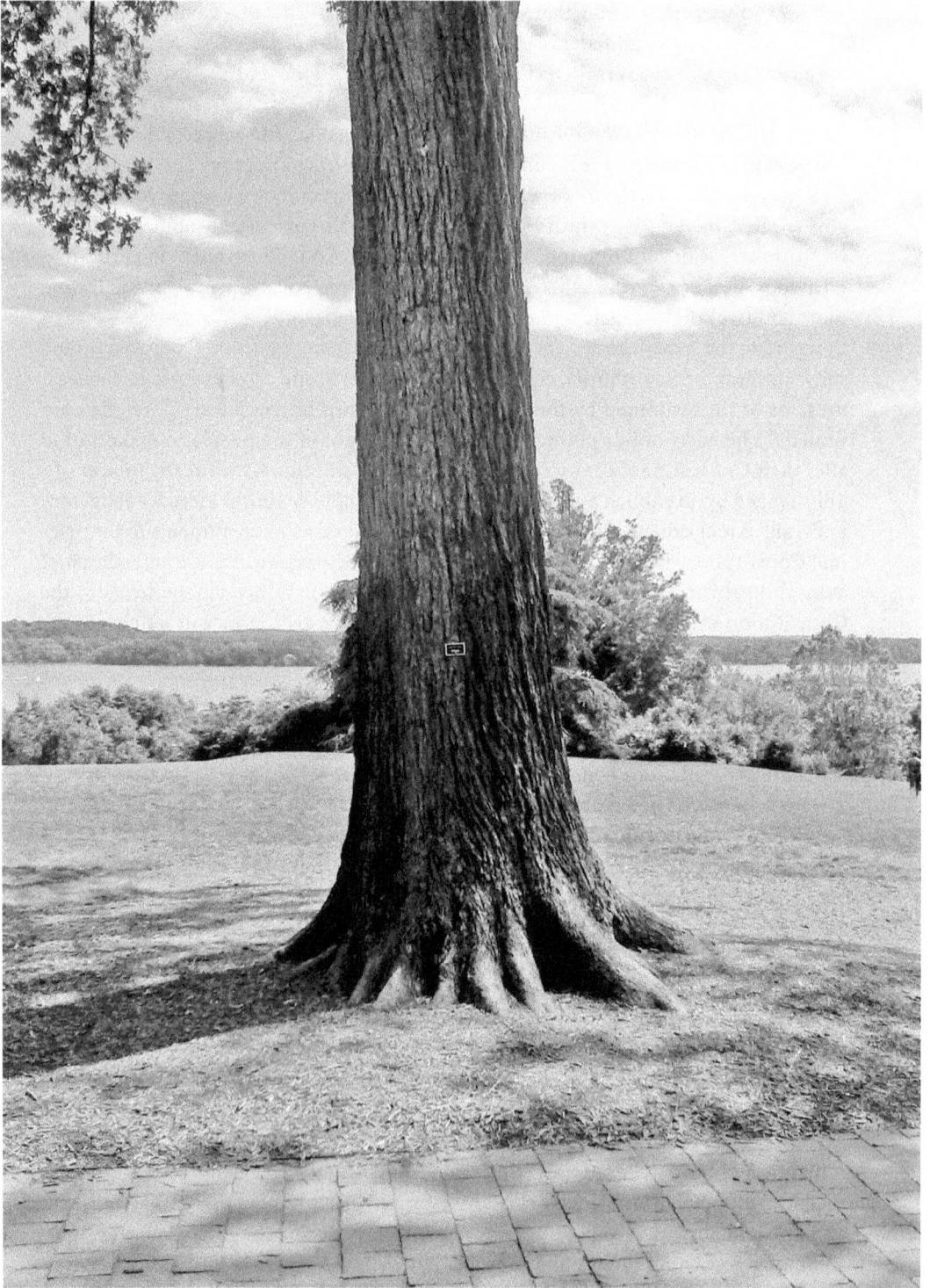

Standing tall as General Washington, Mount Vernon, overlooking the Potomac River, Alexandria, Virginia (photograph by the author).

or guideline within the school or community which might need additional consideration, modification, or amendment. As a class or group, research the issue, form committees and/or subcommittees, propose changes or amendments, debate the validity of differing proposals, reach a consensus, write the new rule or policy, and debate and edit its wording by consensus. Present the proposal to community members or at community/governmental meetings. Review and monitor the consequential actions of the board or body or personnel to whom the proposal was directed.

AASL Standards

1.1.1 Follow an inquiry-based process in seeking knowledge in curricular subjects, and make the real-world connection for using this process in own life

Civic Service: Part I—Patriotism and Courage

As a group or class, hold discussions about which members of your class have proved most adept at political strategy (up to 25 members). Hold fund-raisers throughout the year and/or obtain individual or group sponsors to assist the class or group members selected in attending the well-respected Harvard Model Congress (Boston or San Francisco; http://harvardmodelcongress.org/). Ask members who attend to agree to apply what they learn at the conference in service to the school or public library community upon their return, leading civic action projects such as the one listed in the preceding "Civic Action" section.

Associated Resources

Choose an Alternate Model Congress: http://en.wikipedia.org/wiki/Model_Congress

AASL Standards

1.1.2 Use prior and background knowledge as context for new learning.

Discussion: Part II—Education of the Head and Heart (pages 133–166)

1. Should we endeavor to study the character of our governmental leaders? Should their family lives and childhood experiences be scrutinized? Their record and private lives carefully examined? How do we best allow our leaders to remain human while also expecting strength in character? Which human fallacies are acceptable within a leader? Do fallacies ever make our leaders stronger in the end?

2. Why did John Adams believe the study of Greek and Latin was important to the formation of exemplary American citizens? How did the Greeks' historical forms of government and political philosophies contribute to our current form of government? Why are Cicero (Tully) and his works important to know if a citizen wishes to understand our system of government? Did Greek republics serve as a design model for the government our Founding Fathers instituted by means of the U.S. Constitution? What was the end the Founders had in view in regard to our system of government, and from which philosophy did this end flow? Who were the role models or enlightened

thinkers who influenced the Founders, and how are the philosophies of these models reflected in our current system of government?

3. Sam Adams stated, "For no people will tamely surrender their liberties, nor can any be easily subdued when knowledge is diffused and virtue is preserved." What did this statement mean in Adams's day? Does it carry the same meaning today? In 21st-century America, is knowledge about our government, its workings, and its leaders properly shared by the public? If not, how might such knowledge become more transparent and widely disseminated? Are today's American citizens easily subdued? How might the original radical spirit of our Founding Fathers be preserved? Does it need to be? Is the extent of rebellion exhibited by the Founding Fathers necessary to each generation? What was Adams's idea of virtue? How are virtues best preserved within a society? How are they preserved in 21st-century America? How might we work for their continual preservation?

4. What is an American citizen's duty to his or her fellow men and women? To the government? Which sorts of action make a person proud of the service he or she has rendered to other citizens? To the government? How is a strong character best instilled within our youth? Is it the duty of the government to ensure civic and character education is a mainstay and a requirement within public schools and other responsible public institutions? Benjamin Rush and Noah Webster believed the purpose of education was to inculcate the principles of liberty and government, as well as the obligations of patriotism. Is this still true today? How is a respect for these principles best nurtured?

5. Our Founding Fathers repeatedly lauded the quality of reason. How did they define reason? Why was it important to the perpetuation of a sound republic government? Does reason demand a respect for law and order? By what reasoning did the Founding Fathers ignore and defy English law? Are there instances in our day when laws should be scrutinized and reform be demanded? What is an example and what is your reasoning?

6. Which primary, current, or to-be-written resource should be included in the textbook to which Noah Webster spoke: "A selection of essays, respecting the settlement and geography of America; the history of the late revolution and of the most remarkable characters and events that distinguished it; a compendium of the principles of the federal and provincial governments." Which courses should be instituted to teach the ethics, law, commerce, money, and government of our country so that, as suggested by Montesquieu, the yeomanry is well versed in civic concerns.?

Associated Resources

Political Philosophy:
http://www.iep.utm.edu/cicero/
http://www.britannica.com/EBchecked/topic/117565/Marcus-Tullius-Cicero
http://www.iep.utm.edu/locke/
http://fee.org/the_freeman/detail/john-locke-natural-rights-to-life-liberty-and-property
http://www.iep.utm.edu/rousseau/
http://plato.stanford.edu/entries/rousseau/
http://www.ushistory.org/declaration/signers/adams_s.htm

http://www.history.com/topics/american-revolution/samuel-adams
http://press-pubs.uchicago.edu/founders/documents/v1ch18s30.html
http://www.ushistory.org/declaration/signers/rush.htm
https://www.noahwebsterhouse.org/discover/noah-webster-history.htm
http://press-pubs.uchicago.edu/founders/documents/v1ch18s26.html

AASL Standards

1.1.3 Develop and refine a range of questions to frame the search for new understanding.

1.1.4 Find, evaluate, and select appropriate sources to answer questions.

1.1.9 Collaborate with others to broaden and deepen understanding.

1.3.2 Seek divergent perspectives during information gathering and assessment

Civic Action: Part II—Education of the Head and Heart

Celebrate the best of humanity! Begin a "My Hero" project in which students choose a "most remarkable character" of the American Revolution to study in depth. Which character trait and resulting action(s) do you admire most in your chosen historical figure? Establish a hero a day (or week, or however often the class or group meets) session in which one or several students/patrons prepare(s) a 30-minute presentation dramatizing a particular adventure experienced by the hero during the American Revolution.

Next, as a class or group, decide on a civic action project which would best utilize the talents and character strengths exhibited by the "heroes." Use the guidelines found at the Constitutional Rights Foundation (http://www.crf-usa.org/school-violence/implementing-a-civic-action-project.html) to implement a quarterly or semester-long project which considers the six steps of an action project: (1) select a problem to work on, (2) research the problem, (3) choose a project, (4) plan the project, (5) do the project, and (6) evaluate what you have done. Once the project is accomplished and evaluated, enter the CRF CAPFolio Contest (http://www.crfcap.org/mod/page/view.php?id=6).

AASL Standards

2.1.1 Continue an inquiry-based research process by applying critical-thinking skills (analysis, synthesis, evaluation, organization) to information and knowledge to construct new understandings, draw conclusions, and create new knowledge.

2.1.3 Use strategies to draw conclusions from information and apply knowledge to curricular areas, real-world situations, and further investigations.

Civic Service: Part II—Education of the Head and Heart

As a six-month to year-long project, compile a textbook that would have been well respected by Noah Webster—one that includes the "best of the best" with regard to primary resources, articles, readings, images, excerpts, speeches, writings, diary entries, journals, and letters, and that would engage a learner in delving into civic literacy requirements: the settling and geography of America, the history of the American Revolution and its distinguishing characters, and the principles of the federal and provincial governments. Make sure the choices included are within the public domain. Visit local printers to determine if they will sponsor printing several copies, so that each school and public library (including branches) within the county served can circulate at least one copy each to the general public and/or stakeholders.

Associated Resources

http://www.loc.gov
http://www.archives.gov

AASL Standards

2.1.2 Organize information so that it is useful.

2.1.4 Use technology and other information tools to analyze and organize information.

3.3.5 Contribute to the exchange of ideas within and beyond the learning community.

3.3.6 Use information and knowledge in the service of democratic values.

National Cathedral at sunrise, Washington, D.C. (photograph by the author).

Discussion: Part III—Justice

1. Jefferson personified *truth* in his "Bill for Establishing Religious Freedom." He wrote that she was "great" and was certain she would "prevail if left to herself." Of which principle was he really speaking? In which venue or venue is this "truth" enacted in our modern day? What are the natural weapons of "truth"? How do these weapons actually lead to justice and peace and freedom from erroneous decisions? Can you give an example in your lifetime as to when this "turnabout" occurred—that is, when open communication, argument, and debate led to a solid answer, reconciliation, or the truth of the matter?

2. Washington believed citizens should look to government for protection. Do you feel protected by the U.S. government? Why or why not? If not, how does the government need to change to provide necessary protection to its citizens? In return, each citizen is to give the government its "effectual support." What does Washington mean by that phrase? How would you like to support your government to the greatest effect? Which actions will you take to guarantee the success of your government and the manner in which it protects each citizen? Which amount, degree, actions, or decisions of government best lead to a "national prosperity"? Which part of government does not lead to prosperity? Does this part need to be extinguished? How will such culling be accomplished? Would our Founding Fathers be proud of the workings and administration of the current U.S. government? Why or why not?

3. Have you ever considered the rights afforded by our Bill of Rights as property? Were you aware of your rights before reading this book and the documents found at the end of the book? Are you ready to express your opinion more freely after reading the powerful writings of our Founding Fathers? Were you aware it is in fact your civic duty to express your opinion? In which ways do you exercise your reason? Which topics can you discuss in small groups or as a class that require targeted reasoning skills? Do our current leaders utilize the same degree of reason as our Founding Fathers? How may we insist reason is used by our leaders in decision-making processes, rather than cronyism or emotionality?

4. Which eyes around the world, in the 21st century, are opening to the rights of man? Which struggles are these peoples experiencing and are there ways we may help these "revolutions" succeed? Should our eyes, as American citizens, also be open? Which of our rights, at this point in time, need vigilant and watchful eyes to ensure their perpetuation? (Are any of our rights under attack?)

Associated Resources

Jefferson and Religious Freedom:
http://founders.archives.gov/documents/Jefferson/01-02-02-0132-0004-0082
http://www.vahistorical.org/collections-and-resources/virginia-history-explorer/thomas-jefferson

AASL Standards

3.1.5 Connect learning to community issues.

3.3.7 Respect the principles of intellectual freedom.

Civic Action: Part III—Justice

Thomas Jefferson said, "Let the annual return of this day forever refresh our recollections of these rights and an undiminished devotion to them." As a group or class, think of ways in which Independence Day should be celebrated for the purpose of refreshing recollections of rights in your community or school and enhancing the devotion we demonstrate to them. How might individuals who are unaware of the importance of protecting such rights be motivated to learn more about them? How can you expose circumstances in which these rights are not honored and protected?

Organize and develop classes, presentations, online interactive experiences, posters, blogs, radio broadcasts, videos, local TV interviews, theater productions, and other creative events which will spread the word about the rights we are truly celebrating each July 4. After the July 4 events, hold follow-up biweekly civic discussions at the library which invite class or group members, as well as citizens who participated in the events (be sure to have sign-up sheets), to "argue and debate," express opinions, and make reasonable decisions about the means of ensuring justice is served within the local community.

Associated Resources

July 4:
http://www.history.com/topics/holidays/july-4th
http://www.constitutionfacts.com/us-declaration-of-independence/fourth-of-july/

AASL Standards

3.3.4 Create products that apply to authentic, real-world contexts.

3.3.5 Contribute to the exchange of ideas within and beyond the learning community.

3.3.6 Use information and knowledge in the service of democratic values.

Civic Service: Part III—Justice

Are there voices within your students' or patrons' community that are not heard? Select one such group and determine how to assist the unheard group in voicing its concerns. For example, are female county governmental workers paid less than male workers at the same level? Can the women be interviewed as a group and an editorial be written and placed in the local newspaper? Are the homeless within the community receiving necessary medical care? Can you discover an instance in which medical care was denied and the patient's health was affected permanently? Can you produce a *60 Minutes* type of exposé which will bring awareness to the issue?

AASL Standards

3.1.4 Use technology and other information tools to organize and display knowledge and understanding in ways that others can view, use, and assess.

3.1.5 Connect learning to community issues.

3.3.6 Use information and knowledge in the service of democratic values.

The Astonishing Life of Octavian Nothing: Traitor to the Nation by M.T. Anderson

Octavian would have been a prince in his native land. Yet, in the American colonies, he is an experiment—a slave, not fully alive, not fully dead, yet fully human. He breaks crayons in anger, cherishes his mother and his ability to read, feels sorrow so great he wishes to no longer live, and warms his heart to those who truly model, exhibit, and offer their very lives for liberty and freedom, all in service to another experiment, the American Revolution.

Discussion

1. This account provides a counter-narrative to the "glory" often associated with the American Revolution, yet provides hope despite cruelty, hypocrisy, and greed. What is the hope provided within the pages of this award-winning book? Provide instances from within the text which support this hope. How does this same hope present itself within our Constitution, its amendments, and the Bill of Rights? Within the Universal Declaration of Human Rights? How has this hope improved our nation? Our world? Was the American Revolution, despite its hypocrisy based in economic circumstances, worth the effort? Have the precepts and values and beliefs which resulted from the Revolution helped to free both men and women during the past (almost) 240 years?

2. Was Octavian right to freely speak his mind to Mr. Sharp at the end of the book? How is this courage reflected in the time he spent with kind friends who believed in the rights of man—that is, Bono and Private Evidence Goring? How do we encourage freedom of speech in today's age? How might speaking your opinion freely, first among friends, help you demonstrate this same courage when it is required to fight injustice?

3. Did this book pique your interest in the virtues of liberty and freedom, or were you discouraged by its content? How did both hope and destitution help Octavian recognize the human enlightenment which would follow an American victory? If your interest in American values was heightened by this book, how will you act upon this interest? If the content was upsetting, how will you rise above the injustices found in your own life, find those who are kind, and rely upon the strength of our rule of law to achieve a civic purpose and advocate for those rights due to all, as described by Mr. Anderson: "tinkers, cordwainers, shopkeepers, doctors, farmhand, coopers, goose-boys, innkeeps, sawyers, cobblers, freemen & Slaves" (291).

4. On page 170, Octavian narrates: "Empedocles claims that in utero, our backbone is one long solid, and that through the constriction of the womb and the punishments of birth it must be snapped again and again to form our vertebrae; that for the child to have a spine, his back must first be broken." Provide examples of how America's "vertebrae" (infrastructure or circumstances) have been snapped again and again to form a stronger and stronger backbone. Which shackles have been endured and unlocked? How did American citizens participate in the unshackling of the chains of injustice? Do today's American citizens need—like Octavian or those Americans living

The Supreme Court Building, where decisions such as *Island Trees v. Pico* were debated and decided by our country's highest court, Washington, D.C. (photograph by the author).

in prior epochs—to become aware of their shackles, and find means of loosening the country from such chains? If so, what are these shackles (inconsistencies or injustices), and how might each citizen work to free our arms from the burden, once again feeling the lightness and ease as arms lift high to celebrate our freedoms?

5. Are America's minority groups still struggling to realize their freedoms? Which laws currently protect minority groups? Have these laws been recently compromised? How can each citizen learn about, embrace, and demand justice for all the diverse groups within the United States' borders? How does cooperation among diverse groups strengthen our nation and ensure the continuation and perpetual health of the Republic?

AASL Standards

3.2.2 Show social responsibility by participating actively with others in learning situations and by contributing questions and ideas during group discussions.

3.3.3 Use knowledge and information skills and dispositions to engage in public conversation and debate around issues of common concern.

Civic Action

Octavian would have died for the freedom to read as he wished. The American Library Association and the American Civil Liberties Union work diligently today to ensure this right is protected. In association with the ALA's Banned Book Week, host a celebration that, as found in Octavian's account, denounces the tragedy of book banning (throughout history and in all parts of the globe), yet heralds the hope present in each American's freedom to read (see the ALA's Freedom to Read statement—Appendix B, Exhibit 3). Global banning incidences to "uncover," for the purpose of exposing censorship's dangers, might include Hitler's book burnings, Socrates's demise, banning under China's emperors, the burning of the Library of Alexandria, Athanasius's burning of early Christian documents, and multiple instances of Bible banning. Organize and host seminars which instruct other faculty or library members, as well as students and interested parents, about the dangers associated with, and precipitated by, these events (i.e., mass murders, oppression). Invite librarians who have fought censorship, a member of the state chapter of the ACLU, and a constitutional rights attorney to speak about American liberties, the laws and cases which support those rights, means of protecting our rights, and instances in which individuals can take action to fight against censorship of reading or other civil liberties abuses. Hold book talks about banned books throughout the event, specifically pointing out the literary value of each book as well as its thematic importance. Make sure sessions are held that point out cases which protect educators, librarians, and students' right to read (e.g., *Island Trees v. Pico* and *Tinker v. Des Moines*).

Associated Resources

ACLU:
https://www.aclu.org/about-aclu-0
https://www.aclu.org/aclu-history
History of Book Censorship: http://viking.coe.uh.edu/~wmasterson/cuin7337/history.htm
Banned Book Week:
http://www.bannedbooksweek.org/about
http://www.ala.org/bbooks/bannedbooksweek:
Island Trees v. Pico: http://www.oyez.org/cases/1980–1989/1981/1981_80_2043

AASL Standards

4.1.8 Use creative and artistic formats to express personal learning.

4.4.3 Recognize how to focus efforts in personal learning.

Civic Service

Begin a "Reading Hero" program, organized and implemented by your class or discussion group, in which students provide read-alouds, reading guidance, and reading interpretation to elementary students who are struggling with reading. Ask local schools for help in identifying candidates for the program (obtain parental and school permission). Visit the school of the child on a weekly basis to provide reading assistance. Also, determine which factors within your community are contributing to reading struggles among elementary school students. Present your findings to the local school board, organize trips to the state capital to advocate for increased funding for reading programs, and write editorials and give public speeches that decry our nation's current practice of funding prisons appropriately, but not reading programs; insist that funding for reading literacy programs be mandated and legislated.

Associated Resources

http://www.ascd.org/publications/books/104428/chapters/the-struggling-reader.aspx

http://www.readingrockets.org/article/who-are-children-who-have-reading-difficulties

A Sentence of Their Own: http://www.doc.nv.gov/sites/doc/files/pdf/education/Education_Services_Spring_2012_Newsletter.pdf

Why Are Prisons More of a Priority Than Schools?: http://www.huffingtonpost.com/kevin-p-chavous/why-are-prisons-more-of-a_b_1611956.html

AASL Standards

3.2.1 Demonstrate leadership and confidence by presenting ideas to others in both formal and informal situations.

3.1.1 Conclude an inquiry-based research process by sharing new understandings and reflecting on the learning.

3.2.3 Demonstrate teamwork by working productively with others.

Chapter XIII

Civics-Related Reading
Promotion Plans

"Our children should learn the general framework of their government and then they should know where they come in contact with the government, where it touches their daily lives and where their influence is exerted on the government. It must not be a distant thing, someone else's business, but they must see how every cog in the wheel of a democracy is important and bears its share of responsibility for the smooth running of the entire machine."
—Eleanor Roosevelt

Utilize the reading promotion plans provided in this chapter to engage students in reading material which spurs civic discourse, action, and service opportunities. Plans will be divided into grade levels K-2, 3-4, 5-7, 8-10, and 11-12. Overarching themes will be as follows:

K–2 Serving Others
3–4—America's Natural Resources and the Environment
5–7 American Women's History
8–10 How Do I Define a Model Citizen?
11–12 How Do I Wish to Serve My Country?

* * *

K–2 Americans Helping Americans:
Service Encourages Freedom!

Thematic Reading Material

The Three Questions: Based on a Story by Leo Tolstoy, written and illustrated by Jon J. Muth (Scholastic, 2002)

Abe Lincoln: The Boy Who Loved Books, written by Kay Winters, illustrated by Nancy Carpenter (Simon & Schuster, 2003)

A Worn Path, written by Eudora Welty (Creative Education, 1991)

Moses: When Harriet Tubman Led Her People to Freedom, written by Carole Boston Weatherford, illustrated by Kadir Nelson (Hyperion, 2006)

Program Description: This thematic program is based on one full school library academic year (August–May). (Public libraries using the plan for a summer reading program will divide the program into two-week units; that is, one public school nine-week activity will constitute one two-week summer reading program activity.) Each nine weeks, the principal will visit K–2 students for the purpose of reading and discussing a designated story (picture book). (In the case of the public library, the library director shall visit story hour.) Thereafter, students will be asked to read at least eight other books (either individually or with a parent) and, with the assistance of parents, dictate a one-paragraph summary and one-paragraph evaluation to be turned into the reading program's monitoring librarian for accounting. Each nine weeks (two weeks for public library), the student, if the eight-book goal is met, will be allowed to participate in a fun civics-based activity.

Year-Long Program Goals: The goals of this K–2 reading promotion plan are civic service oriented. The books shared with students will reveal the characteristics of a model citizen—that is, one who considers the best interests of others. All of the role models found in the books "look out" for the welfare of those in need or the group as a whole, using their talents, grit, fortitude, intellect, patience, and heart-filled values to assist others. The books and activities shared through the implementation of this reading promotion plan will answer the following questions, which are contained in the National Council of Social Studies Civics Standards:

- How do we exercise the responsibilities associated with our rights as American citizens?

- What does a model American citizen look or act like?

- What is civic participation?

- How do citizens become involved?

- What is the role of the citizen in the community and the nation, and as a member of the world community?

This plan connects summer reading program patrons with community issues which necessitate individual service work as well as group problem-solving efforts.

Objectives for First Nine Weeks: Given the book *The Three Questions*, K–2 students will discover the challenges faced by vulnerable elderly citizens within the community. They will find a way to help beautify the grounds of the nearest resthome (to match the story). (Who are the elderly citizens who need to be served in the here and now?) K–2 students will also find a way to directly assist the persons assigned as their elderly civics buddies on the day of the visit, and will provide a "tip" of some sort to each elderly citizen's health worker.

First Nine-Week Activity and Implementation: Those students who earn the right (reading eight books in nine weeks, turning in paragraph summaries to the librarian) will be allowed to enjoy a field trip to visit a local resthome or assisted living facility for the purpose of providing service to the home, including both its elderly citizens and its workers. Prior to the visit, the librarian will inform the students who have earned this right about the letter-writing relationship between Adams and Jefferson during their twilight years. Abridged excerpts from their letters will help children realize the manner in which these Founding Fathers served and honored each other in their later years.

(See http://nationalhumanitiescenter.org/pds/livingrev/religion/text3/adamsjefferson-cor.pdf.)

The librarian will also detail the problems associated with residing in an assisted living facility or resthome, such as immobility, lack of exercise, lack of individualized care, and service by workers who are not even paid the minimum wage. Working with the resthome, each student will be assigned a civics buddy. During the visit, the student will talk with the buddy about what he or she likes and does not like about the manner of care received. The student will ask how he or she might brighten the day of the buddy and perform the task if able (e.g., retrieving tissues, watering flowers, retrieving a book or magazine). The student will deliver a handmade gift of his or her choosing (completed or created in the library prior to the visit) to the worker who checks on the elderly buddy that day. A group gardening improvement project will be preapproved with the library and the resthome, and students will complete the project on the day of the visit. Elderly citizens will be allowed outside to monitor or watch the work, and encouraged to provide gardening tips.

Back at the library, the children will (K–1) consider what they would include in a letter to a Congressional representative about how to improve care for the elderly or (2–3) actually compose a letter to a good friend giving their opinion about how care for the elderly could be improved. Students will stay in touch with the elderly buddy as parents see fit.

Objectives for Second Nine Weeks: Given the book *Abe Lincoln: The Boy Who Loved Books,* the student will discover the power of words in a democratic society.

The Jefferson Memorial flanked by cherry blossoms, Washington, D.C. (photograph by the author).

Second Nine-Week Activity and Implementation: Students who meet the reading goal will be allowed to join a field trip to the nearest presidential library. If such a library is not available in your area, visit a presidential home site, museum, or commemorative site associated with a particular president's term in office. At the library or site, ask personnel to tell stories that reveal the manner in which the president in question was influenced by words, stories, and community literacy efforts (President Lincoln is a good example). Upon their return home, students who met the goal will gather in the library on specially designated days to talk about ways in which the library could promote the love of books within the school or public library community. From these ideas, students will vote on the one to be implemented. Students will discover one way to share a story or book with someone who did not make the reading goal.

Objectives for Third Nine Weeks: Given a reading of *A Worn Path*, by Eudora Welty, students will discover the manner in which environmental factors, improper medical care associated with poverty, and disease left unattended can lead to birth defects and disabilities in children.

Third Nine-Week Activity and Implementation: Students meeting this nine-week reading goal will participate in a March of Dimes state-based event or the March for Babies. Prior to the event, a local March of Dimes representative will visit the library to speak with the group of students achieving the reading goal, specifically addressing the political efforts needed to assure the health of mothers and newborn babies. In age-based groups, and in association with art teachers and community artists, students will create signs to carry during the March of Dimes event; the signs will inform voting-age adults about programs which need to be supported by governmental officials. Example: Support the Women's, Infants', and Children's (WIC) program (picture of milk, bread, and cheese).

Objectives for Fourth Nine Weeks: Given a reading of *Moses: When Harriet Tubman Led Her People to Freedom*, written by Carole Boston Weatherford and illustrated by Kadir Nelson, students will examine the character and fortitude required of a model citizen, participating in interdisciplinary discussions exploring, as well as video renderings demonstrating, civic-minded individuals.

Fourth Nine-Week Activity and Implementation: Plan, gather, setup, and invite students who have met the fourth nine-week reading goal to a Harriet Tubman Day in the library that provides centers associated with the subjects found in *Moses*. Utilize the discussion guide created for the book to develop discussion, language arts, math, music, art, science, author, and Underground Railroad centers (http://wildgeeseguides.blogspot.com/2010/01/moses-when-harriet-tubman-led-her.html). Make sure the discussion center questions address the incredible sacrifice Tubman made for fellow American citizens, as well as the courage and bravery required for civic action and service, as exhibited by the children during the past 36 weeks. Also, have a "You Took Action; What Now?" center in which each student who met all four reading period goals will be allowed to videotape his or her thoughts on the following reflection: How do you plan to "use your gifts to break chains" in your lifetime? Present the compiled and edited video of student response at a PTA or library board meeting.

* * *

Grades 3–4: Environment First! Influencing Public Policy

Thematic Reading Material

Giving Thanks: A Native American Good Morning Message, written by Chief Jake Swamp, illustrated by Erwin Printup, Jr. (Scholastic, 1995)

Brother Eagle, Sister Sky: A Message from Chief Seattle, paintings by Susan Jeffers (Penguin, 1991)

M Is for Majestic: A National Parks Alphabet, written by David Domeniconi, illustrated by Pam Carroll (Sleeping Bear Press, 2003)

Freedom River, written by Doreen Rappaport, illustrated by Bryan Collier (Hyperion, 2000)

Program Description: This thematic program is based on one school library academic year (August–May). (Public libraries using the plan for a summer reading program will divide the program into two-week units; that is, one public school nine-week activity will constitute one two-week summer reading program activity.) Each nine weeks, the principal will visit grade level 3–4 students for the purpose of reading and discussing a designated story (picture book). (In the case of the public library, the library director will visit either

The Old North Bridge, Minuteman National Park, Concord, Massachusetts (photograph by the author).

story hour or after-school programming.) Thereafter, students will be asked to read at least six other books on an appropriate reading level (chapter to middle-grade books) and write a one-paragraph summary and one-paragraph evaluation to be turned into the reading program's monitoring librarian for accounting. Each nine weeks (two weeks for public library), the student, if the six-book goal is met, will be allowed to participate in a fun civics-based activity.

Year-Long Program Goals: The goals of this grade 3–4 reading promotion plan are (1) to develop an awareness of environmental issues in America, (2) to recognize the importance of America's natural lands, and (3) to develop an awareness of public policy which needs to be legislated or amended to protect America's natural resources. The books shared with students will reveal the characteristics of a model citizen—that is, one who considers the well-being of the environment as a means of ensuring the well-being of all Americans. (The role models found in the books "look out" for the welfare of the environment and/or use natural resources in a civic-minded manner.) The books and activities shared through the implementation of this reading promotion plan will address the following standards, contained in the National Council of Social Studies C3 Framework:

1. Identify the beliefs, experiences, perspectives, and values that underlie their own and others' points of view about civic issues.
2. Explain how rules and laws change society and how people change rules and laws.
3. Illustrate historical and contemporary means of changing society.

It will also connect public library summer reading patrons with community issues that require individual civic dispositions as well as group problem-solving efforts. Throughout the school year, students participating in the reading program will be allowed to visit a nearby river for a few hours (with adult supervision and predetermined inquiry), noting the river flow, riverbank animals (if possible), aquatic life, plant life, and human activity. Visits will occur during each season, and students are to make note of any observed changes, comparing river life from season to season. Notes should be saved until the completion of the fourth nine-week reading program, at which time an opportunity to participate in a culminating project will be offered as an award. (Please read *Fourth Nine-Week Activity and Implementation*.")

Objectives for First Nine Weeks: After reading the book *Giving Thanks*, 3–4 grade students will understand the connectedness of earth, sky, water, moon, and sun to the well-being of humanity.

First Nine-Week Activity and Implementation: Those students who earn the right (reading six chapter or middle-grade books in nine weeks, turning in paragraph summaries to the librarian) will be allowed to enjoy a field trip to visit a local organic farm and the local agricultural extension agent office. Students will prepare questions to ask of the farmers and agents ahead of time—specifically, questions about environmental issues that affect local farming and gardening efforts. (Share national issues as well, to aid in questions formation, by previewing http://www.nrdc.org/issues/.) Once the questions have been asked, another half-day will be set aside for students to determine how the immediate library environment (inside or outside) might be improved in ways that promote the clean, sustainable environment necessary to local agriculture. Students will write letters at this event asking school board members or County Commission members to provide funding for such improvements. Students should indicate they will be glad to assist in any projects requiring service work (e.g., growing a library garden, planting herbs, placing recycle bins in offices).

Objectives for Second Nine Weeks: Given the book *Brother Eagle, Sister Sky,* the grade 3–4 student will find his or her significance in the web of life and understand how to care for the resources necessary to human survival.

Second Nine-Week Activity and Implementation: Students who meet the reading goal will be allowed to join a field experience (hike with a ranger) hosted by the library at the nearest national forest reserve. During the hike and ranger talk, students will each find one natural item in the air, on the land, or flowing in a body of water, which they will fall in love with and "love as we have loved it," per Chief Seattle's entreaty. The students will be allowed to visit the library during specified, set-aside hours to research how best to preserve and care for the animate or inanimate part of the Earth. Students may choose to enter an essay contest which exposes their feelings and findings regarding a love and care for the natural resource or creature. The library's Media Advisory Committee will judge the essays submitted. The winner will receive a collection of civics-related, age-appropriate reading material worth $200, to be funded by the library or a library benefactor.

Objectives for Third Nine Weeks: Given a reading of *M Is for Majesty* by David Domeniconi, students will discover the manner in which they may advocate for the National Park Service and become involved in policy formation efforts, also understanding the environmental benefits associated with "our NPS."

Third Nine-Week Activity and Implementation: Students meeting this nine-week reading goal will participate in a trip to the nearest National Park Service site, whether a park, memorial, or place of historical significance. Upon return, hold a library "Your NPS: Get Involved" Day, during which students explore ways to continue supporting the National Park Service. Centers will be arranged in the library that indicate means of involvement, and local park service rangers or federal employees may be invited into the library to speak to service and advocacy opportunities. Use the National Park Service website (http://www. nps.gov/getinvolved/index.htm) to organize the centers. Invite parents to attend the event and especially learn how to comment on National Park Service policy considerations, involving children in discussions of the issues associated with policy additions and amendments (http://www.nps.gov/getinvolved/index.htm). Ask students to keep a log of their service and advocacy efforts associated with what is learned during the field trip and the "Your NPS" Day. Students who log ten significant efforts throughout the year will be awarded a seedling to plant in commemoration of America's majestic national parks.

Objectives for Fourth Nine Weeks: Given a reading of *Freedom River* by Doreen Rappaport, students will understand how rivers and other bodies of water have helped humans, throughout history, escape oppressive situations.

Fourth Nine-Week Activity and Implementation (School children only, first paragraph): Students who meet the nine-week goal(s) will visit a local river on one occasion during each of the four seasons, noting the change in the river, its inhabitants, and its plant and insect life during each visit. They will also note the human activity on the river from season to season. As a culminating activity at the end of the year, students will reflect on and respond to the visits, either by creating art, writing, telling digital stories, blogging, acting out, or documenting (via photography or video) what they have learned about the river (both positive and negative). If the student has noted any environmental concerns during the visits, they will somehow depict these concerns in the artwork or productions. The artwork and productions will be displayed in the library, with public comment kiosks placed beside significant works portraying environmental concerns.

For the public library only, patrons meeting the reading goal will be offered an opportunity to participate in a lazy raft expedition. Also, the public library, during the summer months, will be asked to display the public school students' artwork and productions created as a result of visiting a river during each season of the year. Again, public comment kiosks will be placed beside the works. From these public comments, the public library will plan and hold public forums whose purpose is to raise awareness of the issues, in an attempt to seek political, economic, and science-based solutions.

Grades 5–7: All by Herself: American Women's Struggle for Equality

Thematic Reading Material

A Is for Abigail by Lynne Cheeny
All by Herself by Ann Whitford Paul

Program Description: This program will promote bravery and fortitude during a reading program that encourages development of introspective reading habits designed to build character. Each individual reader will be singled out and honored with the intent of sparking the bravery and sense of civic responsibility inherent in each and every child. Gender equality will serve as the thematic strand conducive to the development of a civic-oriented personal core within each reader. Introspective reading among all genres will be encouraged.

Program Goal: The reading program will divulge the history of women's struggle in the United States as well as the manner in which women have combated gender inequality by demonstrating persistence and courage, heralding the fact our nation's rule of law is applicable to all peoples and all times. American Association of School Librarians Standards 4.1.4 and 4.4.6 will be targeted:

- Seek information for personal learning in a variety of formats and genres.

- Evaluate own ability to seek resources that are engaging and appropriate for own personal needs and interests.

Objective: Given a special, "quiet time" reading of *A Is for Abigail* and *All by Herself,* the student will discover women who have sacrificed and/or are sacrificing all for gender equality and personifying those freedoms contained within the Bill of Rights. Students will recognize and internalize the need for at least a moderate amount of sacrifice (civic action and service) on the part of each individual American citizen (for the good of the Republic as a whole). Reading as a means of building character via vicarious experience, reaction, and response will be emphasized. The intrinsic and life-sustaining rewards associated with personal sacrifice and the unselfish giving of one's talents (for the benefit of those in present times and in the future) will also be discovered.

Activity and Implementation: Each student or patron participating in the program will visit the library on an individual basis and be given a quiet corner or reading nook in which to read, without any interruption or rush, both thematic reading materials listed above. Upon reading the books, each student or patron will be provided with a journal in which to capture thoughts and ideas about the readings, as well as all readings subsequently completed for the program. Before leaving the individualized reading session, the librarian(s) will provide an individualized reading guidance session in which the student asks for a book on a subject which most impressed or touched them while reading the material. The student/patron and librarian will find a book in this vein which may be checked out as the first "read" of the program. Students/patrons will be asked to specifically reflect upon the need for civic action and service by all American citizens as they read hand-picked selections over the next few months. They will also reflect upon how reading serves as a catalyst for the perpetuation of democratic principles and civic-mindedness amongst the general population.

During each two-week period for the next ten weeks, students will visit the library as classes or discussion groups to hear a special "book talk" for selected titles associated with the program's theme—women who serve as catalysts for civic action—in addition to special historical talks from local historians. Following the book talks, students will be provided with a 30-minute exclusive browse and check-out time. The students should find a book

Plaque honoring Jonathon Harrington, who died at Lexington Green, April 19, 1775 (photograph by the author).

in the same genre as that covered in the book talk to read and reflect upon over the next two weeks. The book should target the theme of social responsibility and advocating for human rights. Genres to be highlighted include (may need to be rotated among classrooms or discussion groups because of the sheer volume of check-outs):

First week: biography
Second week: myth
Third week: fairytale
Fourth week: historical fiction
Fifth week: biography

Upon completing the reading strand, students will have a personal consultation with a librarian and converse about how the reading program contributed to the student/patron's understanding of courage and bravery exhibited by humans throughout history, as well as his or her own ability to exhibit courage and bravery. Students/patrons will also discuss their most significant reading, their most poignant and/or most memorable reading, and, perhaps most importantly, what they have learned about the critical charge of knowing one's rights and developing one's inner ability to act upon those rights. (Librarians can use these conversations to assist with the development of additional programming and/or instructional plans.) As the discussion ends, students/patrons will be allowed to choose a civics-related book as found in a "special-order" catalog developed by the librarian. The librarians will order these books for the students and distribute them upon receipt. The purchases will be funded by library, PTO, grant, special benefactor, or fund-raising monies.

Grades 8–10: Lights, Camera, …: Reel Action Helps Discern a Real Model Citizen

Thematic Reading Material

The Notorious Benedict Arnold: A True Story of Adventure, Heroism, and Treachery by Steve Sheinkin (Roaring Brook Press, 2010)

Sophia's War: A Tale of the Revolution by Avi (Beach Lane [Simon & Schuster], 2012)

Program Description: This program will use both nonfiction and fiction to reveal the character of a model American citizen, first investigating a character who did not rise to the model, and then delving into the traits of a character who put her life on the line, not for fame and glory, but rather to protect, defend, and protect the life of her fellow countrymen. Students will read both novels and participate in library-held discussions like those found near pages 168–172 of *Sophia's War*. Thereafter, those meeting the reading goal—reading the two selections and participating in library discussions—will be allowed the privilege of researching other model citizens in American history during specially held library research sessions (librarians will have associated pathfinders prepared). These students will be allowed to place their newfound understanding of a model citizen into a three-minute video that creatively answers this question: "What (or who) constitutes a model American citizen?" The videos, produced by either individual readers of groups of readers, per student or patron choice, will be entered into the president's White House Student Film Festival (http://www.whitehouse.gov/filmfestival). Librarians and technology experts will assist students with questions about the ethical inclusion of content, arrangement, editing, and uploading.

Program Goal: The goal of this reading promotion is to assist in the development of the reader's desire to act as a model American citizen and recognize the dispositions and character traits associated with such a citizen, most especially viewpoints based in reason, not sentiment; moderation of personal behavior and habits; persistence; observation; sacrifice; and willingness to support and encourage social justice. The American Association of School Librarian Standards attached to the plan include the following:

> 2.1.5 Collaborate with others to exchange ideas, develop new understandings, make decisions, and solve problems.
>
> 3.3.6 Use information and knowledge in the service of democratic values.
>
> 3.1.1 Conclude an inquiry-based research process by sharing new understandings and reflecting on the learning.
>
> 3.1.6 Use information and technology ethically and responsibly.

Program Objective: Student/patron readers will recognize the oftentimes quiet, unassuming, yet extremely involved, reason-based, and resilient characters who eventually reach the limelight as model American citizens. They will first recognize the inevitable psychological struggles and material temptations which may stand in the way of upright, committed citizenship (as portrayed in the character of Benedict Arnold). They will then observe the steady, persistent, and altruistic nature of civic action based on a commitment to collective well-being, human rights, and social justice (as portrayed by the character of Sophia Calderwood).

Activity and Implementation: Student/patrons will, from mid–August to mid–September, read *The Notorious Benedict Arnold* by Steve Sheinkin, entering into the following discussion at allotted times scheduled by the library:

1. Benedict Arnold at one point stated he could no longer serve his country with honor. Was it honorable for Arnold to enjoy the pleasures of Boston while his country was still at war, taking into consideration the trials he had just passed through? How do we balance our country's needs against our own personal needs as human beings?

2. What inspires you most about your country? Does that inspiration make you want to share your talents in service to the country? If you have not found your inspiration to serve your country to date, how will you go about trying to find it?

3. Should one's passion for civic action and advocacy ever be tempered? In which instances? Are the passions of our present leaders overboard? Underdeveloped? Inappropriate? On target? Why did Benjamin Franklin believe moderation was the key to a successful government? How can we moderate our passions for action and make them effective and productive? How might our leaders do the same? In the book, which leader displayed the most productive course of action based upon his or her passions?

Next, from mid–September to mid–October, student/patrons will read and discuss *Sophia's War: A Tale of the Revolution*. Questions include the following:

1. What was happening in the colonies that forced Nathan Hale (and fictional character Sophia) to put his or her life on the line at such a young age? Would you have acted the same way as Nathan Hale (or Sophia)? Why or why not? Is there any cause in our country today for which citizens should be putting their lives on the line?

2. Do citizens act on behalf of the country before or after traumatic experiences? Does an injustice have to become personal for one to act on behalf of others? Do human beings have a natural tendency to recognize terms of social justice, or must the call to honor human rights be inculcated by experience and education?

3. How might sentimentality or sensationalism blind one to the truth of a particular situation or issue? What is one's responsibility in discerning the truth of a particular report or happening? How does one go about finding the truth about governmental actions in today's world?

4. Which historical character within *Sophia's War* do you most admire, and why? How do you believe this character developed the traits of fortitude, courage, bravery, and contemplative action?

5. Compare and contrast the character, personality, attitudes, and strengths of Benedict Arnold and Sophia Calderwood. How do their inner journeys coincide? How do they differ?

From mid–October to mid–November, students/patrons who participated in the readings and discussions will be allowed time in the library to research other civic heroes, both historical and living. (Librarians will have pathfinders available to ensure reliability and quality of resources.) Students may visit individually or in groups, depending on whether they will be filming their eventual entry as a solo project or as a group. As they research, students/patrons will envision utilizing the information found to support their answer within the film as to "What (or who) constitutes a model American citizen?" Students will be allowed four two-hour research sessions within the library and will be allowed to check out print material conducive to the study. At the last research session (last hour), the librarian will provide instruction about the ethical use of information sources.

From mid–November to mid–January (or up to the entry deadline—check the White House website), students/patrons will film, edit, and critique a three-minute clip that answers the thematic question about a model citizen. Rubrics of exemplary film production techniques and the ethical use of information will be provided to students as they begin work. They will be encouraged to inquire about the ethical use of material, editing practices, and YouTube loading. Technology experts will be on hand in the library at certain specified times to assist students/patrons.

The films will be entered into the contest by the deadline. All participating students will receive a 128-GB flash drive, to be purchased by the library (through its budget, friends, benefactor, parents, or fund-raisers). Also, each student will enter a drawing to receive a collection of either Steve Sheinkin's or Avi's books, with two winners to be drawn (one Avi Winner, one Sheinkin winner).

Grades 10–12: How Do You Hope to Serve America?
Thematic Reading Material

John Adams by David McCullough (Simon & Schuster, 2002)

1776 by David McCullough (Holt McDougal, 2006)

Program Description: Students/patrons will be introduced to the narrative nonfiction of David McCullough, the Pulitzer Prize–winning author of bestselling titles whose subject is the American Revolution. Readers will enter book discussions found in publisher reading guides as well as self-created guides. The discussions will center on the contributions and service offered to America by John Adams, George Washington, Nathanael Greene, and Henry Knox. Thereafter, discussants will develop an artistic portfolio of the student/patron's choosing that addresses this question: "How do I hope to serve America in my lifetime?" The portfolio may be based in the following artistic genres: theater, film, essay, oral presentation (such as a TED talk), art, creative writing, or dance. Upon completion, the portfolio will be presented during a school assembly or specified public library–sponsored event. As a reward, the school or library will plan a 12th-grade (reader and portfolio creators only) trip to one of the following historical locations, chosen by student vote (the locales are conducive to further study of the men featured in McCullough's books): Savannah, Georgia; Mount Vernon (Alexandria, Virginia); Hudson Valley Knox Trail; or Boston/Quincy, Massachusetts.

Program Goal: The goal of the program is similar to the portfolio mandate required by the state of Tennessee, as mentioned in Chapter III: "an inquiry process which results in carefully designed products and tasks." In this instance, the reading promotion will allow an emerging adult to consider his or her civic duties and responsibilities and the contributions, based on his or her talents, that a student/patron might make to his or her country during adult life. The program will also encourage creative, critical thinking, production, and information literacy skills (21st-Century Learner Framework; http://www.p21.org/our-work/p21-framework) necessary to college and career readiness. It will serve as a catalyst for lifelong civic engagement and will target the following AASL Standards:

> 2.1.1 Continue an inquiry-based research process by applying critical-thinking skills (analysis, synthesis, evaluation, organization) to information and knowledge to construct new understandings, draw conclusions, and create new knowledge.
>
> 2.4.4 Develop directions for further investigations.
>
> 3.4.4 Create products that apply to authentic, real-world contexts.
>
> 3.3.6 Use information and knowledge in the service of democratic values.

Objective: Students/patrons will familiarize themselves with the extreme sacrifice of "heroes" (and Founding Fathers) of the Revolutionary War: John Adams, George Washington, Nathanael Greene, and Henry Knox. Students/patrons will develop a habit of consulting the wisdom of Revolutionary giants as they strive to "keep the Republic" during their lifetime via civic engagement, work, observation, and service, and will cherish the opportunity for self-expression provided by our forefathers. Participants in the reading program will also visit and pay their respects to historical markers, monuments, and parks commemorating not only the men and women of the Revolution, but also the values for which they stood: liberty, freedom, justice, and the observation of basic human rights.

Activities and Implementation

First Nine Weeks: Students/patrons will read McCullough's *John Adams* and enter into a fascinating book discussion per the publisher's reading guide: http://books.simonand-schuster.com/John-Adams/David-McCullough/9780743223133/reading_group_guide. During the discussions, allow additional time for and emphasize these questions: What are your thoughts on the government of the United States? Is the United States realizing John Adams's dream? Why or why not? What do you think was driving the life of John Adams? What were his motivations?

Second Nine Weeks: Readers will delve into McCullough's *1776*. The responsible librarians will divide readers into two groups. The first group will write discussion questions for pages 1–154 like those found in the *John Adams* discussion guide utilized in the first nine weeks, to be delivered to the second group. Alternating students in group 1 will lead the discussions. The second group, upon completing discussions for pages 1–154, will write discussion questions for pages 155–294. Group 2 members will lead discussions, alternating group leaders, for group 1 members. As they write questions, students/patrons will emphasize the vision of our leaders and explore how such vision is exhibited (or not) in the workings of today's government. Discussions about the manner in which the Revolutionary subjects serve as role models for today's American citizen should also be encouraged.

Third and Fourth Nine Weeks: Each individual student/patron participating in the reading promotion will complete an artistic portfolio that answers the key question: "How do I hope to serve America in my lifetime?" The answer can be expressed via any artistic medium of the student/patron's choice: theater, film, essay, creative narrative, oral presentation (such as in the TED talks), art, or dance. Instructors and/or community artists working in such media should be on hand to help each stu-

"Whose shoes will you fill?" Colonial chair and buckled shoes, Old State House, Boston, Massachusetts (photograph by the author).

dent as appropriate. Librarians will provide specified times in the library during which students can gather necessary information and resources that support the student/patron's answer, theme, trajectory of thought, and political/social philosophy. Library and technology professionals will also assist in instructing students/patrons about the ethical use of information/resources and the utilization of production and multimedia tools. During the fourth nine weeks, as students/patrons complete the creative portfolio, "recitals" will be scheduled in which several students exhibit their art during one show, in whatever form. Faculty/staff/fellow students and/or community members should be encouraged to attend.

Culminating Trip: At the beginning of the last nine weeks, 12th-grade reading participants will vote as to which locale should be visited in association with the culmination of their high school years, as tied into the reading promotion activities which honor a segue into responsible, civic-oriented adult years. The choices might include Savannah, Georgia (in honor of Nathanael Greene); Mt. Vernon (Alexandria, Virginia; in honor of George Washington); the Hudson Valley Knox Trail (in honor of Henry Knox); or Boston/Quincy, Massachusetts (in honor of John Adams). Once votes are in and a locale is selected, appropriate library administrators should plan the trip via a reliable travel agency and provide all means of support necessary (e.g., fund-raisers) to ensure any student who cannot afford the trip, yet who participates in the reading plan, may travel with his or her peers.

Hints for Successful Reading Promotion Plan Implementation

1. Tie all plans into civics/social studies/language arts/interdisciplinary curricula, whether offered at a school or public library. Involve members of the business community, revealing how the plans will develop productive, literate workers capable of thinking in critical, creative terms. Ask such members (the Chamber of Commerce might be contacted) for fiscal support of the activities planned.
2. Promote the plan to students/patrons through flyers, video clips on community cable, brochures, local newspaper event listings, and radio/school announcements.
3. Downplay any "educational" benefit or standards listed for professional use only, instead emphasizing the fun and love of learning which will accompany the program.
4. Develop a sense of community among participants, making the event not only a time of learning, but also a social event.
5. Ask for community/parent volunteers who are willing to commit time to the program throughout its duration.
6. Talk to student/patron visitors on a regular basis about their involvement in the program, asking for feedback and methods of improvement, and discussing the books with readers on a one-to-one basis.
7. Provide and display associated titles in the library for reading extension purposes.
8. Involve all stakeholders, ask for their help and solicit additional ideas, to include teachers, administrators, parents, local college faculty, business leaders, and community members.
9. Involve and incorporate art, music, dance, book talks, storytelling, and guest speakers as frequently as possible. Have fun, fun, fun!

Chapter XIV

Lesson Plans in Association with *Foreign-Born American Patriots: Sixteen Volunteer Leaders in the Revolutionary War*

> *"No free government, nor the blessings of liberty, can be preserved to any people, but by ... a frequent recurrence to fundamental principles."*—George Mason

This chapter encourages civic awareness, debate and colloquy, action, and service among high school and college students by providing complete and thorough lesson unit plans fashioned in association with the fresh, ground-breaking revelations found within an American Revolutionary War treatise: *Foreign-Born American Patriots: Sixteen Volunteer Leaders in the American Revolution* by Reneé Critcher Lyons (McFarland, 2013). The profiles from this book that will be used for instructional purposes are Charles Armand, Thomas Paine, John Paul Jones, Thaddeus Kościuszko, and Baron von Steuben.

Lesson Plan: Charles Armand

Title: (Not) Lost to History: Recognizing the Contribution of Revolutionary Frenchman Charles Armand

Student Characteristics: High School American History or Civics students

Objectives: National Council for the Social Studies Standard: Civics and Government

Compare competing historical narratives, recognize the tentative nature of historical interpretations, and hypothesize the influence of the past.

Materials

READINGS

Foreign-Born American Patriots: Sixteen Volunteer Leaders in the Revolutionary War, Chapter 11

National Park Service: Yorktown Battlefield, http://www.nps.gov/york/historyculture/armandbio.htm

Charles Armand Tuffin, Brigadier General in the Continental Army of the American Revolution: http://www.jstor.org/stable/20084323?seq=1

French Wikipedia article (translated): http://www.microsofttranslator.com/bv.aspx?from=&to=en&a=http%3A%2F%2Ffr.wikipedia.org%2Fwiki%2FArmand_Tuffin_de_La_Rou%25C3%25ABrie%23cite_note-73

IMAGES

From French Archives: http://en.wikipedia.org/wiki/Charles_Armand_Tuffin,_marquis_de_la_Rouerie#mediaviewer/File:Armand_La_Rou%C3%ABrie2.jpg

Charles Wilson Peale Portrait: http://impereur.blogspot.com/2014/03/armand-charles-tuffin-de-la-rouerie.html

New York Public Library Digital Gallery: http://digitalgallery.nypl.org/nypldigital/dgkeysearchdetail.cfm?strucID=1943109&imageID=2012036&k=1&print=small

Washington Gallery: http://www.history.com/topics/us-presidents/george-washington/pictures/george-washington/by-gilbert-stuart

VIDEOS

Now or Never: The Tide Turns: http://www.mountvernon.org/animated-washington/yorktown/

The French Revolution: History Channel, http://www.youtube.com/watch?v=LEq_lAx3ssE

QUOTES

Robespierre Quotes: http://izquotes.com/author/maximilien-robespierre

Washington Quotes: http://www.brainyquote.com/quotes/authors/g/george_washington.html

RESEARCH RESOURCE POSSIBILITIES

Queen's Rangers: http://www.jaegerkorps.org/reference/SIMCOEJournal.pdf

Pennsylvania Gazette, 1779: http://archiver.rootsweb.ancestry.com/th/read/AMREV-HESSIANS/2004-10/1097107706

History of County of Westchester: Search under Google Books

Six Nations: National Park Service, http://www.nps.gov/fost/historyculture/the-six-nations-confederacy-during-the-american-revolution.htm

History of French Army, 1750–1820, by Rafe Blaufarb: Search under Google Books

MAPS

Campaigns of the American Revolution, 1775–1781: http://www.lib.utexas.edu/maps/historical/shepherd/american_revolution.jpg

The American Revolution in the Hudson River Valley: http://www.hudsonrivervalley.com/Files/Brochures/109744HudsonRevolution.pdf

New York River Basins: http://www.dec.ny.gov/images/wildlife_images/nysmaprivlu05.jpg

Hudson River Valley: http://www.ridermagazine.com/wp-content/uploads/2009/05/2009-New-York-Favorite-Ride-Dahse-111.jpg

Pennsylvania/New York/New Jersey, 1778: http://www.emersonkent.com/images/campaigns_1778.jpg

Pennsylvania: http://www.lib.utexas.edu/maps/us_2001/pennsylvania_ref_2001.jpg

MOCK UNITED NATIONS

http://www.unausa.org/global-classrooms-model-un/how-to-participate

Essential Questions

1. Who is Charles Armand and why does he need to be recognized in the annals of American Revolutionary War history?
2. Which factors contributed to this military hero not being adequately recognized by posterity?
3. How does the recognition of Charles Armand's contributions enhance the study of social justice policy and philosophy?
4. How might the study of Charles Armand's personality and character strengthen the resolve of future American leaders who fight for social equality?
5. Which lessons does Charles Armand carry for today's military leaders who train soldiers involved in "combat," rather than battle?
6. Which lessons does Charles Armand's decision about logical and reasonable revolution (Armand failing to follow the leaders of the "Reign of Terror") have for international relations in today's world?

Overview and Sequence

This plan constitutes a 7-day (90-minute class periods) back-to-back reflection-based unit in which students will discover the historical figures of Charles Armand, George Washington, Louis XVI, and Robespierre; familiarize themselves with the settings of major Revolutionary War strategic positions; understand the Battle of Yorktown; be introduced to the French Revolution; internalize positive traits of character; and contemplate the psychological make-up of history's great leaders. Modify the plan as appropriate, based on time constraints and class length.

Strategy

Day 1: Introduce Charles Armand while sharing several of the primary images provided under "Materials" (Images). Watch the Mount Vernon Yorktown video provided as a resource. Assign readings.

Day 2: Discussion questions

1. Which factors and life experiences most notably led Charles Armand to cross the Atlantic Ocean to assist America's revolutionary cause?
2. Which factors most notably led to posterity (thus far) failing to acknowledge his contributions?
3. What was Armand's most notable contribution to the Revolution?
4. What is his legacy and why is his memory noble rather than ignoble?

Extension: Ask students to reflect upon this day's discussion in a personal journal as a homework assignment (due day 3), addressing whether their opinion proved reasonable when offered for response or debate, how their opinion changed due to the points of view offered, and what was learned about sacrifice, duty, honor, impetuous behavior, and correcting one's mistakes.

The iconic Mount Vernon weathervane, Mount Vernon, Alexandria, Virginia (photograph by the author).

Day 3: In the library, research the British military guerrilla leaders captured by Armand: Simcoe (Queen's Rangers), Alderman Leggett, Major Baremore, Captain Cruser, and members of the Six Nations. Also, research the significance of the capture of Redoubt 9 at Yorktown and why Armand's act of first crossing the parapet served as an exhibition of extreme courage. With guidance, ask students, as a group, to write a short script in which they act out a scenario in which Jimmy Fallon (or another popular late-night personality) is asking people on the street "Who is Charles Armand?" The "citizen" does not know, so Armand, Simcoe (especially Simcoe), Leggett, Baremore, Cruser, and several Native American leaders appear as either reverent, or not so reverent, immortals on All Hallows Eve to toggle the memory of highly such highly forgetful mortal souls! Assign parts and props and practice for the "theatrical production" on day 7.

Extension: In their journals, ask students to reflect upon Armand's courage and how actions based in such courage continue to affect American life, and the student's life, to this day.

Day 4: Watch a video on the French Revolution. As the video concludes, ask each student to relay one reason why Armand would not have followed that movement. (Be sure and supply the prompt before watching the video.) Students will have to elicit and remember several reasons—when a reason is verbalized, the next student cannot repeat it. Next, ask the following discussion questions:

1. Why would Armand have attempted to defend the king and place him back in power, at least temporarily?
2. Did Armand have any obligation to Louis XVI?
3. Had Louis XVI showed mercy to Armand in the past?
4. Did Armand believe the king should be offered mercy by the Revolutionaries?
5. Why, in your opinion, were the princes ineffective in the French Revolution, yet the planters effective in the American Revolution?
6. Which revolutions occurring today are of a civil nature? A terrifying nature?
7. How long do movements based in terror usually last? Movements based in civility? Can you think of examples to support your answer?

Extension: Ask students to reflect upon the type of leader necessary to effect change while also protecting our country and its Constitution and ensuring social stability. Consider the leader's background, philosophies, actions, and character traits. Does excellent oratory or penmanship or charisma alone supply a great leader? What else is needed?

Day 5: Compare and contrast: How were Washington and the other Founders different than Robespierre and his colleagues? Armand said, "What France lacks is men of judgment, men with any understanding of public welfare. These men we have not, at least none has showed himself." Find quotes from Washington versus Robespierre. Display primary resource images of both Washington and Robespierre for students to examine. Form two reading teams. Alternate, asking members of each team to first read a Washington quote, then a Robespierre quote. Ask the following discussion questions:

1. What is the difference in tone and content within the quotes?
2. What did you both feel and think when viewing the images and hearing the quotes?
3. What do the portraits say about the person's character? The quotes?
4. What are other means of judging character besides looks and words?
5. Define "sound" judgment. Define understanding of public welfare. How did Washington and Armand exhibit these qualities while Robespierre did not?

Extension: Find the context of one of the favorite quotes heard today. Was it included in a letter, a speech, or a document? Why was the entire content important for the time? For today? Report to the class on day 6. Also, evaluate the Model UN site and its worth in association with the "upbringing" of future leaders.

Day 6: Each student will provide a brief report on the content of a quote as provided in day 5. Also, each will be prepared to provide an opinion on the Model UN site.

Next, students will research and discuss these questions:

1. What and who were the King's Guards (Garde du Corps)?
2. How were they trained?
3. As a result, why was Armand an expert at guerrilla tactics?

Using provided materials, point out the areas in Pennsylvania and New York (Hudson Valley) kept safe by Armand's Legion, both on a Revolutionary map and a current map.

Extension: Write a fictional account, complete with descriptive setting and detailed action, of one of Armand's raids to either (1) read to the class or (2) turn in to the teacher—student's choice.

Day 7: Allow students to read fictional accounts of their choice. Perform the theatrical script written on day 2.

Discussion

1. What did Armand endure within his lifetime which contributed to the development of courage, intellect, and a tendency toward proactivity?
2. How do we determine what constitutes a great leader? Sacrifice? Character? What are several examples of great leaders in human history? How did they exemplify these traits? Examples? (e.g., Mandela, Washington, King). Which biographies, autobiographies, and other character-development books are held in your library which will help strengthen the character of our future leaders? Find them, find a quote from the book that attests to this person's character, and share it with the class.
3. Reflection to be written in class: How has the study of Charles Armand helped to develop your own inner character?

Enrichment

• Compare the Wikipedia pages of French and American explanations of Charles Armand. How is Armand portrayed in modern-day France? Is the French viewpoint different, the same, expanded in anyway?

• Watch a caricature of Simcoe in an episode of *Turn* on AMC. Compare it to a real-life biography or biographical excerpt.

Differentiation

• Ask special-education students to serve as interview moderators.

• Allow ADD and ADHD students to be highly involved in acting and/or props.

• Ask the library assistant to help students experiencing difficulties in writing personal reflections with correct grammar, verbiage, and punctuation.

• Make several of the discussion question sessions into think–pair–share activities.

• Ask those who are reluctant to join discussions to bring in songs, video excerpts, books excerpts, or other materials that will amplify their viewpoint.

- AIG: Brainstorm ways in which we might honor Charles Armand in our country. Be proactive and develop a plan and the means of ensuring such honor is instituted.

Assessment

- Participation in discussion

- Journal reflections

- Resource sharing

- Oral presentations

- Appropriate resource gathering

- Appropriate gleaning of information from materials

- Participation in theatrics

- Appropriate usage of dictionaries, maps, and OPAC

- Examination and evaluation of UN site

- Exemplary research skills

Lesson Plan: Thomas Paine

Title: Farmer of Thoughts: Thomas Paine
Student Characteristics: High School American History or Civics students
Objectives: National Council for the Social Studies Standard: Civics and Government
Assist learners in understanding the origins and continuing influence of key ideals of the democratic republican form of government, such as individual human dignity, liberty, justice, equality, and the rule of law

Materials

READINGS

Foreign-Born American Patriots: Sixteen Volunteer Leaders in the Revolutionary War, Chapter 2
Common Sense: http://www.ushistory.org/paine/commonsense/
American Crisis: http://www.ushistory.org/paine/crisis/

IMAGES

http://www.quoteswave.com/picture-quotes/433606
http://www.evolvefish.com/fish/media/G-ToArgueReasonPaineLG.gif

VIDEOS

Thomas Paine: Bill Moyers' Journal, http://www.pbs.org/moyers/journal/06122009/watch2.html

Essential Questions

1. Who is Thomas Paine and why does he need to be recognized in the annals of American Revolutionary War history?
2. What is America's democratic impulse? How is the impulse nurtured?
3. How do life experiences assist in the development of values, ideals, and beliefs? How does a strong value system serve as a call to action?
4. What are the major ideals of a democratic republic form of government? Define such ideals and provide examples of men who have practiced such ideals.
5. Why and how have the ideals of the American government withstood the test of time? Why is it necessary for these ideals to reside in the heart of the American people?
6. Why is it important to refer back to the writings of major political philosophers from time to time? How do these philosophies continue to direct our opinions, policies, and decision making?

Overview and Sequence

This plan constitutes a back-to-back 9-day (60-minute class periods) discussion-based unit in which students will discover the historical figures of Thomas Paine, John Locke, and Masaniello; familiarize themselves with writings which spurred America's turn toward independence; internalize the democratic values and ideals of our Founding Fathers and the American Revolution; understand the character traits required of governmental leaders; and develop an "ardent glow of generous patriotism." Modify the plan as appropriate, based on time constraints and class length.

Strategy

Day 1: Introduce Thomas Paine while sharing several of the primary images provided under "Materials" (Images). Discuss why these quotes are still relevant in today's society. Assign readings as follows:

Days 1–3: Lyons
Days 4–6:0 *Common Sense*
Days 7–9: *American Crisis*

Day 2: Lyons, Video, and Discussion Questions

1. Based on your biographical reading and the video, what is your understanding of how Paine fostered the "American democratic impulse?" What are such impulses? Are they followed in the 21st century?
2. How was Paine's life serendipitous? What is unusual about his historical prominence? Does his story inspire you to rise above circumstances? Either privately or in group discussion, reflect upon how his story has raised your desire to succeed.
3. Which principles did Paine develop as a result of being a witness to injustice? How do these principles stand as mental weapons? Provide examples both in Paine's life and in your own.
4. Paine believed citizens should exhibit the "ardent glow of generous patriotism." Which type of behavior or action was he encouraging? In what ways do these words encourage you to act on behalf of your country?

Fife and drum corps exhibiting an "ardent glow of generous patriotism," Williamsburg, Virginia (photograph by the author).

Day 3: Timeline and Garden

Using an online source (http://www.readwritethink.org/files/resources/interactives/timeline/), complete a trajectory timeline of the life experiences of Thomas Paine which spawned his set of values. Thereafter, sequence the dates of his writings and the earth-shattering actions and documents that came thereafter: Trenton, Saratoga, the Declaration of Independence, the U.S. Constitution and Bill of Rights, and so on.

On a large sheet of poster paper, collectively diagram and draw a Thomas Paine garden. Place the "crops" (Thomas Paine's contributions to the mindset of the American people) in rows labeled (1) checks and balances, (2) representation, (3) power structure, (4) justice, (5) rights of man and woman, (6) self-governance, and (7) viewpoint. Draw representative vegetables and label them based on the American principles, values, and ideals "farmed" by Thomas Paine in association with each "row." Example: Row 3 (power structure) is drawn as corn stalks, and individual stalks might be labeled "accountability," "civil servants," "elections," "divisions," "representative," and "We the People."

Homework: Read *Common Sense.*

Day 4: Diagram, in the fashion of a family tree, the manner in which Paine's pamphlet *Common Sense* is, as Washington stated, a writing of "unanswerable reasoning." In other words, how does this writing win any counterpoint debate? Prepare several diagrams in association with the claims found in the pamphlet.

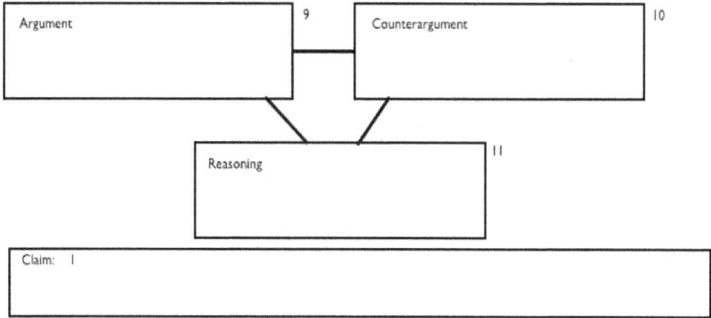

Day 5: Using a Venn diagram, compare and contrast the U.S. governmental organization and electoral scheme with the system proposed by Thomas Paine. Discuss which system is most reasonable and why. Take a vote on which system you would institute and share the results.

Day 6: Consider the points within *Common Sense* which created a "monument within the heart." List these points on a chart or board. Based on these points, as a class discuss and decide which type of monument should be erected to Thomas Paine—or whether, in fact, a monument should be built. Write a collective poem which would be placed on any monument or, if a monument should not be built per class opinion, write a poem of gratitude to Mr. Paine.

Homework: Read *American Crisis.*

Day 7: Study several issues within today's society as found at Idea of America (http://ideaofamerica.org/). Reflect upon how these issues might be addressed by Paine, pursuant to his writings in the *Pennsylvania Gazette, Common Sense,* and *American Crisis.* As a class, write a policy position based on Paine's ideas and share it on the website if possible (you must register).

Day 8: Research the historical figure Masaniello with the discussion promptings provided here in mind. Come back together as a class and discuss his significance in Italian history and the reference Paine made to this figure in *Common Sense:* "It is infinitely wiser and safer, to form a constitution of our own in a cool deliberate manner, while we have it in our power, than to trust such an interesting event to time and chance. If we omit it now, some Massanello may hereafter arise, who laying hold of popular disquietudes, may collect together the desperate and discontented, and by assuming to themselves the powers of government, may sweep away the liberties of the continent like a deluge."

1. Why did Paine use this figure as an example for his readers? How were the leaders of the American Revolution, their character, values, and background, different than this Italian leader?

2. Imagine what Paine might have said about the French Revolution while in prison. Would he have referred to this time period and its chaos as similar to the turn which occurred in Masaniello's character and actions? Would he have agreed French society was not prepared for a revolution, unlike America, which was ripe for a revolution resulting in stability?

Return to research and find what John Locke had to say about Masaniello: "Had [Filmer—another societal philosopher] had the happiness to live under Masniello's government, he could not by this his own rule have forborn to have done homage to him, with O king live forever, since the manner of his government by supreme power, made him properly king, who was but the day before properly a fisherman." Map out how government by supreme power ("might is right"), even if it exists at the hand of the destitute, differs from the philosophy of Paine and our Founding Fathers (discussing life, liberty, and the pursuit of happiness; checks and balances; and reason)? Use historical references as appropriate.

Extension: Reflect within a journal entry about any newfound influences on the beliefs, values, and ideals which form your personal opinion regarding how a government should be organized, instituted, and maintained. Quote significant and meaningful passages from the readings. Write your own philosophy of government.

Day 9: Write poetry in class which "brings to life" Walt Whitman's contention that Paine's contribution to history is "large, containing multitudes." Using think–pair–share strategies, obtain critiques for improvement. Spend time editing the poem. Share poems as time allows.

Enrichment

- Read and discuss Paine's additional writings: http://thomaspaine.org/pages/writings. html.

- Read and discuss Conway's biography of Thomas Paine.

- Watch and discuss *Thomas Paine: Apostle of Freedom*: http://thomaspaine.org/pages/ videos.html.

Differentiation

- Ask special-education students to serve as pollsters and research note takers.

- Allow ADD and ADHD students to be highly involved in typing the timeline, drawing the "Paine garden," governmental diagrams, and Venn diagrams.

- Ask the library assistant to help students experiencing difficulties in writing listings, entries, or poems with correct grammar, verbiage, and punctuation.

- Make several of the discussion question sessions into think–pair–share activities.

- Ask those who are having difficulty in discussion groups to write their opinions or record them on their phones at night.

AIG: Write an essay which details the manner in which America should strive to follow the "dangerous" precepts found in Thomas Paine's writings. Describe the "unanswerable reasoning" ideas which have been followed thus far, and advocate for the institution of those precepts (which, to this day, need to be instituted within our government and societal institutions).

Assessment

- Participation in discussion

- Participation in group writings

- Journal reflection

- Poetry

- Peer review

- Appropriate resource gathering

- Appropriate gleaning of information from materials

- Participation in diagram building, timeline formation, and art activities

- Exemplary research skills

Lesson Plan: Baron Friedrich von Steuben

Title: *The Revolutionary Pedagogy of Drillmaster Baron Friedrich Wilhelm von Steuben*
Student Characteristics: High School American History or Civics students (Massachusetts specific, but other states no doubt have similar standards.)
Objectives: Social Studies Standards—State of Massachusetts
USI.2 Explain the historical and intellectual influences on the American Revolution.
USI.4 Analyze the reasons for the American victory and the British defeat during the Revolutionary war.

Materials

READINGS

Foreign-Born American Patriots: Sixteen Volunteer Leaders in the Revolutionary War, Chapter 16
General von Steuben: NPS, http://www.nps.gov/vafo/historyculture/vonsteuben.htm
Bergen County Historical Society Page: http://www.bergencountyhistory.org/Pages/gnsteuben.html
Stony Point Battlefield: http://www.cr.nps.gov/history/online_books/colonials-patriots/sitec33.htm

IMAGES

http://usarmy.vo.llnwd.net/e2/-images/2009/06/14/37867/size0-army.mil-37867-2009-06-15-100613.jpg
http://upload.wikimedia.org/wikipedia/commons/c/cd/Baron_Steuben_by_Peale,_1780.jpg
http://www.bergencountyhistory.org/Pages/gnsteuben.html

Monument Information: http://www.nps.gov/vafo/historyculture/steubenmonument. htm

VIDEOS

Valley Forge: A Winter Encampment: http://www.youtube.com/watch?v=eOOFhGFNT3M

Now or Never: Washington at Yorktown, http://www.mountvernon.org/animated-washington/yorktown/

Battle of Monmouth: http://www.youtube.com/watch?v=TnYTUwhs-v4

RESEARCH RESOURCE POSSIBILITIES

Revolutionary War Drill Manual: http://books.google.com/books?id=njiwFoU3GFoC&q= bayonets#v=onepage&q&f=false

Essential Questions

1. Who is Baron Wilhelm von Steuben and why does he need to be recognized in the annals of American Revolutionary War history?
2. How did Baron von Steuben play a central role in the American victory? Would Yorktown have been possible without the contribution of this historical figure?
3. Which intellectual genius and creative authority measures did von Steuben utilize to ensure the American troops independently *agreed* to improve their lot? How did the troop consensus assist von Steuben in his efforts?
4. How were von Steuben's efforts evident in subsequent Revolutionary War battles?
5. How was von Steuben's demeanor and example of benefit to the morale of the Continental Army?

Overview and Sequence

This plan constitutes a back-to-back 6-day (60-minute class periods) kinesthetic- and research-based unit in which students will discover the historical figure of Baron von Steuben, understand his role in the American victory, embrace von Steuben's well-rounded approach to learning, be introduced to motivational teaching methods, become aware of the duties of an American citizen, and receive background knowledge associated with several battles in which von Steuben was a key player. Modify the plan as appropriate, based on time constraints and class length.

Strategy

Day 1: Introduce Baron von Steuben by sharing the National Park Service's page on the history of the Valley Forge National Park monument to Baron von Steuben; see "Materials" (Monument Information). Discuss first impressions of the Baron based on an understanding of the monument.

Homework: Lyons reading, NPS (Steuben) reading, Bergen Historical Society reading.

Day 2: Lyons Reading and Discussion Questions:

1. What most impressed you about von Steuben's training method? Have you ever been involved in a train-the-trainer scenario? How did this method improve the skills of all persons involved?

Baron von Steuben (1730–1794) drilling the troops at Valley Forge, winter 1777–1778 (Edwin Austin Abbey, artist [1852–1911], Library of Congress).

2. How did von Steuben's drill practice improve the abilities of the Continental Army? Would von Steuben have been as understanding of the deficiencies of the troops if not for his prior experience? Why would von Steuben, who was trained in a rigid European army, have attempted to understand the mindset of the soldiers at Valley Forge? Why was he willing to explain why his methods were best?

3. Consider why humor might be a mode of survival in dark times. How did humor allow von Steuben to reach his goals and contribute to the cause of the American Revolution in a manner which used his expertise to the greatest extent?

4. How was von Steuben, as the author states, the "great teacher of the American Revolution"? Which types of "art" and creative art were part of his training practices? How were the remaining battles of the American Revolution an example of von Steuben's stamp upon the psyche of his troops? How did this common sense of pride help the Americans prevail in battle and eventually win the war?

5. In accordance with von Steuben's pedagogical philosophy, which strengths were apparent in the Continental Army? Which examples did he provide to training officers? How did he encourage the soldiers? Enable them? Allow them to become independent, confident soldiers?

6. How did von Steuben's dress, appearance, demeanor, and humanity demand that he be listened to and followed? How can mere presence motivate a group and spur proactivity? Why is a combination of sternness and kindness necessary to effective leadership? Why is it important to understand the characteristics of those who are being led?

Day 3: ROTC Kinesthetic Exercises

Invite the ROTC candidates at your high school to demonstrate a drill for the class. Ask the ROTC officer to discuss how the drill as exhibited was similar to the means of drill taught by von Steuben (comparison). Ask the officer to discuss how von Steuben contributed to the development of the military's most important officers, drill sergeants. Next, ask students to line up in rows of four with flag poles or slim and long wood pieces to substitute as weapons. Ask the ROTC officer to call a drill without any training. Thereafter, ask the ROTC candidates, who have been trained by the trainer, to teach the drill provided by the officer to the groups. Come back together as a line and note the difference in abilities.

Extension: Write a journal reflection in which you describe your reaction to the drill before any training versus your feelings and thoughts upon receiving training. Write your thoughts about how this shift probably lifted the soldiers at Valley Forge out of their sense of desperation and hopelessness.

Day 4: Research the Prussian honor known as the Order of Fidelity (as well as the meaning of the insignia) and/or the term "knighthood." List the qualifications, attributes, and qualities of character of someone who received this honor. Break into groups of four and ask students to identify four examples of how von Steuben exhibited such a quality while stationed at Valley Forge and/or as Inspector General of the Continental Army. Come back together as a class and complete a character map of moments of honor, quotes, beliefs and opinions, and morality. Discuss how you might teach these qualities to another class within the building.

Extension: In your personal journal, describe how von Steuben fulfilled a knight's charge—to always and everywhere be right and good against evil and injustice—by volunteering to serve the cause of the American Revolution.

Homework: Read the NPS Stony Point material.

Day 5: Watch the videos on the Battle of Monmouth and the Battle of Yorktown. How did Steuben's ability to motivate, inspire, and train the Continental Army reveal itself at the Battle of Monmouth? Could the troops have performed at Stony Point or Yorktown in a professional manner if not for Steuben's training? What did Rochambeau mean when he said, "You must have formed an alliance with the King of Prussia. These troops are Prussian!" Is there a reason why Redoubt 10 was easier to overcome than Redoubt 9? Why did Steuben feel vindicated in being the first to place an American flag atop the conquered redoubt?

Extension: Imagine you are von Steuben upon the capture of the redoubts and the surrender of Cornwallis. In your journal, write what you are feeling and thinking as you climb the redoubt and place the American flag atop the fortification.

Day 6: Ask students to share any thoughts, feelings, or comments from the extension assignment. Based on these promptings, write a collective newspaper editorial that expounds on von Steuben's love for America, urging citizens to renew their own love for country in his honor.

Von Steuben allowed a soldier with the last name of "Arnold" to take his name (see the Lyons chapter—and remember that Benedict Arnold accepted British bribes). With this example in mind, what would von Steuben say about the amount of money spent on campaigns in modern-day America? How would he have "trained" a modern-day American politician? A modern-day American citizen in "fast time"? Due to the urgency associated with the need for campaign finance reform, create a "training" strategy which will assist Americans in fighting the battle against "big money" interests.

Enrichment

- Write a poem that would be placed on von Steuben's gravestone along with this epigraph: Indispensable to the Achievement of American Independence.

- Plan a "Von Steuben" Field Day with the physical education teacher.

Differentiation

- Allow ADD or ADHD students to create a diorama depicting the trenches at Yorktown and/or the multiple trenches in which von Steuben was involved during his military career.

- Allow special-education students to collect and pass out the rods or other materials needed for the ROTC candidates drill.

- Allow artistic learners to create a "knighthood" chart in which the class discusses and votes for any peers they wish to be knighted as an honorary American citizen. The chart will creatively describe and point out the virtues associated with knighthood. The award will be an Order of Fidelity badge created by the art students.

- Allow linguistic learners to take the lead in writing the classroom editorial.

- AIG: Begin a "Steuben blog" in which students periodically post musings about reasons to renew our love for American values, principles, and ideals.

Assessment

- Participation in discussion

- Participation in kinesthetic drill

- Participation in creation of editorial, charts, models, and/or listings

- Journal reflections

- Appropriate resource gathering

- Appropriate gleaning of information from materials

- Participation in completion of a character map

- Exemplary research skills

Lesson Plan—John Paul Jones

Title: Going in Harm's Way: The Adventures of John Paul Jones
Student Characteristics: College Undergraduates
Objectives: Objectives for college-based courses (multiple disciplines):
Familiarize students with key personalities of the American Revolution.
Consider how the Revolutionary generation, as well as subsequent generations, have remembered the American Revolution.

Materials

READINGS

Foreign-Born American Patriots: Sixteen Volunteer Leaders in the Revolutionary War, Chapter 7

John Paul Jones: Sailor, Hero, Father of the American Navy by Evan Thomas

John Paul Jones by James Fenimore Cooper: http://www.history.navy.mil/bios/jones_jp_cooper.htm

John Paul Jones Naval Biography, with Chronology: http://www.history.navy.mil/bios/jones_jp.htm

MUSIC

John Paul Jones by Johnny Horton: http://www.youtube.com/watch?v=9s58mlY1R6k

MOVIE

John Paul Jones (1959): http://www.youtube.com/watch?v=ugsFLq1SxEg&list=PL4554A8E464758431

Monument Information: C-SPAN Talk on John Paul Jones Monument, http://www.c-span.org/video/?309248-1/john-paul-jones-memorial

VIDEOS

C-SPAN *Booktalk* on Evan Thomas's Biography:http://www.c-span.org/video/?176683-1/book-discussion-john-paul-jones-sailor-hero-father-american-navy

Essential Questions

1. Who is John Paul Jones and why does he need to be recognized in the annals of American Revolutionary War history?
2. How does the legacy of John Paul Jones remain relevant to 21st-century American naval officers?
3. How is John Paul Jones's bravado (and his definition of bravery) displayed and exemplified by the U.S. Navy SEALs?
4. Why was Theodore Roosevelt interested in the contributions of John Paul Jones to the American cause during the Revolutionary War? What are the similarities in character between these two American leaders?
5. How is John Paul Jones recognized in 21st-century America?
6. How did Jones free and provide for American prisoners of war (in the Revolutionary War)? What was his opinion of slavery? Why was Jefferson eager to provide Jones with a command to free American prisoners in Nigeria following the war?

Overview and Sequence

This plan constitutes a module within a college undergraduate course, whether the discipline core constitutes American studies, history, international studies, or interdisciplinary studies. The undergraduate student will recognize the contributions of John Paul Jones to the cause of the American Revolution, the annals of American naval history and performance, and the mindset of today's naval officers.

Strategy

Lecture: Ask students to provide their knowledge of the historical figure, John Paul Jones. Ask them if they are aware he has drifted in and out of popular culture; share the song and movie from the 1950s provided in "materials." After a brief discussion of Jones's contributions, ask students to ponder why a person who attacked British naval ships in British waters during the Revolutionary War is not more highly recognized in middle school and high school textbooks. Reveal Jones's geographical route (and raids) during Revolutionary sea battles in which he served as captain. Share several of Jones's quotes and discuss the prophetic nature of his declarations:

- "When the enemy's land force is once conquered and expelled from the continent, our Marine will rise as if by enchantment and become, with the memory of persons now living, the wonder and envy of the world."

- "Without a respectable Navy— alas America!"

Share the video provided in the "Materials" and assign readings and group assignments, to be presented at a later date in the semester.

Group 1: Research Theodore Roosevelt's interest in the return of John Paul Jones's remains to American soil. What was this president's role in the return, and how would Roosevelt have known a great deal about American naval heroes? How did Roosevelt's experiences mirror those of Jones? Compare the personalities of these two heroes and identify similarities between them. Present findings to the rest of the class in a creative manner and provide handouts as appropriate.

John Paul Jones (1747–1792) (portrait by George Bagby Mathews [1857–1943]).

Group 2: Research the manner in which the personalities, bravery, fortitude, bravado, mindset, professionalism, and success of America's Navy SEALs mirror the legacy of John Paul Jones. Predict how Jones would both congratulate and critique these officers. Present findings to the class in a creative manner and provide handouts as appropriate.

Group 3: Research the crypt of John Paul Jones at the Naval Academy in Annapolis, Maryland. Explain the symbols, etchings, materials, and figurines that appear in his crypt.

Provide information about how the crypt was constructed, as well as the ceremony during which Jones was finally laid to rest on American soil. Would Jones have been proud of the crypt and the service? Present findings to the rest of the class in a creative manner and provide handouts as appropriate.

Group 4: Research the professional values, demeanor, and dispositions required of naval officers as well as Jones's letters and writings regarding the conduct of a naval officer. How do Jones's qualifications mirror the behavioral and personality traits, as well as the skills and qualifications, of 21st-century American naval officers? Present findings to the rest of the class in a creative manner and provide handouts as appropriate.

Upon making assignments and, after students have read the print materials, enter the following discussion.

1. What were Jones's ideas about destiny? Do you believe great leaders always appear in times of trial? What were some of the amazing "firsts" in Jones' life which signify the workings of serendipity?
2. Why were Jones's childhood experiences crucial to the development of his passion and ambition for the American cause?
3. In what manner did the "exertions" of John Paul Jones ensure that "the great American naval power" did not disappear after the close of the Revolutionary War? To answer this question, reflect upon Jones's quote: "The first beginning of our Navy was, as navies now rank, so singularly small that I am of opinion it has no precedent in history."
4. How did Jones's feats bear out a biographer's contention: "No more appropriate name for a ship commanded by John Paul Jones could have been devised" (referring to Jones's first ship, *The Ranger*).
5. After studying the battles won by Jones, do you, like one biographer, believe Jones was an "imponderable human force"? Why or why not? Jones never surrendered in battle, but what did he surrender in his personal life for the benefit of American liberty?
6. Comment on the quote under the French engraving by J. B. Fosseyeux: "Rarely are such men made, but when they fall from the sky, the faint enjoy."
7. How will you apply Jones's quotes to your choice of careers: "Men mean more than guns in the rating of ships." "I am not calculating risks, but estimating the chances of success." "The sources of success are quick resolve and swift stroke."

Culminating Assignment

In a personal journal, to be turned in, students will reflect upon how the learning provided by this module has contributed to their appreciation of this naval hero and the larger cause for which he fought: universal human rights. Also, reflect upon this quote from Herman Melville: "Intrepid, unprincipled, reckless, predatory, with boundless ambition, civilized in externals but a savage at heart, America is or may yet be the Paul Jones of nations."

Enrichment

- Visit the Naval Academy at Annapolis during spring break. Visit the tomb of John Paul Jones.

- Visit the John Paul Jones Museum in Scotland.

- Visit the John Paul Jones Memorial in Washington, D.C.
- Visit the John Paul Jones Memorial Park in Kittery, Maine.
- Visit the Garden of the Heroes art museum in Philadelphia, Pennsylvania.

Differentiation

- Ask groups to "scout" individual talents among group members. For example, those excelling in technology skills might fashion the form of presentation and ensure appropriate technology is utilized. Artistic students might graph the form of presentation or illustrate props for the presentation.

- Students who do not enjoy speaking before the class might assist their group by becoming the group wordsmith or completing a major portion of the required research.

Assessment

- Substantive participation in discussion
- Journal reflections
- Appropriate resource gathering
- Appropriate gleaning of information from materials
- Balanced participation in group work and presentations
- Exemplary research skills

Lesson Plan—Thaddeus Kosciuszko

Semester and/or Academic Year Portfolio Project: Thaddeus Kościuszko
Title: Thaddeus Kościuszko: Prince of Tolerance
Student Characteristics: High School American History or Civics Students
Objectives: National Standards for Civics and Government
Which civic dispositions or traits of private and public character are important to the preservation and improvement of American constitutional democracy?
Tennessee Law (TCA, Section 49–6–1028): http://www.tn.gov/sos/acts/107/pub/pc1036.pdf

Materials

READINGS

Foreign-Born American Patriots: Sixteen Volunteer Leaders in the Revolutionary War, Chapter 10
The Peasant Prince: Thaddeus Kościuszko and the Age of Revolution by Alex Storozynski
History Channel Article: http://www.history.com/topics/american-revolution/tadeusz-kosciuszko
Kościuszko Foundation: http://www.thekf.org/kf/

IMAGES

Monument in Philadelphia: http://www.nps.gov/thko/planyourvisit/images/khouse1.jpg

Monument in Chicago: http://www.waymarking.com/gallery/image.aspx?f=1&guid=ebdc8214–4890–444b-8ae7–7eba6a14575a&gid=3

Videos

Dublin Park: http://dublinohiousa.gov/parks-open-space/thaddeus-kosciuszko-park/
The Man of Mount Kościuszko: http://www.youtube.com/watch?v=y495VFurkDg

Quotes

- "That sound that crashes in the tyrant's ear, Kościuszko!" (Lord Bryon)

- "He is as pure a son of liberty as I have known and of that liberty which is to go to all, not to the few and rich alone." (Thomas Jefferson)

- "One can be independent anywhere, provided one is noble in thought, judgment, and of heart." (Thaddeus Kościuszko)

Maps

National Park Service (also quotes, images, primary documents): http://www.nps.gov/thko/upload/KHouse%20REV%20CompPlan.pdf

Advice to Teenagers (letter to Conrad Zeltner—Swiss family Kościuszko lived with during his later years):

Rising at four o'clock in summer and at six o'clock in winter, your first thought must be directed towards the Supreme Being, worshipping Him for a few minutes. Put yourself at once to work with reflection and intelligence…. Be always frank and loyal … and always speak the truth; never be idle, be sober and frugal and even hard on yourself but indulgent toward others. Avoid selfishness and egotism. Before speaking about something and answering, reflect well and reason…. In all your actions you must be upright, sincere, and open, no dissimulation in any of your talk, never argue, but seek truth serenely and modestly. Be polite and considerate to everyone, agreeable, and obliging in society, always humane, and succor the poor according to your means. Read instructive books to embellish your mind or better your heart. Never degrade yourself by making bad acquaintances, but be always with persons full of morals and of good reputation; and finally, your conduct must be such that everyone approves of it."

Current Human Rights Issues

Morningstar Teachable Moments (Social Responsibility): http://www.morningsidecenter.org/teachable-moment/lessons
PBS News Hour Extra: http://www.pbs.org/newshour/extra/
Student News Daily: http://www.studentnewsdaily.com/
New York Times Question List: http://learning.blogs.nytimes.com/2013/06/13/182-questions-to-write-or-talk-about/?_r=0
Amnesty International: http://www.amnestyusa.org/our-work/issues
Global Issues: http://www.globalissues.org/article/139/the-usa-and-human-rights
Department of State: http://www.state.gov/policy/
Human Rights Watch: http://www.hrw.org/united-states
Human Rights in the United States: http://www.theadvocatesforhumanrights.org/human_rights_in_the_united_states

Human Rights Failings: http://www.theguardian.com/world/2014/mar/13/us-un-human-rights-abuses-nsa-drones

Project Examples and Resources

Tennessee State: http://www.tccle.org/projectcitizen.html

NCLCE: http://www.everystudentacitizen.org/2013/01/advancing-accountability-in-civic-education-florida-tennessee-lead-the-way/

American Bar Association: http://www.americanbar.org/content/dam/aba/migrated/publiced/LabReport_Booklet_August_2010.authcheckdam.pdf

Florida State: http://education.ucf.edu/litsymposium/resources2013/supportingjusticesandradayoconnor.pdf

Essential Questions

1. Who is Thaddeus Kościuszko and why does he need to be recognized in the annals of American Revolutionary War history?
2. Which civic dispositions and traits of public and private character did Kościuszko exhibit that inspired biographers and historians to call him the "Prince of Tolerance"?
3. How does the study of Kościuszko contribute to a tolerant society?
4. In what manner do Kościuszko's dispositions and traits of public and private character contribute to a government based in liberty, freedom, and justice?
5. How does the recognition of Kościuszko's contributions enhance the study of social justice policy and philosophy?
6. How might the study of Kościuszko's personality and character strengthen the resolve of future American leaders who fight for social equality?
7. How does the study of Kościuszko's personality and character strengthen the resolve of American citizens who work to perpetuate a governmental system based in liberty, freedom, justice, and social equality?

Overview and Sequence

This plan constitutes a semester-long study in which the student completes a culminating portfolio for examination by peers and a faculty-based committee. Students will use an example from Kościuszko's life to identify a portfolio theme based on the wide topic of "civic tolerance in American society." Students will associate the actions of Kościuszko with a civic issue in 21st-century America which needs citizen response and proactivity in the form of action, advocacy, awareness building, and service. The issue chosen for inspection, research, analysis, and debate should center on enhancing tolerance within the American citizenry for all groups (i.e., the homeless, impoverished, illiterate, racial minorities, religious minorities, female workers, immigrants, mentally disadvantaged, abused or neglected children, medical patients of any variety, the elderly, LGBT populations, and/or any group or individuals who experience intolerance to some degree within modern societies). Library, history, English, and technology teachers will collaborate to provide the teaching and mentoring required for this project. Committee members will cover all subject areas within the high school, and each student will be assigned an advisor (community professionals and volunteers may also have to be recruited for advisement purposes, depending on the number of students). The final electronic portfolio may include videos or trailers, film productions,

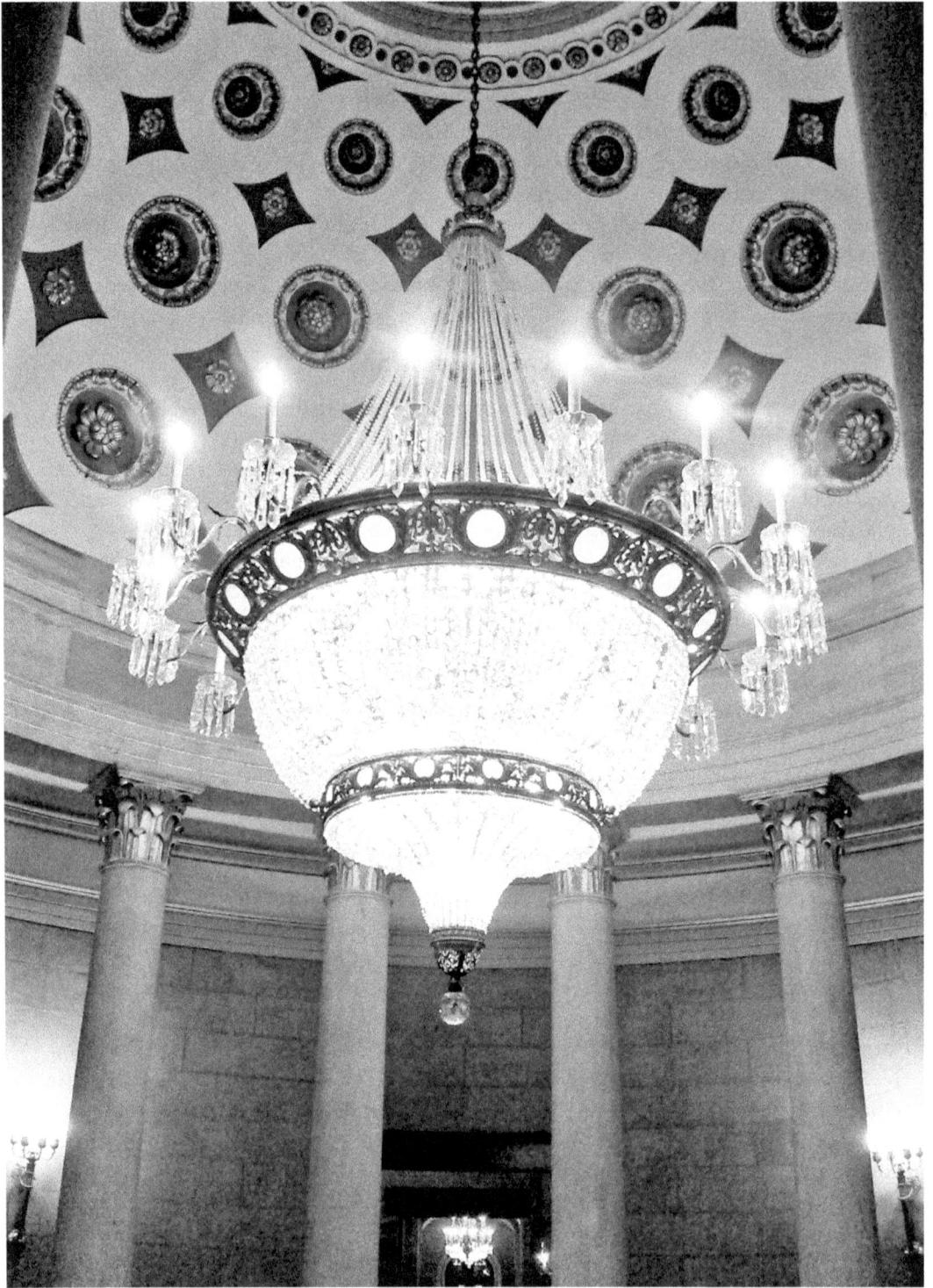

Chandelier at the Library of Congress, Washington, D.C., a reflection of Kościuszko's light (photograph by the author).

digital imagery, audio, timelines, digital plotting applications, digital collage, voice threads, wordles, and required textual reflections, reporting, and information delivery.

Strategy

Step 1: Introduce Thaddeus Kościuszko by assigning all readings and sharing images, maps, websites, and videos. Engage students in the following discussions:

1. Name some instances in which Kościuszko exhibited tolerance for all peoples. Which action(s) exhibited his tolerance? Can you think of examples of men or women exhibiting such proactivity for oppressed groups in today's society?
2. How did Kościuszko's life reflect and represent the four qualities symbolized by his Krakowian hat: duty, honor, liberty, and freedom?
3. How did Kościuszko's intent on obtaining the finest education and training contribute to his ability to serve the causes of liberty and freedom, and how did his education and training help him take action for the downtrodden and the oppressed? Which of Kościuszko's contributions to the American Revolution impresses you the most, and why?
4. How were reflection and silence important to Kościuszko's continuing productivity throughout his lifetime?
5. What "goodwill to humankind" has resulted from Kościuszko's contributions, both in the American and the Polish revolutions?
6. How did Kościuszko bless his country, relatives, friends, benefactors, countrymen— the whole human race? How might you do the same?
7. Reflect upon Kościuszko's prayer, the poems of Coleridge and Keats, and Kościuszko's letter to Conrad Zeltner. What inspires you most in these works, and how will you use this inspiration to direct your portfolio? Your own life and civic action and service?

Step 2: Discuss modern-day issues associated with tolerance and equality for oppressed and/or minority groups. Students will be assigned the readings found under "Issues" and asked to reflect in journals during each night of the readings (to be turned in), addressing the following question:

1. What surprises you about human rights violations in the United States? Around the globe? How will these violations affect your life in a negative manner, in your opinion? How would a reversal affect your life positively? Using Kościuszko as an example, what type of assistance should these groups receive? What is the answer for reform? Which public policy changes are required?

Also, in class, after the assigned readings have been completed, discuss these questions:

1. Which group(s) in the United States are subjected to the highest degree of marginalization? How are their issues being voiced and addressed? Do you see evidence of this marginalization in your own community? How is your community addressing the issue?
2. How are our legislators addressing the issues? How are grassroots organizations addressing the issues?
3. Just as Kościuszko was instrumental in the Race of the Dan, in which time was of the essence, which issues, in today's society, are "of the essence"? In other words, which

issues must be dealt with immediately for the preservation of not just our democracy, but the entire human race?

Step 3: Ask students to reflect anonymously in their journals about which issue touched their heart and/or piqued their interest. Students should schedule an appointment with advisors to debate the worth and value of a chosen portfolio topic. They must also prepare a rationale for their proposed project to present for approval by portfolio committees. Hold approval committee meetings for student presentation of the topic, and obtain approvals.

Step 4: Students will begin work on their projects, following this outline:

A. Overview of topic
B. Viewpoints
C. Debate and current reforms
D. Personal debate and viewpoint based in research
E. Civic action in association with the established group or the action project created by student
F. Service to the population affected, either self-organized or in association with a service group
G. Reflection upon impact of actions and service
H. Creation of a portfolio depicting the issue at hand, majority and minority viewpoints, personal viewpoint, action completed and the impact thereof, service completed and the impact thereof, and future endeavors planned

Students will work directly with librarians, teachers, and advisors while constructing their personal portfolios throughout the semester, meeting on a weekly basis with these professionals to monitor progress.

Step 5: Students will present their portfolios to their peers and librarians/teachers/advisors for critique.

Step 6: Students will make any changes based on the review and critique.

Step 7: Students will present the portfolio presentation to the approval committee.

Step 8: The committee will vote on approval/disapproval of student portfolios. If disapproved, the committee will ask the student for specific improvements.

Step 9: The portfolio is approved. (If initially disapproved, the student will provide improvements and again seek approval.)

Assessment

- Participation in reading and discussion
- Journal reflections
- Resource sharing
- Advisement meetings
- Appropriate resource gathering

- Appropriate gleaning of information from materials
- Participation in self-directed action and service projects
- Exemplary research skills
- Presentations to peers and committee
- Electronic portfolio production—create rubric

Chapter XV

Ask for Support

Civic Organizations, Research Centers, Civic Institutes and Support Networks

"The only title in our democracy superior to that of president is the title of citizen."—Louis Brandeis

To find the time, money, and collaborative colleagues necessary to the implementation of the activities, lessons, action, service, and reading promotion plans found in this book, reach out to librarians in your hometown or community, state library offices, state professional library organizations, American Library Association support networks and professional advocates, as well as the directors and staff of the following organizations, advocating for the return of exemplary, widespread, required, and "taken seriously" civics education and/or literacy.

ACKERMAN CENTER FOR DEMOCRATIC CITIZENSHIP

http://ackerman.education.purdue.edu/

Founded by Purdue University's College of Education, the Ackerman Center strives to provide programs, institutes, activities and resources for educators to implement more powerful citizenship programs and opportunities that result in active student involvement in schools and communities.

AMERICAN ASSOCIATION OF SCHOOL LIBRARIANS (AASL)

http://www.ala.org/aasl/

The American Association of School Librarians is the national organization for librarians working within our nation's public schools. It supports and provides resources for librarians dealing with issues of censorship and intellectual freedom. The organization prepares and updates declarations of a student's right to read (http://www.ala.org/advocacy/intfreedom/statementspols/freedomreadstatement). It also establishes practice guidelines and standards which assist students in sharing knowledge and participating ethically and productively as members of our democratic society (http://www.ala.org/aasl/sites/ala.org.aasl/files/content/guidelinesandstandards/learningstandards/AASL_Learning_Standards_2007.pdf).

American Democracy Project

http://www.aascu.org/programs/ADP/

The American Democracy Project is a multicampus project organized by the American Association of State Colleges and Universities in association with *The New York Times*. It strives to reach today's college student, who will graduate and become tomorrow's "steward of place." Its goal is to train students enrolled in our nation's colleges about the need to be ready to participate in the American form of government and to act within their local communities as knowledgeable, committed, and involved citizens.

American Library Association (ALA) Center for Civic Life

http://centerforciviclife.tumblr.com/

The recently organized ALA Center for Civic Life (2010) hopes to encourage engagement and deliberative action among citizens in local communities across our nation. As such, it trains librarians in the creation of public forums and patron services in which the public library emerges as a nonpartisan, active, conciliatory, and productive participant in the civic life of a given community.

American Revolution Center

http://amrevmuseum.org/

The American Revolution Center is constructing a museum in the heart of historic Philadelphia (to be opened in 2017), near Independence Hall, which will include both a physical and a digital overview of the American Revolution, in an attempt to cure the general citizenry's "historical amnesia."

Annenburg Learner

http://www.learner.org/resources/discipline-social-science.html

This site provides lesson plans based in political science: "Democracy in Action," "Electoral Politics," "Federal Deficits," "Judicial Elections," "Public Trusts; Private Interests," "The Constitution," and "State Government."

Ashbrook Center at Ashland University (Ohio)

http://ashbrook.org/

The mission of the Ashbrook Center is to "restore and strengthen the capacities of the American people for constitutional self-government. To fulfill this mission, [it] offers educational programs for students, teachers, and citizens." As such, the center offers an Ashbrook Scholars' Program for outstanding political science and history majors, the "Teaching American History" and "50 Important American Document" lesson plans for civics teachers, and educational programming for the general citizenry.

Bill of Rights Institute

http://billofrightsinstitute.org/

A nonprofit organization, the Bill of Rights Institute strives to provide educational resources dealing with America's founding documents and principles. The organization's vision is to create a citizenry schooled in the knowledge, values, principles, and dispositions necessary to the perpetuation of a free republic.

Campaign for Civic Mission of Schools

http://www.civicmissionofschools.org/

Along with 60-plus coalition partners, the Campaign serves as the advocacy arm for civics education, operating on two tracks, the national and state levels. Labeled the "Guardian of Democracy," the organization encourages use of its six proven practices in effective civic learning. Supported by Sandra Day O'Connor, the organization is a project of the Lenore Annenburg Institute for Civics. This project, along with CIRCLE, receives high regard among proponents of civics education reform. Educators are provided with online resources, civic competencies, research findings, best practices, criteria for success, and assessment tools.

Center for Civic Education

http://www.civiced.org/

Founded on the campus of the University of California, Los Angeles, the Center publishes model national civics standards and resources conducive to the instruction thereof. It also produces the following programs: "We the People: The Citizen and the Constitution," "We the People: Project Citizen," and "Foundations of Democracy."

Center for Democracy and Citizenship

http://www.augsburg.edu/sabo/programs/center-democracy-citizenship/

Augsburg College's (Minneapolis) lessons focus on the role and character of citizenship in a vibrant democracy, guiding the Center's practice:

- Civic engagement is a result of good citizenship.
- A successful political process depends on deliberative practice.
- Political leadership is a vocation in democracy.
- The art of politics is about how to get things done.
- Good decisions should be guided by values.

Center for Engaged Democracy Merrimack

http://www.merrimack.edu/academics/education/center_for_engaged_democracy/

Acting as a central hub, Merrimack College's (Massachusetts) Center strives to develop, coordinate, and support academic programs across the country which provide majors, minors, or certificates focusing on civic and community engagement; sponsor symposia and conferences; and provide research opportunities for such academic programs nationwide.

Center for Information and Research on Civic Learning and Engagement (CIRCLE)

http://www.civicyouth.org/

CIRCLE, a project based at Tufts University's College of Citizenship and Public Policy, provides reliable data and analysis cited by civics education advocates nationwide, as well as major publications such as *The New York Times* and *The Washington Post*. It is highly recommended for librarians who are striving to justify civics-based programming.

Center for Teaching the Rule of Law

http://www.thecenterforruleoflaw.org/

Located on the campus of Roanoke College in Salem, Virginia, the Center for Teaching the Rule of Law recognizes the general citizenry must understand both the philosophy behind and the governmental structure provided by the U.S. Constitution. All online resources provided by the Center, as well as its sponsored face-to-face projects, are based in the belief that "the rule of law cannot be appreciated without knowing its history and evolution, and the vital role citizens play in the democratic process which enables its systems to work and endure." The Center's signature project brings lawyers and judges together with teachers to enhance instruction in the rule of law within public and private elementary, middle, and high schools in the United States.

Chronicling America

http://chroniclingamerica.loc.gov/

This site is a digital archive of America's major newspapers, providing primary resources conducive to civics discussion.

Civic Action Project

http://www.crfcap.org

This project provides a bundle of project-based learning plans for today's civic educator. Archiving student lessons which provide students with the "key content and skills they need to choose an issue and begin taking civic actions," CAP also helps students "understand the connections between their CAP issue, civic actions, and public policy."

Constitutional Rights Foundation

http://www.crf-usa.org/

Supporting state-based programming, the Foundation educates and empowers tomorrow's citizens, connecting students with ideals crucial to our democracy through the use of mock trials, civic action projects, appellate court experiences, and teaching American history resources.

Constitutional Rights Foundation—Chicago (CRFC)

http://www.crfc.org/

CRFC believes being a citizen is a participatory sport; thus it provides "interactive, classroom-tested curricula designed for use in government, Constitution, civics, and other

The Old State House, site of the Boston Massacre and one of the first public readings of the Declaration of Independence (photograph by the author).

social studies classes. Curricula provide students with background on our legal and political systems and challenge them to apply this knowledge through case studies, mock trials, discussions, and other interactive means."

CORE KNOWLEDGE FOUNDATION

http://www.coreknowledge.org/

E.D. Hirsch's approach to curriculum—a return to foundational knowledge, to include instruction based in the civic ideals of our Founding Fathers—is featured at this website.

CQ RESEARCHER

http://www.cqpress.com/researcher

Published by the CQ Press, and a favorite of librarians, this weekly report, housed within an available digital database, highlights today's major issues with 12,000-word exposés and extensive bibliographies.

C-SPAN CIVICS CLASSROOM

http://www.c-spanclassroom.org/

C-SPAN provides social studies teachers with free primary source "teachable moment" current issues videos (timely, teachable videos), "On This Day" resources, and classroom deliberation prompts.

DAVID MATHEWS CENTER FOR CIVIC LIFE

http://mathewscenter.org/

Honoring the president of the Kettering Foundation, the Center's purpose is to "foster infrastructure, habits, and capacities for more effective civic engagement and innovative decision making." Offerings include webinars, lesson plans, and a teacher's institute.

DISCOVERING JUSTICE (BOSTON)

http://discoveringjustice.org/

Based in the cradle of democracy, Boston, Massachusetts, Discovering Justice's mission is to "prepare young people to value the justice system, realize the power of their own voices, and embrace civic responsibility by connecting classrooms and courtrooms." As such, it offers in-school, after-school, and field-trip experiences based in courtroom scenarios. Specifically targeting the disadvantaged, the nonprofit offers the following programming: "Children Discovering Justice," "Stand Up for Your Rights," "Mock Trials," "Discovering the Bill of Rights," and "Courthouse Tours."

ENGAGE! PICTURING AMERICA THROUGH CIVIC ENGAGEMENT

http://www.programminglibrarian.org/engage#.VIShl8nQqlk

Piloted at the Chicago Public Library in the summer of 2010, this innovative programming effort engages civic discourse via dynamic discussions utilizing the visual arts as a springboard. Webinars and a program guide are available for youth service librarians wishing to implement Engage! programming within a particular local community.

Jack Miller Center

http://www.jackmillercenter.org/

This Center is dedicated to improving education based on America's founding ideas and principles. As such, it provides summer institutes, library and postdoctoral fellowships, videos, sample syllabi, Jeffersonian seminars, and higher education summits for civics education stakeholders.

Kettering Foundation

http://kettering.org

The Kettering Foundation strives to answer this question: What does it take to make a democracy work as it should? The Foundation's research is based in "what people can do collectively to address problems affecting their lives, their communities, and their nation." Findings are published in three journals: *Connections, Higher Education Exchange*, and *Kettering Review*. Papers and videos are also published.

Leonore Annenberg Institute for Civics

http://www.annenbergpublicpolicycenter.org/political-communication/leonore-annenberg-institute-for-civics/

The Annenberg Institute creates flagship civic programming for high school students, to include award-winning videos on the U.S. Constitution, Annenburg Classroom.org, Student Voices Speak Out, Fact Check, and Flack Check.

Mikva Challenge Center

http://www.mikvachallenge.org/

An example for every American city, community, and state, Chicago's Mikva Challenge is a center serving 6,000 high school students and 130 teachers, providing programming which encourages students to become active participants in the political process. Using the byline "Democracy Is a Verb," the Center challenges students to find their "civic voice" by means of active learning projects centered on the teachings of John Dewey and Jane Addams.

MIT's Benjamin Franklin Project

http://cheme.scripts.mit.edu/bfranklin-project/

A branch of Massachusetts Institute of Technology's undergraduate engineering program, this project, using Franklin's experiences as a model, seeks to inculcate within MIT's engineering students the concept of the profession serving as a tool for the common good. Calling upon ethical, philosophical, political and historical contexts, the goal is to allow students to "understand engineering as it fits into the whole."

National Children's Book Literacy Alliance (NCBLA)

Formed by award-winning children's and young adult authors, the NCBLA strives to (1) inform the American public about the reality of literacy levels; (2) build alliances with organizations, institutions, and businesses working to solve literacy issues; (3) share opportunities for action; and (4) inspire action. The Alliance supports and maintains a website dedicated to civics education (http://www.ourwhitehouse.org/civicedpage.html).

NATIONAL COMMISSION ON CIVIC RENEWAL

http://www.cpn.org/crm/essays/1stpanel1.html

The purpose of this network, sponsored by the Pew Charitable Trust, is to "assess the condition of civic engagement in the United States today and to propose specific actions— to be undertaken by the public, private, and voluntary sectors as well as by individuals— that could improve this condition." As such, this site provides essays, findings, case studies, reports, practical tools, and other resources reporting on the state of civics education in America.

NATIONAL CONSTITUTION CENTER

http://constitutioncenter.org/about

Situated within Independence Mall in Philadelphia, Pennsylvania, the National Constitution Center is a nonprofit, nonpartisan civics education headquarters dedicated to Constitutional education and debate. Students and civics educators may visit the "We the People" museum located at the Center; utilize online, interactive programming (live chats and webcasts); listen to podcasts; and even sign the Constitution.

NATIONAL ENDOWMENT FOR THE HUMANITIES (NEH)

http://www.neh.gov/NEH50years

NEH offers grants, special events, and projects targeting humanities education across the nation. For example, one current program focuses on the enduring question: What is good government?

NATIONAL ISSUES FORUM EDUCATOR CENTER

https://www.nifi.org/en/educators-center#edu_k-12_head

The Center provides a space in which civics educators "learn more about deliberation and its use in the classroom and other educational communities." Networks are available online, and educators may share their experiences (what works and what does not) when integrating deliberation strategies into the K–12 curriculum, after-school programs, and college courses.

NATIONAL PARK SERVICE (NPS)

http://www.nps.gov/index.htm

The National Park Service preserves locales important to America's story, also providing both local and digitally accessed resources associated with National Historic Landmarks and environs included in the National Register of Historic Places and Buildings. Both teacher and student resources may be accessed.

NBC's iCue

http://www.nbclearn.com/portal/site/learn/about

Containing archives of 12,000 news stories broadcast by NBC since 1920, this site correlates such stories to K–12 learning, including instruction based on civic standards.

New York Times in Education

http://events.nytimes.com/learning/teachers/NIE/

New York Times in Education connects current news stories with instruction in all subjects, to include national political issues. The wealth of resources found at this site includes articles, multimedia material, websites, and archival materials. The "Issues in Depth" and "This Day in History" components serve as instructional materials.

Rooney Center for Study of American Democracy

https://rooneycenter.nd.edu/

Notre Dame's Rooney Center holds conferences, workshops, and round tables—and sponsors research grants and thesis competitions—to encourage undergraduate students' participation in civic life.

September Project

http://theseptemberproject.org/

Answering the question "What is it?", the September Project, active since 2004 across the globe, states: "The September Project is a grassroots effort to encourage events about freedom in all libraries in all countries during the month of September. These events explore and exercise freedom, justice, democracy, and community and include book displays, community book readings, children's art projects, film screenings, theatrical performances, civic deliberations, voter registrations, gardens, murals, panel discussions, and puppet shows. September Project events are free and open to the public."

Socrates Café

http://www.philosopher.org/Socrates_Cafe.html

Supporting organizations around the world that wish to hold events in which people of all viewpoints discuss ideas and experiences, for the purpose of reaching reasonable decisions and/or promoting human progression, Socrates Café now works under the auspices of Democracy Café, a nonprofit organization dedicated to coming to a greater understanding of the nature and future of democracy (http://www.democracycafe.org/).

Thomas Jefferson Center for the Study of Core Texts and Ideas

http://www.utexas.edu/cola/centers/coretexts/about/About1.php

This undergraduate program at the University of Texas–Austin allows for student immersion (discussion and debates) in the core texts and ideas consulted by our Founding

Fathers. It also sponsors book discussions open to all university students, lecture webcasts, a junior fellows program, and resources for teachers, such as http://www.utexas.edu/cola/centers/coretexts/resources-for-teachers/Essential-Documents.php.

URBAN LIBRARIES COUNCIL: "INSPIRING LIBRARIES, TRANSFORMING COMMUNITIES"

http://www.urbanlibraries.org/

The Urban Libraries Council shares and inspires innovative library projects, including the institution of services which work at the local community level to engage people in civics discussion, problem solving, and policy development, "creating opportunities for community service and enhancing civic life."

YOUTH LEADERSHIP INITIATIVE

http://www.youthleadership.net/

A project of the University of Virginia Center for Politics, the Initiative creates free "education resources designed to assist civics teachers, and encourage students to participate in the political process," to include lesson plans, e-Congress (online legislative simulations), mock elections for real candidates, and democracy corps (a service learning program).

Find other civics education related sites at http://www.annenbergclassroom.org/page/best-civics-sites-for-teachers and http://www.civiced.org/resources/civic-education-links.

Chapter XVI

Closing Thoughts and Tips

"As citizens of this democracy, you are the rulers and the ruled, the lawgivers and the law-abiding, the beginning and the end."—Adlai Stevenson

As a final helpmate, the following technology tools may be conducive to the modification of many of the activities or suggestions contained in this book:

- Google Lit Trip: Take students on a virtual journey, pinpointing locales of note (including activities as links): http://www.googlelittrips.com/GoogleLit/Home.html.

- Wordsmyth: Create a civic glossary at this site: http://www.wordsmyth.net/?mode=gm.

- Timelines: Students may wish to create timelines in association with a historically significant period: http://www.readwritethink.org/files/resources/interactives/timeline/.

- Collage: A digital collage of primary resource images may be developed at Photovisi: http://www.photovisi.com/.

- Plot Landmarks: A Fodor's application allowing the plotting of historically significant landmarks may be found at http://www.fodors.com/news/download-now-plotter-app-6571.html.

- Oral History: Record interviews and oral histories at http://www.kid-cast.com/.

- Digital Storytelling: "Discover the threads connecting peoples' lives across time and place" with MemoryMiner: http://memoryminer.com/.

As I finish this manuscript, schools are letting out for Christmas across the nation. Thanksgiving has just been celebrated by all. We are still free to worship as we wish, work where we will, and pursue happiness in many forms. I will use this special season, and now a bit more free time, to hope and pray that those who determine what these same school children will study and learn upon their return in January 2015 will remember America's gifts and think how each and every right earned by our forebears benefits not only the young and vulnerable, but also the proud and strong. I will ask for a return to education which serves to internalize, among America's students, (1) the life-threatening sacrifices made by our forebears; (2) the incredible gifts bestowed by our form of government, as

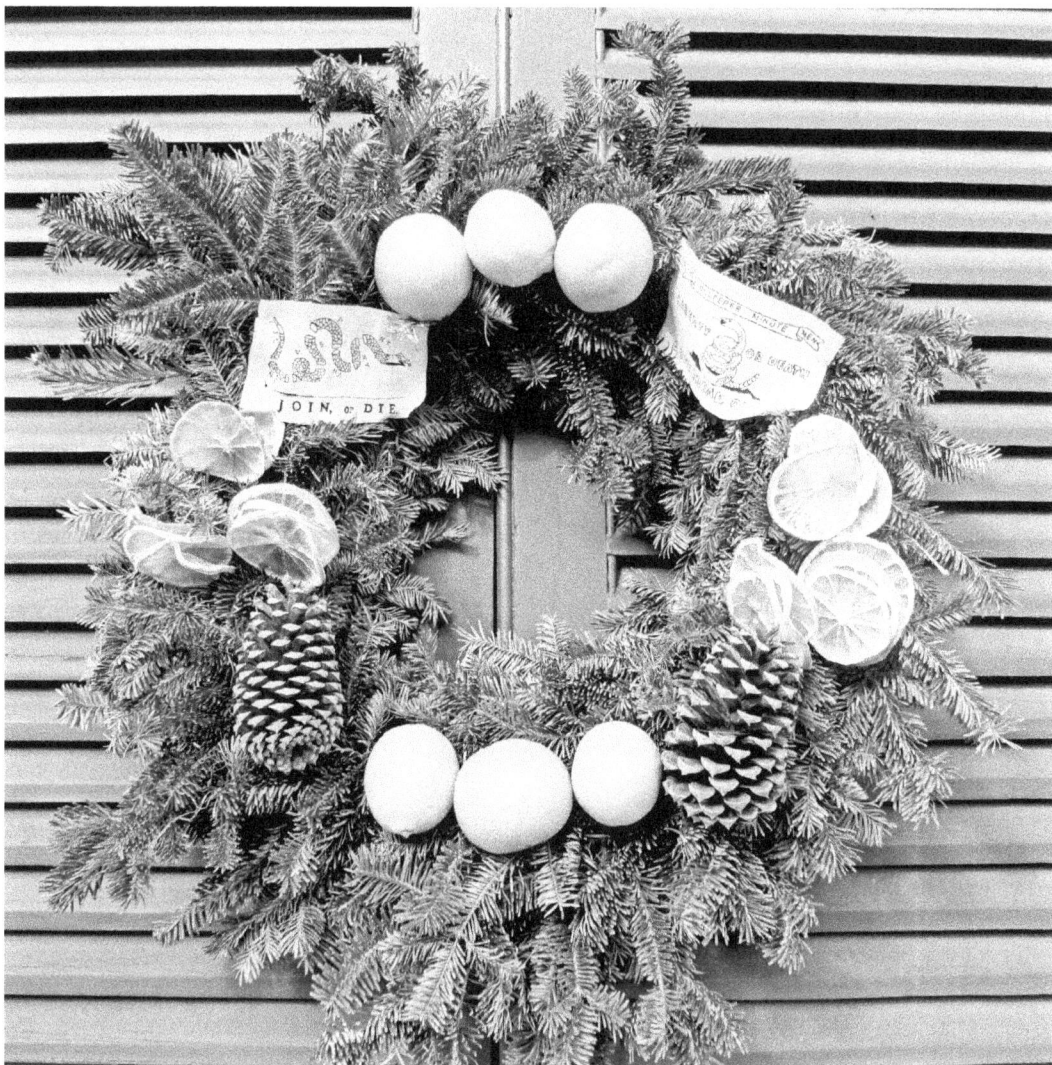

Christmas wreath as displayed in Colonial Williamsburg, Virginia (photograph by the author).

articulated within our rule of law; (3) the necessity of learning more about our freedoms and the philosophies encouraging these rights; and (4) the urgency of preserving these freedoms at all costs. Just as John Adams spoke to posterity, describing the pains he endured for its benefit, so I have honored these sacrifices, and our freedoms and rights as American citizens, by sharing facts, contentions, opinions, and civics education suggestions with American educators, administrators, proponents, and politicians. I hope and pray the action and service I have rendered to America's cause (a cause now shared across the globe) will, in some small way, be added to the action and service of millions, helping us to return, once more, to what Jimmy Carter would label "a functional democracy."

Appendix A
Discussion

Exhibit 1

Outline of American Flag Graphic Organizer

Exhibit 2

LIBERTY TREE

by Thomas Paine

In a chariot of light from the regions of day,
    The Goddess of Liberty came;
Ten thousand celestials directed the way,
    And hither conducted the dame.
A fair budding branch from the gardens above,
    Where millions with millions agree,
She brought in her hand as a pledge of her love,
    And the plant she named Liberty Tree.
The celestial exotic struck deep in the ground,
    Like a native it flourished and bore;
The fame of its fruit drew the nations around,
    To seek out this peaceable shore.
Unmindful of names or distinctions they came,
    For freemen like brothers agree;
With one spirit endued, they one friendship pursued,
    And their temple was Liberty Tree.
Beneath this fair tree, like the patriarchs of old,
    Their bread in contentment they ate
Unvexed with the troubles of silver and gold,
    The cares of the grand and the great.
With timber and tar they Old England supplied,
    And supported her power on the sea;
Her battles they fought, without getting a groat,
    For the honor of Liberty Tree.

But hear, O ye swains, 'tis a tale most profane,
    How all the tyrannical powers,
Kings, Commons and Lords, are uniting amain,
    To cut down this guardian of ours;
From the east to the west blow the trumpet to arms,
    Through the land let the sound of it flee,
Let the far and the near, all unite with a cheer,
    In defence of our Liberty Tree.

Exhibit 3

Universal Declaration of Human Rights (Abridged)

1. We Are All Born Free and Equal. We are all born free. We all have our own thoughts and ideas. We should all be treated in the same way.
2. Don't Discriminate. These rights belong to everybody, whatever our differences.
3. The Right to Life. We all have the right to life, and to live in freedom and safety.
4. No Slavery. Nobody has any right to make us a slave. We cannot make anyone our slave.
5. No Torture. Nobody has any right to hurt us or to torture us.
6. You Have Rights No Matter Where You Go. I am a person just like you!
7. We're All Equal Before the Law. The law is the same for everyone. It must treat us all fairly.
8. Your Human Rights Are Protected by Law. We can all ask for the law to help us when we are not treated fairly.
9. No Unfair Detainment. Nobody has the right to put us in prison without good reason and keep us there, or to send us away from our country.
10. The Right to Trial. If we are put on trial, it should be in public. The people who try us should not let anyone tell them what to do.
11. We're Always Innocent Until Proven Guilty. Nobody should be blamed for doing something until it is proven. When people say we did a bad thing, we have the right to show it is not true.
12. The Right to Privacy. Nobody should try to harm our good name. Nobody has the right to come into our home, open our letters, or bother us or our family without a good reason.
13. Freedom to Move. We all have the right to go where we want in our own country and to travel as we wish.
14. The Right to Seek a Safe Place to Live. If we are frightened of being badly treated in our own country, we all have the right to run away to another country to be safe.
15. Right to a Nationality. We all have the right to belong to a country.
16. Marriage and Family. Every grown-up has the right to marry and have a family if he or she wants to. Men and women have the same rights when they are married and when they are separated.
17. The Right to Your Own Things. Everyone has the right to own things or share them. Nobody should take our things from us without a good reason.
18. Freedom of Thought. We all have the right to believe in what we want to believe, to have a religion, or to change it if we want.
19. Freedom of Expression. We all have the right to make up our own minds, to think what we like, to say what we think, and to share our ideas with other people.
20. The Right to Public Assembly. We all have the right to meet our friends and to work together in peace to defend our rights. Nobody can make us join a group if we don't want to.
21. The Right to Democracy. We all have the right to take part in the government of our country. Every grown-up should be allowed to choose his or her own leaders.

22. Social Security. We all have the right to affordable housing, medicine, education, and child care; enough money to live on; and medical help if we are ill or old.
23. Workers' Rights. Every grown-up has the right to do a job, to a fair wage for his or her work, and to join a trade union.
24. The Right to Play. We all have the right to rest from work and to relax.
25. Food and Shelter for All. We all have the right to a good life. Mothers and children; people who are old, unemployed, or disabled; and all people have the right to be cared for.
26. The Right to Education. Education is a right. Primary school should be free. We should learn about the United Nations and how to get on with others. Our parents can choose what we learn.
27. Copyright. Copyright is a special law that protects one's own artistic creations and writings; others cannot make copies without permission. We all have the right to our own way of life and to enjoy the good things that art, science, and learning bring.
28. A Fair and Free World. There must be proper order so we can all enjoy rights and freedoms in our own country and all over the world.
29. Responsibility. We have a duty to other people, and we should protect their rights and freedoms.
30. No One Can Take Away Your Human Rights.

Exhibit 4

THE DECLARATION OF INDEPENDENCE
IN CONGRESS, JULY 4, 1776

The Unanimous Declaration of the Thirteen United States of America

When in the Course of human events, it becomes necessary for one people to dissolve the political bands which have connected them with another, and to assume among the powers of the earth, the separate and equal station to which the laws of nature and of nature's God entitle them, a decent respect to the opinions of mankind requires that they should declare the causes which impel them to the separation.

We hold these truths to be self-evident: that all men are created equal; that they are endowed by their Creator with certain unalienable rights; that among these are life, liberty and the pursuit of happiness; that, to secure these rights, governments are instituted among men, deriving their just powers from the consent of the governed; that whenever any form of government becomes destructive of these ends, it is the right of the people to alter or to abolish it, and to institute new government, laying its foundation on such principles and organizing its powers in such form, as to them shall seem most likely to effect their safety and happiness. Prudence, indeed, will dictate that governments long established should not be changed for light and transient causes; and accordingly all experience hath shewn [sic], that mankind are more disposed to suffer, while evils are sufferable, than to right themselves by abolishing the forms to which they are accustomed. But when a long train of abuses and usurpations, pursuing invariably the same object evinces a design to reduce them under absolute despotism, it is their right, it is their duty, to throw off such government, and to provide new guards for their future security. Such has been the patient sufferance of these colonies; and such is now the necessity which constrains them to alter their former systems of government. The history of the present King of Great Britain is a history of repeated injuries and usurpations, all having in direct object the establishment of an absolute tyranny over these States. To prove this, let facts be submitted to a candid world.

- He has refused his assent to laws, the most wholesome and necessary for the public good.

- He has forbidden his Governors to pass laws of immediate and pressing importance, unless suspended in their operation till his assent should be obtained; and when so suspended, he has utterly neglected to attend to them.

- He has refused to pass other laws for the accommodation of large districts of people, unless those people would relinquish the right of representation in the legislature, a right inestimable to them and formidable to tyrants only.

- He has called together legislative bodies at places unusual, uncomfortable, and distant from the depository of their public records, for the sole purpose of fatiguing them into compliance with his measures.

- He has dissolved representative houses repeatedly, for opposing with manly firmness his invasions on the rights of the people.

- He has refused for a long time, after such dissolutions, to cause others to be elected; whereby the legislative powers, incapable of annihilation, have returned to the people at large for their exercise; the state remaining in the mean time exposed to all the dangers of invasion from without, and convulsions within.

- He has endeavoured to prevent the population of these States; for that purpose obstructing the laws for naturalization of foreigners; refusing to pass others to encourage their migrations hither, and raising the conditions of new appropriations of lands.

- He has obstructed the administration of justice, by refusing his assent to laws for establishing judiciary powers.

- He has made judges dependent on his will alone, for the tenure of their offices, and the amount and payment of their salaries.

- He has erected a multitude of new offices, and sent hither swarms of Officers to harass our people, and eat out their substance.

- He has kept among us, in times of peace, standing armies without the consent of our legislatures.

- He has affected to render the military independent of and superior to the civil power.

- He has combined with others to subject us to a jurisdiction foreign to our constitution, and unacknowledged by our laws; giving his assent to their acts of pretended legislation:

    o For quartering large bodies of armed troops among us:

    o For protecting them, by a mock trial, from punishment for any murders which they should commit on the inhabitants of these states:

    o For cutting off our trade with all parts of the world:

    o For imposing taxes on us without our consent:

    o For depriving us in many cases, of the benefits of trial by jury:

    o For transporting us beyond seas to be tried for pretended offences:

    o For abolishing the free System of English Laws in a neighbouring province, establishing therein an arbitrary government, and enlarging its boundaries so as to render it at once an example and fit instrument for introducing the same absolute rule into these colonies:

    o For taking away our charters, abolishing our most valuable Laws, and altering fundamentally the forms of our governments:

    o For suspending our own legislatures, and declaring themselves invested with power to legislate for us in all cases whatsoever.

- He has abdicated government here, by declaring us out of his protection and waging war against us.

- He has plundered our seas, ravaged our coasts, burnt our towns, and destroyed the lives of our people.

- He is at this time transporting large Armies of foreign mercenaries to compleat [*sic*] the works of death, desolation and tyranny, already begun with circumstances of cruelty & perfidy scarcely paralleled in the most barbarous ages, and totally unworthy the head of a civilized nation.

- He has constrained our fellow citizens taken captive on the high seas to bear arms against their country, to become the executioners of their friends and brethren, or to fall themselves by their hands.

- He has excited domestic insurrections amongst us, and has endeavoured to bring on the inhabitants of our frontiers, the merciless Indian savages, whose known rule of warfare, is an undistinguished destruction of all ages, sexes and conditions.

In every stage of these oppressions we have petitioned for redress in the most humble terms: Our repeated petitions have been answered only by repeated injury. A Prince whose character is thus marked by every act which may define a tyrant, is unfit to be the ruler of a free people.

Nor have we been wanting in attentions to our British brethren. We have warned them from time to time of attempts by their legislature to extend an unwarrantable jurisdiction over us. We have reminded them of the circumstances of our emigration and settlement here. We have appealed to their native justice and magnanimity, and we have conjured them by the ties of our common kindred to disavow these usurpations, which would inevitably interrupt our connections and correspondence. They too have been deaf to the voice of justice and of consanguinity. We must, therefore, acquiesce in the necessity, which denounces our separation, and hold them, as we hold the rest of mankind, enemies in war, in peace friends.

   We, therefore, the representatives of the United States of America, in General Congress, assembled, appealing to the Supreme Judge of the world for the rectitude of our intentions, do, in the name, and by authority of the good people of these colonies, solemnly publish and declare, that these United Colonies are, and of Right ought to be Free and Independent States; that they are absolved from all allegiance to the British crown, and that all political connection between them and the state of Great Britain, is and ought to be totally dissolved; and that as free and independent states, they have full power to levy war, conclude peace, contract alliances, establish commerce, and to do all other acts and things which independent states may of right do. And for the support of this Declaration, with a firm reliance on the protection of divine Providence, we mutually pledge to each other our lives, our fortunes and our sacred honor.

Appendix B
Civic Action

Exhibit 1

Native American Reservation Facts (courtesy of National Relief Charities)

1. Altogether, 566 federally recognized Native American tribes exist in the United States.
2. The overall living conditions on some reservations have been cited as "comparable to the Third World."
3. Access to jobs is limited on the reservations. Unemployment ranges from 35 percent to 85 percent, depending on the community. Overall unemployment for American Indians is about 49 percent.
4. Many American Indians work full-time, yet still fall below poverty level. Poverty ranges from 38 percent to 63 percent of the population on Navajo, Rosebud, Pine Ridge, Lower Brule, Crow Creek, and other reservations.
5. From 30 percent to 43 percent of American Indian children are living in poverty.
6. The high school dropout rate for American Indian students ranges from 30 percent to 70 percent, depending on the reservation and the state. About 9 percent of American Indians have a college degree, compared to 19 percent of their Caucasian peers.
7. Some 23 percent of American Indian households experience low food insecurity—more so than other families in the United States. Low food security means uncertain or limited access to enough food for an active healthy life, typically because of a lack of money or access.
8. Suicide rates for American Indians between the ages of 15 and 24 are three times the national average—and the second leading cause of death for their age group.
9. Life expectancy for American Indians has improved, yet still trails that of other Americans by a few years. American Indians are experiencing a diabetes epidemic—they have the highest rate of diabetes in the United States. The tuberculosis rate for American Indians is seven times higher than that for the general U.S. population. Cancer-related disparities for American Indians are higher than for any minority group in the United States, mainly due to poverty and lack of access.
10. There is a housing crisis in Indian country. About 90,000 American Indian families are homeless or under-housed, and 40% of on-reservation housing is considered inadequate.

Exhibit 2

The Ten-Minute Guide to the U.S. Constitution

https://www.mindflash.com/wp-content/uploads/2011/01/110128-MIND-CONSTITU-TION1.png

Exhibit 3

American Library Association's Freedom to Read Statement

The freedom to read is essential to our democracy. It is continuously under attack. Private groups and public authorities in various parts of the country are working to remove or limit access to reading materials, to censor content in schools, to label "controversial" views, to distribute lists of "objectionable" books or authors, and to purge libraries. These actions apparently rise from a view that our national tradition of free expression is no longer valid; that censorship and suppression are needed to counter threats to safety or national security, as well as to avoid the subversion of politics and the corruption of morals. We, as individuals devoted to reading and as librarians and publishers responsible for disseminating ideas, wish to assert the public interest in the preservation of the freedom to read.

Most attempts at suppression rest on a denial of the fundamental premise of democracy: that the ordinary individual, by exercising critical judgment, will select the good and reject the bad. We trust Americans to recognize propaganda and misinformation, and to make their own decisions about what they read and believe. We do not believe they are prepared to sacrifice their heritage of a free press in order to be "protected" against what others think may be bad for them. We believe they still favor free enterprise in ideas and expression.

These efforts at suppression are related to a larger pattern of pressures being brought against education, the press, art and images, films, broadcast media, and the Internet. The problem is not only one of actual censorship. The shadow of fear cast by these pressures leads, we suspect, to an even larger voluntary curtailment of expression by those who seek to avoid controversy or unwelcome scrutiny by government officials.

Such pressure toward conformity is perhaps natural to a time of accelerated change. And yet suppression is never more dangerous than in such a time of social tension. Freedom has given the United States the elasticity to endure strain. Freedom keeps open the path of novel and creative solutions, and enables change to come by choice. Every silencing of a heresy, every enforcement of an orthodoxy, diminishes the toughness and resilience of our society and leaves it the less able to deal with controversy and difference.

Now as always in our history, reading is among our greatest freedoms. The freedom to read and write is almost the only means for making generally available ideas or manners of expression that can initially command only a small audience. The written word is the natural medium for the new idea and the untried voice from which come the original contributions to social growth. It is essential to the extended discussion that serious thought requires, and to the accumulation of knowledge and ideas into organized collections.

We believe that free communication is essential to the preservation of a free society and a creative culture. We believe that these pressures toward conformity present the danger of limiting the range and variety of inquiry and expression on which our democracy and our culture depend. We believe that every American community must jealously guard the freedom to publish and to circulate, in order to preserve its own freedom to read. We believe that publishers and librarians have a profound responsibility to give validity to that freedom to read by making it possible for the readers to choose freely from a variety of offerings.

The freedom to read is guaranteed by the Constitution. Those with faith in free people will stand firm on these constitutional guarantees of essential rights and will exercise the responsibilities that accompany these rights.

We therefore affirm these propositions:

1. It is in the public interest for publishers and librarians to make available the widest diversity of views and expressions, including those that are unorthodox, unpopular, or considered dangerous by the majority.

    Creative thought is by definition new, and what is new is different. The bearer of every new thought is a rebel until that idea is refined and tested. Totalitarian systems attempt to maintain themselves in power by the ruthless suppression of any concept that challenges the established orthodoxy. The power of a democratic system to adapt to change is vastly strengthened by the freedom of its citizens to choose widely from among conflicting opinions offered freely to them. To stifle every nonconformist idea at birth would mark the end of the democratic process. Furthermore, only through the constant activity of weighing and selecting can the democratic mind attain the strength demanded by times like these. We need to know not only what we believe but why we believe it.

2. Publishers, librarians, and booksellers do not need to endorse every idea or presentation they make available. It would conflict with the public interest for them to establish their own political, moral, or aesthetic views as a standard for determining what should be published or circulated.

    Publishers and librarians serve the educational process by helping to make available knowledge and ideas required for the growth of the mind and the increase of learning. They do not foster education by imposing as mentors the patterns of their own thought. The people should have the freedom to read and consider a broader range of ideas than those that may be held by any single librarian or publisher or government or church. It is wrong that what one can read should be confined to what another thinks proper.

3. It is contrary to the public interest for publishers or librarians to bar access to writings on the basis of the personal history or political affiliations of the author.

    No art or literature can flourish if it is to be measured by the political views or private lives of its creators. No society of free people can flourish that draws up lists of writers to whom it will not listen, whatever they may have to say.

4. There is no place in our society for efforts to coerce the taste of others, to confine adults to the reading matter deemed suitable for adolescents, or to inhibit the efforts of writers to achieve artistic expression.

To some, much of modern expression is shocking. But is not much of life itself shocking? We cut off literature at the source if we prevent writers from dealing with the stuff of life. Parents and teachers have a responsibility to prepare the young to meet the diversity of experiences in life to which they will be exposed, as they have a responsibility to help them learn to think critically for themselves. These are affirmative responsibilities, not to be discharged simply by preventing them from reading works for which they are not yet prepared. In these matters values differ, and values cannot be legislated; nor can machinery be devised that will suit the demands of one group without limiting the freedom of others.

5. It is not in the public interest to force a reader to accept the prejudgment of a label characterizing any expression or its author as subversive or dangerous.

   The ideal of labeling presupposes the existence of individuals or groups with wisdom to determine by authority what is good or bad for others. It presupposes that individuals must be directed in making up their minds about the ideas they examine. But Americans do not need others to do their thinking for them.

6. It is the responsibility of publishers and librarians, as guardians of the people's freedom to read, to contest encroachments upon that freedom by individuals or groups seeking to impose their own standards or tastes upon the community at large; and by the government whenever it seeks to reduce or deny public access to public information.

   It is inevitable in the give and take of the democratic process that the political, the moral, or the aesthetic concepts of an individual or group will occasionally collide with those of another individual or group. In a free society individuals are free to determine for themselves what they wish to read, and each group is free to determine what it will recommend to its freely associated members. But no group has the right to take the law into its own hands, and to impose its own concept of politics or morality upon other members of a democratic society. Freedom is no freedom if it is accorded only to the accepted and the inoffensive. Further, democratic societies are more safe, free, and creative when the free flow of public information is not restricted by governmental prerogative or self-censorship.

7. It is the responsibility of publishers and librarians to give full meaning to the freedom to read by providing books that enrich the quality and diversity of thought and expression. By the exercise of this affirmative responsibility, they can demonstrate that the answer to a "bad" book is a good one, the answer to a "bad" idea is a good one.

   The freedom to read is of little consequence when the reader cannot obtain matter fit for that reader's purpose. What is needed is not only the absence of restraint, but the positive provision of opportunity for the people to read the best that has been thought and said. Books are the major channel by which the intellectual inheritance is handed down, and the principal means of its testing and growth. The defense of the freedom to read requires of all publishers and librarians the utmost of their faculties, and deserves of all Americans the fullest of their support.

We state these propositions neither lightly nor as easy generalizations. We here stake out a lofty claim for the value of the written word. We do so because we believe that it is possessed of enormous variety and usefulness, worthy of cherishing and keeping free. We realize that the application of these propositions may mean the dissemination of ideas and manners of expression that are repugnant to many persons. We do not state these propositions in the comfortable belief that what people read is unimportant. We believe rather that what people read is deeply important; that ideas can be dangerous; but that the suppression of ideas is fatal to a democratic society. Freedom itself is a dangerous way of life, but it is ours.

Appendix C
Civic Service

Exhibit 1

THE NATIONAL GUEST
(HONOR BE TO HIM TO WHOM HONOR IS DUE)
by Thomas Hope (Tune: Hail to the Chief)

1

Hail, Hail, Hail to the Patriot Chief, Heaven granted
to aid with life's peril, in Washington's Band;
Long may the Tree—the Heroes have planted,
Flourish the boast—and the pride of our Land.
"heaven send its happy dew";
Time still its strength renew,
O'er Nations to spread—o'er Millions to grow;
While every heart shall throb,
LIBERTY—the gift of God
Shall blossom in splendor—in bloom ever blow.

2

Columbia, the soil—where Freedom for ages
Shall flourish, be sacred, of Freemen the pride;
The home of the Hero, the cradle of sages,
Where Liberty lives—and Tyranny died.
Anchored in our hearts' core,
Liberty shall ever more
Stem Kingly power—vain, idle theme.
And while our Eagle flies
To—or from its native skies,
Free shall be our Land—honor'd be its name.

3

Sound, Clarions, sound! Let Fame spread the story,
The brave Volunteer, who in youth sought our shore,
To aid in our cause—share Washington's glory,
The guest of the nation is with us once more.
Each independent State—laud, then, the Hero great.
GREET Lafayette, with National praise.
May he long happy be,
Patriot, Friend of Liberty,
And in our Love and Land spend all his days.

Bibliography

American Association of School Librarians. *Empowering Learners: Guidelines for School Library Media Programs*. Chicago: American Library Association, 2009.

_____. "21st Century Learning Standards." Chicago: American Library Association, 2010. Web. April 22, 2014.

American Library Association. "Engaging Teens at Chicago Public Libraries." The Campaign for America's Libraries. Chicago: American Library Association, 2012. Web. July 22, 2014.

Campbell, David, Meira Levinson, and Frederick M. Hess. *Making Civics Count: Citizenship Education for a New Generation*. Cambridge, MA: Harvard Education Press, 2012.

Center for Civics Education. "Preface." National Standards for Civics and Government. 2014. Web. June 1, 2014.

Center for Engaged Democracy. "Core Competencies in Civic Engagement." Merrimack, MA: Merrimack College, Center for Engaged Democracy, 2014. Web. April 2, 2014.

Cocciolo, Anthony. "Public Libraries and PBS Partnering to Enhance Civic Engagement: A Study of a Nationwide Initiative." *Public Library Quarterly* 32, nos. 1–16 (2013): 1–20.

Ditzion, Sidney. *Arsenals of a Democratic Culture: A Social History of the American Public Library from 1850 to 1900*. Chicago: American Library Association, 1947.

Edwards, Julie Biando, Melissa S. Robinson, and Kelley Rae Unger. *Transforming Libraries and Building Communities: The Community Centered Library*. Lanham, MD: Scarecrow Press, 2013.

Feith, David. *Teaching America: The Case for Civic Education*. Lanham, MD: Rowman & Littlefield Education, 2011.

Gould, Jonathon. "Guardian of Democracy: The Civic Mission of Schools." Leonore Annenburg Institute for Civics and Campaign for the Civic Mission of Schools. (2012): 1–56.

Hirsch, E. D. *The Making of America: Democracy and Our Schools*. New Haven, CT: Yale University Press, 2009.

Kranich, Nancy. "Libraries and Civic Engagement." *Library and Trade Book Almanac: Information Today* (2012): 75–97.

Martin, Lowell A. *Enrichment: A History of the Public Library in the United States in the Twentieth Century*. Lanham, MD: Scarecrow Press, 1998.

Murray, Stuart A. P. *The Library: An Illustrated History*. New York: Skyhorse Publishing, 2009.

National Council of Social Studies. "The Themes of Social Studies." National Curriculum Standards for Social Studies (2013). Web. May 5, 2014.

Ptacek, Bill. "The Library as Catalyst for Civic Engagement: Reinventing Libraries." *Library Journal* (September 4, 2013): n.p.

Putnam, Robert. *Bowling Alone: The Collapse and Revival of American Community*. New York: Simon & Schuster, 2000.

Rubin, Richard E. *Foundations of Library and Information Science*. New York: Neal-Schuman Publishers, 2010.

Urban Libraries Council. "The Engaged Library: Chicago Stories of Community Building." ABCD Institute, 2005. Web. July 7, 2014.

_____. "Library Priority: Community Civics Engagement." ULC Leadership Brief, (2011). Web. August 8, 2014.

Index

Page numbers in **bold italics** indicate pages with illustrations.

www.ingramcontent.com/pod-product-compliance
Lightning Source LLC
Chambersburg PA
CBHW080553270326
41929CB00019B/3292